ASPECTS OF EUROPEAN CULTURAL DIVERSITY

Contributors

Konrad Schröder • Bob Moon • Hans J. Kleinsteuber •
Torsten Rossman • Volkert Wiesner • Wolfgang Kaschuba

Edited by Monica Shelley and Margaret Winck

The Open University, Deutsches Institut für Fernstudien an der Universität
Tübingen, European Association of Distance Teaching Universities

London and New York

A note for the general reader

Aspects of European Cultural Diversity forms part of a second level course in the humanities and social sciences. The English language version of the *What is Europe?* course is produced by the Open University in conjunction with the European Association of Distance Teaching Universities. Open University students are provided with supplementary teaching material, including a *Course Guide*, which gives a complete list of all printed and audio-visual components.

What is Europe?

Book 1   *The History of the Idea of Europe*

Book 2   *Aspects of European Cultural Diversity*

Book 3   *European Democratic Culture*

Book 4   *Europe and the Wider World*

First published in 1993 by
The Open University, Walton Hall, Milton Keynes, MK7 6AA
Revised edition first published in 1995 by
The Open University, Walton Hall, Milton Keynes MK7 6AA
                        and
Routledge
11 New Fetter Lane, London EC4P 4EE
Simultaneously published in the USA and Canada by
Routledge
29 West 35th Street, New York, NY 10001

Edited, designed and typeset by the Open University
Printed in the United Kingdom by Bell and Bain Ltd., Glasgow
British Library Cataloguing in Publication Data
A catalogue record for this book is available from the British Library
Library of Congress Cataloguing in Publication Data
A catalogue record for this book has been requested
ISBN 0-415-12416-6
ISBN 0-415-12417-4 (pbk)

The other institutions which participated in the creation of *What is Europe?* were:

Open universiteit,
Valkenburgerweg 167,
PO Box 2960,
6401 DL Heerlen,
The Netherlands

Jysk Åbent Universitet,
Nordre Ringgade 1,
DK – 8000 Århus C,
Denmark

Deutsches Institut für Fernstudien an der Universität Tübingen,
Post Fach 1569,
7400 Tübingen 1,
Germany

Fédération Interuniversitaire
de l'Enseignement à Distance,
l'Université Paris X
200 Avenue de la République,
92001 Nanterre,
France

Contents

NOTE: Where there is no English-language published version, the quotations from German authors that appear in these essays have been translated by Monica Shelley; quotations from other foreign authors have been translated by the author or editor.

General preface to 'What is Europe?'

Kevin Wilson, Chair of the European Association of Distance Teaching Universities (EADTU) Humanities Programme Committee

The four books in the *What is Europe?* series are the product of a collaborative enterprise under the direction of the Humanities Programme Committee of the European Association of Distance Teaching Universities (EADTU). The universities involved in the project are:

- The Open universiteit, The Netherlands
- Jysk Åbent Universitet (the Jutland Open University)
- The Deutsches Institut für Fernstudien an der Universität Tübingen
- The Centre d'Analyse des Savoirs Contemporains at the Université des Sciences Humaines de Strasbourg on behalf of the Fédération Interuniversitaire de l'Enseignement à Distance
- The UK Open University

The Humanities Programme Committee of the EADTU was established in late 1988 with a brief to promote joint course development. The four books in this series were designed as the academic core of its first course which was first presented by the Open University in 1993. For this new edition, the course team have revised and updated the original materials so that they can be made available to students of European Studies at universities and colleges not involved in the EADTU programme in Europe, the United States and beyond.

Starting to plan a course on Europe in the heady year of 1989 was both a challenge and an opportunity. With Europe in a state of flux, we quickly rejected as too narrow the idea of a course focused only on the European Community. We dismissed just as quickly the idea of a European history course, not on grounds of irrelevance, but because numerous such courses were already available. Instead we agreed to write a course on European identity in its various historical, cultural, social, political and economic aspects. This topic was at the centre of the debate on Europe, called for a wide-ranging approach across academic boundaries and stood to benefit from the different national perspectives that could be harnessed to the project.

The course has four objectives:

1 To provide a context for the understanding of contemporary European developments through a consideration of the history of the idea of Europe.

2 To consider aspects of European cultural diversity through investigations into language, education, mass-media and everyday culture.

3   To examine the theory, function and practice of democracy as, arguably, fundamental components of European culture.

4   To locate Europe as a political and economic entity in a context of global change.

These objectives – and the European nature of the course – are reflected in the titles and provenance of the respective books:

1   *The History of the Idea of Europe* is a Dutch–Danish collaboration.

2   *Aspects of European Cultural Diversity* emanates from Germany, though one of the authors is British.

3   *European Democratic Culture* is a French product, though there are Italian, German and British, as well as French, contributors to the book.

4   *Europe and the Wider World* comes from the UK.

We have framed the title of the series as a question – *What is Europe?* – yet we are under no illusion that there is a simple, straightforward answer, or even a series of agreed definitions that satisfy. Nor are we making the assumption that Europe is stamped with a unique identity, or that it has a manifest destiny, or that a singular meaning is revealed in its history.

We follow in the footsteps of Hugh Seton-Watson, who tells us that 'the word "Europe" has been used and misused, interpreted and misinterpreted in as many different meanings as almost any word in any language. There have been and are many Europes…'[1] The question, then, is a provocative device to set you thinking, and to prompt further questions. Instead of rushing into definitions we have approached the topic from a number of points of view and from the standpoint of various methodologies, raising questions as we go about how 'Europe' has been conceptualized, organized, structured and utilized, both in the past and in the present. The contributors to this series do not have any particular axes to grind. The essays are not propaganda pieces for a 'European spirit', cultural unity, a single market, political union, or any other European project. On the contrary, they are scholarly explorations designed to enhance our understanding of the many facets of European identity.

So, the essays cover a wide canvas. They deal with various ideas of Europe in the past and present; with different aspects of everyday life and associated tensions making for cultural uniformity or accentuating cultural difference; with a political culture founded on public opinion, law and democracy; and with Europe's relationship with the United States, Russia and the developing countries and with its place in the world economy.

The series as a whole presents Europe as a work in progress rather than a finished product, a construction yard rather than a museum. As a project Europe can never be completed. It will always need to be re-made, emancipated from the past, re-invented.

---

[1]   SETON-WATSON, H. (1985) 'What is Europe, where is Europe?: from mystique to politique', *Encounter,* July/August, vol. LX, No. 2, p. 9.

Introduction to Book 2

Nur durch Aneignung fremder Schätze entsteht ein Großes.

(Goethe)

It is only possible to become great by appropriating foreign treasures.

The first book in this series dealt with the idea of Europe mainly from an historical perspective and included discussion of Europe as a set of ideas or as a continuing process of construction. Europeans-in-the-street, though, confronted daily by the word 'Europe' on TV screens, in newspapers and on advertising hoardings have a much more concrete idea of what Europe means – a place where they live, work, or take their holidays. The boundaries of this geographical space may be hazy, but the space itself is perceived as a jigsaw-puzzle of very disparate political and cultural entities, a perception accentuated by familiar coloured maps and reinforced by commonly-held stereotypes of other European countries and their inhabitants. But with or without Maastricht, or the many other treaties which bind European states in politcial, economic and cultural networks, the homogenization of our market economies, with the movement of people, goods and services on a vast scale and all the contacts between cultures that this involves, must have an effect on those cultures. We are, perhaps, not always consciously aware of the degree of 'Europeanization' in our everyday lives, its effects on our choice of material goods and leisure pursuits, on our attitudes or on the very language we use. Business, academic, tourist and political connections have increased significantly within Europe in the last few years and from 1994 are set to increase further. As Europe's borders become less relevant as physical barriers it seems appropriate to take stock of the effects of converging economic and social policies on our everyday lives and to consider in what subtle and various ways we may all have become more European over the past two decades.

Many European citizens feel that their national culture is threatened by moves towards economic and political unification. Some cultural communities in Europe, however, welcome this trend since their particular identities have not always been respected by nation-states. We are exhorted to preserve the variety of cultures in Europe, whilst at the same time urged to recognize commonalities, collaborate, integrate and unify for the common good. Is this a paradox? Can we preserve our identification with local, regional or national cultures whilst still embracing European integration? The idea of any local, regional or national culture as an isolated, unassailable entity is simply untenable today in a continent with such excellent communications. Also, historically, no region can claim cultural or ethnic 'purity'. All European cultures have been ready to take on Goethe's 'foreign treasures', to adapt and refine them before passing them on again. One of the aims of this book is to increase the readers' sense of the continuous cross-currents and confluences in Europe's cultures, and appreciation of the ways in which external influences past and present have affected their 'own' culture. The phenomena chosen to exemplify these processes are within the ambit of any European, so that readers can bring their own experience to bear on what is described here.

The authors have taken a close look at four aspects of contemporary Europe. These have been chosen for their particular significance in affecting the socializa-

9

tion of individuals and because they loom large in any discussion of European culture. The four essays deal with language, education, the mass media and everyday life. The authors range widely over their respective topics, exploring similarities and differences in values and lifestyles in western Europe and showing how recent European legislation bears on social issues.

The approach to culture adopted by the authors of these essays can be likened to that of the anthropologist, who takes culture in its broadest sense as the totality of everyday life, with all the acquired behaviour patterns, common knowledge, conventions, and identification markers, which are shared by members of a given community and passed on either consciously or unconsciously.

In the first essay Konrad Schröder of Augsburg University in Bavaria looks at languages in Europe. The language we speak, the accent we adopt, the vocabulary we use – these are major determinants of our identity, of the way we categorize the world, and of how others categorize us. In a wider perspective, the problems created by the variety of languages spoken in Europe are undeniable, but the author urges that we should strive to maintain this variety as a source of cultural richness. Repressive policies with regard to minority languages are unacceptable since they lead to cultural deprivation, and educational disadvantage and reduce equality of opportunity. Supporting language variety is seen as a factor contributing to political stability in Europe. Schröder maps out the linguistic characteristics and geographical distribution of the European languages (showing that linguistic and political maps of Europe look quite different) and discusses the emergence of the major languages and loss of minority languages from an historical perspective. He looks at the problems of migrants, linking linguistic, cultural and educational aspects. He also discusses the feasibility and desirability of the use of English as the single accepted *lingua franca* in Europe. Finally, he argues strongly for a particular model of language provision in European schools in order to overcome the barriers between different linguistic communities.

Education is another major factor in the formation of our individual and collective identity. A shared curriculum, calculated to enhance our sense of belonging to a particular nation and including a more or less hidden set of attitudes and values, makes it much easier to communicate and feel at ease with people educated in the same tradition. An understanding of the factors determining our own education and that of our European counterparts, as well as practical knowledge of the systems in which we have been educated may help us to be more sensitive to variations in value-judgements, styles of argument and tastes.

In the second essay Bob Moon of the UK Open University looks in particular at patterns of provision in the secondary sector across Europe. Taking an historical perspective, he shows that education has always encouraged the crossing of political or cultural boundaries. Yet, despite their common roots, the various systems of national education now display considerable differences with regard to provision across the ability range, final qualifications, teaching styles and patterns of control.

The author also addresses the question of the democratization of education in Europe, noting how the diversity of European secondary and higher education began with the spread of universal education. Attending school in another country has its own difficulties. At a very practical level, bringing structures and content closer together would at the very least remove a barrier to mobility of workers with families within Europe and contribute towards comparability of qualifications. A little more flexibility on the part of school bureaucracies might also help since, as the author shows, European curricula share the same philosophical background and there is broad consensus on the major strands.

Education is high on the political agenda in many European countries; there is a tendency to insist that schools provide remedies for social problems, whilst at the same time producing a highly-skilled workforce. Some educationists are responding by observing practice in different countries within Europe, looking for solutions to what are seen to be problems on a common agenda. The author identifies many common concerns, for example, the ways and means of ensuring equality of opportunity for all, in all sectors from higher to vocational education (including special provision for girls); questions of how to measure the effectiveness of schools in societies expecting efficient use of declining public resources; the provision of adequate and equitable opportunities for life-long learning, including open/distance education.

Finally a brief overview is given of the many European action programmes designed to encourage exchange in this sector, from students in school to university professors.

Europe is on the way to becoming the biggest single media-market in the world and the fight is on to corner the largest share of that market. In the world of TV and radio, where, historically, public provision has been the order of the day, there has been a resistance in some quarters to privatization, invoking a dread vision of American commerical practices in Europe. Furthermore, over the last decade or so, there has been a revolution in the capacity to transmit visual and verbal messages and information. The traffic is such that there is an increasing concern about quality.

The authors of the third essay, co-workers at the Media Institute of Hamburg University, take stock of the present situation in Europe, looking first at the development of the mass media in Europe since Gutenberg. The reader is introduced to some key questions of media research today; for example, the question of the effects of mass communication, selectivity of reception, agenda-setting by the media, stereotyping, and the intercultural role of the media in Europe. The authors describe the present media structures within Europe, the ownership and networking of the multinational media companies and the attempts to provide multinational programming. They discuss the effects of commercialization on European TV film production and of American dominance of this market on European culture.

Critical themselves of the concept of a European cultural identity, they attempt to assess the contribution the mass media might make to the integration of culture in Europe. They look at the problems of overcoming linguistic boundaries in the conception of multinational programmes, but also at how to preserve the rich diversity of media provision in Europe.

A recurrent feature is the tension between tendencies towards integration or unification and the seemingly opposite tendencies towards the preservation of diversity and difference. The former can lead to improvements in mutual understanding or greater equality. The latter can promote cultural variety and an awareness of different cultural contexts. Both are possibly creative and problem-solving strategies, depending on how far a given situation is dictated by tradition, political opportunism, or economic necessity – factors which on the one hand tend to affect the convergence of cultural phenomena or on the other hand accentuate differences thereby creating new levels of differentiation. This theme is also a *leitmotif* of the last essay by Wolfgang Kaschuba, of the Humboldt University in Berlin, who discusses those day-to-day rituals and routines which govern so much of our waking lives.

Professor Kaschuba investigates the minutiae of everyday living in Europe. His aim is to provide the reader with the tools to perceive and understand their own and foreign *cultural practice*, that is to say the forms and conventions of day-to-day life. The essay is not intended to be merely a European family album of so many carefully arranged snapshots; but more a collection of optical instruments which should help us to focus better when observing our own and other cultures. The all-pervading 'hidden' socialization imparted to each and every one of us, day in, day out, by our immediate environment leads to deep-seated habits and assumptions of whose origins we are no longer aware. Few of our daily actions are performed by chance. On the contrary, the majority of our actions follow a strict everyday logic, conforming to a set of habits, experiences and conventions which we share with those in our immediate surroundings and which we take for granted. Naturally, in most respects, these patterns follow very general rules applicable to any civilized society, but there are subtle variations which can cause misunderstandings when we move into different social, ethnic or national groups.

The essay begins with an introduction to ways of perceiving and categorizing the substance of day-to-day life. This should help us to assess the significance of everyday culture and to understand better the actions and reactions of ourselves and our European neighbours and to realize where – and why – we share common assumptions and where we differ. This is followed by a wide range of examples of cultural practice mainly from western Europe, which reveal both variety and commonality in everyday life and culture. It is hoped that readers will relate these examples to their own daily experiences and go on to reflect on the significance of these practices in their own cultural settings.

Essay 1
Languages

*Prepared for the Course Team by Konrad Schröder,
Professor of English, University of Augsburg.
Translated by Dinah Cannell*

> It is impossible to translate the idiosyncrasies of each language; every
> word, from the most arcane down to the simplest, is permeated by the
> particular nature of the nation, be it in character, outlook or
> circumstances.
>
> *Goethe: Italienische Reise, I*

Many languages, one world

Multilingualism as the rule

A superficial look at a map might suggest that the world is made up of monolingual blocks: in the west, the Anglo-Saxon countries; in the east, the mighty empires of China and what was the Soviet Union, with Spanish-speaking Central and South America flanked by yet more vast English-speaking territories in the shape of South Africa, Australia, New Zealand and even India, where English is spoken by the ruling classes everywhere and is the major language of higher education. Yet appearances can be deceptive. Whilst large areas of the world officially proclaim themselves monolingual, in practice many of their inhabitants speak a variety of minority languages. Minorities generally speak more than one language and those who come into contact (in whatever fashion) with minority communities are increasingly called upon to speak more than one language themselves. In the United Kingdom, the motherland of English, large numbers of British citizens speak a huge variety of minority languages such as Urdu, Gujarati, Creole, Turkish, Italian and Welsh. Afro-Asian 'community languages' are spoken by rapidly growing numbers of people, a phenomenon paralleled by a process of ghettoization. In the United States, Spanish is the language making most rapid advances, whereas native Indian languages are gaining prominence in South America. The non-Russian peoples of the former Soviet Union are no longer willing to accept Russian as the dominant language. On the Indian subcontinent, ethnic and linguistic rivalry is on the increase, where Hindi and the Tamil languages are the major opponents and English – as a post-colonial bridge between these cultures – is not attacked. What will the linguistic map of South Africa look like once human rights can no longer be withheld from the black majority and major tribal languages become important ethnic and political factors? And how linguistically pure are those far-flung areas of white settlement (as seen from the traditional European perspective) such as Australia and New Zealand?

Many languages

Some 3000 languages are now spoken around the world; exact figures cannot be advanced, since the transition from dialect to recognized language is a fluid one. What is beyond doubt is that only 155 of these languages (5.2 per cent) are mother tongue to more than a million people and only 55 languages (1.8 per cent) are spoken by more than ten million native speakers.

In an increasingly intermeshing, centralized world there is a strong possibility that 95 per cent of the languages spoken today will have no long-term prospects of survival:

> A language is generally thought to be thriving if its speakers can be educated, administered, judged and informed in it. Providing these services in minority languages is an expense which many countries cannot, or do not wish to afford. To provide a single text-book for Rhaeto-Romanic speakers in Switzerland, for instance, costs around SF200,- per copy because of the very small numbers involved. For commercial providers of information, small linguistic communities are an unattractive economic proposition, so market forces tend to operate against variety here. Threatened languages in Europe include Corsican, Galician, Occitan, Ladino and Sard. Although the fates of languages can sometimes be dramatically reversed, as seen in the case of Catalan after the end of the Franco era, a Bulgarian researcher into lesser-used languages, Svetoslav Kolev, fears that some fifteen of Europe's tongues – and the civilization of the ethnic minorities which speak them – will be extinct within the next hundred years.
>
> *(The European, 20–26 February 1992)*

An illustration of what this means for the earth's cultural heritage, drawing on the example of Europe, will be given later in this essay.

Reliable statistics on the spread of languages across the world are hard to come by and there are flagrant inconsistencies between the standard sources. Time-lapses between data collections in different countries are seldom synchronized, so this distorts figures too. Linguists nevertheless hazard a 'league table' of the world's major languages. Table 1 was compiled in 1990 on the basis of plausible data from a variety of accepted sources and official statements. Languages are ranked according to numbers of native speakers and several interesting factors emerge.

A non-European language, mandarin Chinese, tops the table (770 million), followed by English (415 million). Only three other European languages have more than 100 million native speakers: Spanish (285 million), Portuguese/ Brazilian (160 million) and Russian (115 million) – all with lower teaching priority in western Europe than, say, French. Non-European languages, learnt only by a handful of exotic students in Europe, are, however, up in the 100 million-plus bracket; Hindi (290 million), Arabic (170 million), Bengali (165 million) and Indonesian (125 million).

Table 1   Numbers of (mother-tongue) speakers of selected languages spoken around the world

Current world ranking	*Million*	*Language*	*Countries*
1	770	Mandarin	China
2	415	English	Great Britain, North America, Australia, South Africa, Ireland, Commonwealth countries
3	290	Hindi	India
4	285	Spanish	Spain, Central and South America
5	170	Arabic	(all Arab countries)
6	165	Bengali	India and Bangladesh
7	160	Portuguese	Portugal, Brazil, Angola, Mozambique
8	125	Bahasa	Indonesia, Bahasa
9	120	Japanese	Japan
10	115	Russian	former USSR (Russian-speaking areas)
11	92	German	Germany, Austria, Switzerland
12	55	French	France, (former French colonies)
15	55	Italian	Italy
22	50	Turkish	Turkey
26	42	Ukrainian	Ukraine
27	34	Polish	Poland
38	23	Romanian	Romania, Moldavian Republic
40	20	Dutch	Netherlands, Belgium
42	18	Croatian/Serbian	Yugoslavia (Croatia, Serbia)
55	11	Czech	Czechoslovakia
61	9	Bulgarian	Bulgaria
63	9	Greek	Greece
65	9	Swedish	Sweden
89	5	Albanian	Albania
91	5	Danish	Denmark
92	5	Finnish	Finland
94	5	Norwegian	Norway
112	4	Slovak	Slovenia
131	3	Lithuanian	Lithuania
177	1.2	Estonian	Estonia
205	0.7	Irish	Ireland
206	0.5	Welsh	Great Britain
212	0.7	Basque	Spain

Source: Finkenstaedt and Schröder, 1990, p. 14. See also Haarman, 1975 and Decsy, 1986. On the problem of correlating linguistic data, see Haarman, 1983, p. 102.

German (92 million), next to Russian, is Europe's 'biggest' language (only 60 million Europeans have English as their mother tongue) and ranks number 11 worldwide, well ahead of French and Italian (each with 55 million). Yet the 'smallest' of the currently recognized EC languages, Danish, is nevertheless spoken by 5 million native speakers, whereas Irish Gaelic, one of the two official languages of the Republic of Ireland and the supreme embodiment of independent Irish-Celtic culture, counts indisputably, with a mere 0.7 million speakers, as one of the world's 'endangered languages' now threatened with extinction.

Minority languages

Even in a world of clearly circumscribed, historically unified nations, matched by a range of culturally-specific national languages, communication between states would be difficult enough. The situation is, however, more complex than that. The lesser-used languages in the EC countries tend to be concentrated in mountainous or coastal areas; a map of the dissolving socialist states in the east would be dotted with small linguistic communities. Table 2 gives comparative numbers of speakers in the larger minority groups across northern and western Europe. Sometimes such languages are given tender loving care, as in the case of Sorb in the former GDR; elsewhere the reaction to them is one of hatred – witness the fate of Serbian in pockets of Croatia now (in 1992) that the latter is on the road to autonomy.

Centrally-administered France, with its 54.6 million inhabitants, is home to an unrecorded figure of native speakers of Occitan, 1.5 million Alsatian speakers, 1.4 million Breton speakers, 0.4 million Flemish speakers, around 0.3 million Catalan speakers and 90,000 Basque speakers. Central government language policies remain controversial. Neither Occitan nor Alsatian have been granted the status of autonomous languages. Demoted to the level of *patois* (a local dialect overlaid by the majority language) the socially explosive potential presumably inherent in those idioms will be defused. The exercise has proved much more difficult in the case of Basque, Breton, Flemish and Catalan.

There is also the well-known Belgian phenomenon. Europe has almost learned to live with the age-old language battle between Flemish and Walloon – or, another way of looking at it, between Dutch and French. Dutch versus French means Germanic culture versus Romance culture, with the attendant struggle for influence within the state. The language conflict was not to be solved by the introduction of German as the third official language – harking back to the German past of the administrative districts of Eupen and Malmedy which belonged to the German *Reich* until 1918.

The languages of immigrant communities

Not all languages spoken by minority groups count, however, as *bona fide* minority languages. Around the world, and more especially in the EC countries, immigrant communities are speaking languages which will not become genuine *minority* languages until a generation or two has passed. The Spanish spoken in the United States, for example, is still an immigrant language. In contrast to the true minorities, immigrants lack the centuries-long contact with the majority culture and with the majority language of the nation or nations in which they live. The first few generations of immigrants characteristically finish up speaking two languages only half competently. Mother-tongue proficiency fades alarmingly fast in the absence of proper links with the home culture and, in many cases, as a result of dispersion within the host community. Equally, acquisition of the language of the host country is deficient, a handicap compounded by the fact that schooling frequently leaves much to be desired. The result is social disadvantage and ghettoization. To an outsider the United Kingdom might seem to be monolingual, but quite apart from the Welsh and Scottish Gaelic languages, around one hundred languages are in fact spoken within its borders as the mother tongues of immigrant groups. Some of these have become genuine minority languages; when the Patient's Charter was published, the government thought it necessary to publish it in nine languages for minorities with considerable numbers of speakers – Bengali, Gujarati, Hindi, Punjabi, Urdu, Chinese, Vietnamese, Greek and Turkish.

The only minority languages playing an official role in schools in the Federal Republic of Germany are Danish (with 50,000 native speakers recorded in official statistics) and Sorb (no official data available on the number of native speakers). North Frisian, another minority language (with 60,000 native speakers) does enjoy recognition, but exists very much in a backwater. As for Low German, the biggest minority language in the country, its fate is similar to that of Occitan in France; notwithstanding the federal structure of Germany, the number of mother-tongue speakers does not figure in the official statistics. The powers-that-be tend to view Low German as no more than a dialect of the standard idiom. Furthermore, as many as 8.2 per cent of the citizens of the former (pre-1991) eleven West German *Länder*[1] are in fact the *Gastarbeiter*[2] and their dependants. The cultural ties between these groups and the population of the host country are often tenuous, as is certainly the case with Germany's largest contingent of *Gastarbeiter*: the 1.5 million Turks, with their very different native culture. Over the past thirty years, a spirit of *laissez-faire* has pervaded the Federal Republic's cultural and educational attitudes towards these immigrant workers. There has been no coherent policy in the schools, nor have any consistent efforts been made in the direction of acculturation. For far too long, the authorities have simply assumed that, after a spell working in Germany, the *Gastarbeiter* and their families would go back to their countries of origin. The consequences of this approach have already been hinted at: a second generation which is semi-competent in two languages, plus a marked trend towards ghettoization in the big cities.

Such examples reveal how, in the course of this century, well-nigh monolingual European states (in particular) have, often imperceptibly, turned multilingual. The implications of this shift have yet to become clear.

---

[1] *Translator's note:* Germany consists of 16 *Länder*, a *Land* being a state within the Federal Republic with a considerable degree of autonomy, especially in educational and cultural affairs.

[2] *Translator's note:* Immigrant workers from Southern Europe 'invited' into Germany as 'guests' in order to take up employment contracts, the idea being that they should return home upon termination of those contracts.

If we look at the behaviour of individual human beings, we soon discover that, more often than not, they feel perfectly at home expressing themselves in different ways. Whilst still speaking in their mother tongue, people are able to operate in several 'keys', correctly employing different 'codes' according to the circumstances. They might speak sometimes in dialect, sometimes in the standard idiom; they will use professional jargon at work and, in social intercourse, the language of their particular social group.

English as international language

'As the twentieth century winds down, English is the closest thing to a world language the earth has ever had ...', proclaimed the leader article in the May 1992 edition of British Airways *Highlife* magazine (pp. 102–12). All very fine for native speakers of English, but alongside the 415 million people world-wide who have English as their mother tongue, there are 800 million whose English is no more than a *lingua franca*,[3] an instrument of basic communication.

English is second language to a further 800 million, whose command is near-native. Apart from Latin, English is probably the only language in the history of mankind where the number of non-mother tongue speakers outstrips the number of native speakers. Time alone will tell whether English is destined to share the fate of Latin, i.e. to become progressively splintered, ultimately serving as a springboard for the development of new languages (a possibility in post-colonial Africa and Asia). Like Latin, English has a 'neutral' form (the old King's/Queen's English), plus at least two accepted standard forms (British and American English). Latin made way for Vulgar Latin, which in turn provided the foundation for the Romance languages. In the case of English, too, centrifugal forces are to be found alongside centripetal tendencies. Native speakers of English would, for instance, be hard pressed to understand the popular creolized forms of the language which have evolved in West Africa.

One world speaking one language is a Utopian dream. We should not even discuss the idea of having a single language in Europe as the language of some kind of constituted ruling power; such an idea would be the beginning of the end of the possibility of a united Europe. For better or worse, what we have in this post-Babel world is linguistic diversity. Even in our 'new Europe', the concept of nationhood will continue to thrive in the shape of identification with a culturally autonomous European region. Charles de Gaulle coined the phrase '*l'Europe des patries*' and it is no coincidence that people are picking up that idea again today. Interpreters are certainly necessary, but in the end must be considered an inadequate aid. There is only one way towards a widespread polyglottism in Europe, a way which is achievable by means of a lifelong acquisition of foreign languages, whose starting point must be more intensive and diverse language teaching at an early age.

---

[3] *Lingua franca:* literally, language of the Franks. This was the language used since the early Middle-Ages in the Mediterranean area, mainly to facilitate trade between Christians and Arabs. It has subsequently been used as a description of a language used for communication between several different linguistic communities.

Table 2, compiled largely from official documents, sheds light on the picture regarding Europe's minority communities and immigrant workers, illustrating just how many languages coexist within national borders. We should keep in mind, of course, that different languages do have affinities with one another, as the following section will reveal. Most Europeans – even those with no prior language training – are capable of understanding a certain amount of what is said or written in languages close to their own. In addition, more and more 'international' terms are being used across the languages. When we watch foreign parliamentary coverage on TV, we may even find ourselves picking up the odd word in, say, Russian – if the original is allowed to break through the voice-over.

Table 2   European states: inhabitants, minority-language speakers, immigrant workers

State	*Inhabitants*	*Minority-language speakers*		*Immigrant workers*		
Belgium	9,888,000	German	100,000		885,700 = 9%	(1982)
		Flemish	5,300,000			
		Walloon	3,200,000			
Denmark	5,150,000	German	20,000			
Germany	78,000,000	Danish	50,000		4,630,000	(1987)
		North Frisian		Greek:	300,800	(1982)
				Italian:	601,600	(1982)
				Spanish:	173,500	(1982)
				Turkish:	1,580,700	(1982)
				Yugoslav:	631,700	(1982)
					4,459,100 = 8.2%	
Finland	5,844,000	Lappish	3,800			
		Swedish	345,000			
France	54,613,000	Occitan-speakers	3,500,000			
		Breton	1,400,000			
		Catalan	280,000			
		Alsatian	1,500,000			
		Flemish	400,000			
Great Britain	55,681,000	Welsh	503,549	+ 100 languages spoken by		
		Scottish Gaelic	–	immigrants		
Italy	56,753,000	Sardinian	1,450,000		542,600 = 3.8%	
		South Tyrolian	235,000			
		Occitan-speaker	100,000			
		Greek	36,000			
		Corsican	200,000			
Netherlands	14,531,000					
Norway	4,158,000	Lappish	38,000			
Austria	7,525,000	Croat	37,828			
		Slovenes	25,472			
		Hungarian	4,141			
Sweden	8,353,000	Lapp	8,500		405,500 = 4.9% (1982)	
Spain	38,865,000	Catalan	7,500,000			
		Basque	525,000			
		Galician	2,619,615			

Source: Finkenstaedt and Schröder, 1990, p. 16.

Tower of Babel (undated) (credit: Mansell Collection, London).
The Tower of Babel has been a popular theme throughout the history of art.
These two representations present very different interpretations of that theme.

Notwithstanding all this diversity, English will continue to assert its role as a common language within Europe, although there will be limiting factors – time doubtless being one of them. Europe should certainly not construct its language policy around the assumption of English dominance.

Tower of Babel (1928) by M. Escher (credit: Escher Foundation, Haags Gemeentemuseum, The Hague; ©1928 M.C. Escher/Cordon Art, Baarn, Holland).

Bearing all this in mind, a critical look needs to be taken at certain current theories of language teaching. It has been claimed in some quarters that a broader spectrum of foreign-language teaching overloads the curriculum and leads to discrimination; students can end up being deprived of the chance to gain early mastery of the *lingua franca* or 'world language'. Throughout Europe, the overall success of English-language teaching has been rather modest, despite wide-ranging efforts in the schools, and this of course could lead people to conclude that even more money and energy needs to be poured into promoting English.

More English tuition is not the answer, however, even in terms of practical language competence. This leads rather to an absolutely one-sided orientation on one specific culture, namely the Anglo-Saxon, or to a negation of the link between language and culture, both in the classroom and in society in general, a tendency which prepares the ground for cultural alienation. All that happens is that people become caught within specifically Anglo-Saxon cultural parameters. A tendency develops, both in the classroom and in everyday life, to suppress the link between language and culture, thus preparing the ground for cultural alienation – the corollary of the denial of regional identity. We have already seen the negative repercussions of this cycle.

As we shall see in the following pages, multilingualism is a political imperative in our multicultural world; educating young people to become multilingual adults may prove much more important than a lot of things which now rank as sacrosanct on the syllabuses of Europe's schools.

On the history and geography of European languages

Indo-European languages

Nearly all of the languages found in Europe today are of Indo-European origin; working back from characteristics they share in common, it is possible to reconstruct an initial parent language. In reality, this parent language probably comprised a group of several primitive and interrelated dialects, spoken by people living around 4000 BC in the Caspian Sea area. Offshoots of these dialects spread as far as India (Hindi) and out across the whole of Europe. The Celtic settlers who occupied large parts of the continent during the last millenium BC would have spoken an idiom derived from one of the Indo-European language branches. Henceforward, Celtic dialects were to become superimposed upon the pre-Indo-European languages (whose origins remain unknown) spoken in the Alps, the Rhineland, the British Isles and also in France and Spain; Basque is possibly the only idiom that can be traced back to this language group. Other significant Indo-European branches are: Germanic (initially spoken in Scandinavia and the Baltic); Latin and its derivatives: the Romance languages (spoken from the Danube delta to the west coast of Portugal); Slavonic (spoken throughout eastern Europe and across to the rivers Elbe and Main and the Adriatic coast); Albanian;

other Indo-European languages – Baltic (Latvia, Lithuania); and, lastly, Greek, which would prove so important for the future linguistic development of Europe. A mere glance at this list is enough to ascertain that the Indo-European languages have been uneven in their geographical spread right from the very beginning, with further shifts taking place as history has moved on. Take Albanian or the Baltic languages, for example, and compare their influence with that of the Germanic and Slavonic groups. Celtic used to be the most important Indo-European language in Europe, yet now it survives in purely residual form (Breton and Welsh representing the southern branch, Irish and Scottish Gaelic the northern).

Despite their common European origins, the different language families have grown apart to the extent that, for most people, they seem to be totally disparate and mutually unintelligible. Language experts see this rather differently: the American linguist, Benjamin Lee Whorf, for instance, examining the differences between Hopi languages and comparing these with the differences between the major European languages in 1939, coined the term Standard Average European (SAE!) to denote the group of West-European Germanic and Romance languages, which he found to be much more similar, according to various linguistic criteria. Within the same branch major similarities can be observed even by non-linguists, although the distance between individual languages can vary considerably. Spanish and Portuguese, for example, are closer to one another than Spanish and French. German dialects spoken near the Dutch border are very like the Dutch dialects spoken near the German border; people understand each other without needing to learn their neighbour's idiom. Dutch and German-speakers, however, find the languages of the Scandinavian branch of the Germanic group virtually incomprehensible, particularly in their spoken form. Nevertheless, closer examination uncovers many parallels in vocabulary and syntax. Anyone who manages to master a West Slavonic language (Czech, say), is able to understand other West Slavonic tongues (Polish, Sorb, Slovak, etc.). Russian and Bulgarian might not prove quite so easy, but something will filter through even here.

It is not always easy to distinguish between a dialect and a language; the boundaries tend to be blurred. Until a standard or official language emerges, or a national tongue, we find regional dialects mutually coexisting. These can be classified into groups and charted genealogically, but once a particular dialect is upgraded to language status (for economic or political reasons), it will henceforth dominate all the other dialects within its sphere of influence and they will degenerate into patois. What characterizes a patois is that it is subservient to an overlying idiom, be it standard, official or national. Patois forms thus enjoy lower social prestige than dialects. Established languages can become relegated to the rank of patois in the wake of national unification or as part of a move towards centralized political organization. Sad examples of this process of attrition are the dialects of northern England, which gave way to Queen's (Standard) English; Low German idioms (Low German was the language of the Hanseatic league and has its own specific literary tradition, but since the seventeenth century it has been increasingly superceded by High German, thereby losing its position as an official language); and the various forms of the *langue d'oc* in southern France, where several closely related – and competing – regional languages fell victim in the early part of the modern period to the centralizing tendencies first of Versailles, then Paris. In our times, regionalization and the rise of New Ethnicity – a re-emphasizing of identification with a relatively small ethnic group or regional culture, irrespective of political boundaries or allegiances – have led to the revival of local idioms or even to the creation of new languages; witness the development and growing social acceptance of Modified Standard (i.e. English spoken with a northern accent, in particular). Letzeburgesh (the language of Luxembourg) is really no more than a variant of the German Moselle-Franconian dialect and is readily understood by any German from the central Rhineland or Moselle area. Yet the Grand Duchy of Luxembourg is an independent state, with a separate sense of national identity, so its particular dialect was upgraded and now enjoys full language status. In Alsace the locals regard Alsatian as a language, although from a strictly linguistic point of view it is really no more than an Alemannic dialect of High German. The point is that they feel more French than German, despite the fact that their cultural roots and language lie in the Germanic world. As the Yugoslav Federation collapses so will the artificial linguistic creation, Serbo-Croat, which held the state together. For although Serbian and Croatian are in reality closely-related dialects of South Slavonic, in some ways closer to one another than the patois of New York is to that of Edinburgh, in the wake (once again) of moves towards national independence, each is being upgraded to national language status. This artificial differentiation is further underscored by the fact that the Croats use Latin script whilst the Serbs are opting with more determination than ever for the Cyrillic alphabet.

More will be said later about language and identity, picking up on what has been touched on here.

The following list gives a rough breakdown of the Indo-European languages found in Europe, classified according to language family:

Germanic languages

North Germanic branch: all the Scandinavian languages, with the exception of Finnish and Lapp and including Faroese and Icelandic

West Germanic branch: Low German, High German, Dutch, Frisian, English

Romance languages

West Romanic branch: Italian, Rhaeto-Romanic, French, Catalan, Spanish, Portuguese

East Romanic branch: Romanian

Slavonic languages

East Slavonic branch: Russian, Ukrainian, Bulgarian

West Slavonic branch: Polish, Sorb, Czech, Slovak

South Slavonic branch: Slovene, Croatian, Serbian, Macedonian

Celtic languages: Breton, Welsh, Irish Gaelic, Scottish Gaelic

ARCTIC CIRCLE

ICELAND

Faeroes

NORWAY

SWEDEN

FINLAND

Helsinki

St. Petersburg

THE
RUSSIAN
FEDERATION

Oslo

Stockholm

ESTONIA

LATVIA

LITHUANIA

BELARUS

UNITED
KINGDOM

EIRE

DENMARK

Copenhagen

NETHER-
LANDS

London

BELGIUM

Berlin

Warsaw

POLAND

UKRAINE

Paris

GERMANY

Prague

CZECHOSLOVAKIA

FRANCE

SWITZERLAND

Vienna

AUSTRIA

Budapest

HUNGARY

SLOVENIA

CROATIA

ROMANIA

Bucharest

PORTUGAL

Lisbon

Madrid

SPAIN

ITALY

CORSICA

Rome

SARDINIA

Belgrade

YUGOSLAVIA

ALBANIA

BULGARIA

GREECE

SICILY

	Celtic		Romance		Slavic		Germanic		Albanian

Other Indo-European Languages   Basque   Finno-Ugric

The different language groups in Europe.

25

Baltic languages: Lithuanian, Latvian (Lettish)
Albanian
Greek
This list is not exhaustive; several of the more minor languages have been omitted and the status of a series of idioms has not been established.

Non-Indo-European languages

A few non-Indo-European languages are also to be found in Europe; Basque has already been mentioned in this context. Numerically-speaking, however, the Finno-Ugric group is of greater significance, comprising (from north to south): Lapp, Finnish, Estonian and Hungarian. Unlike Basque – the sole surviving idiom from the European Neolithic age – the Finno-Ugric language family is of Asiatic, i.e. Ural-Altaic origin. The ancestors of today's Finns and Hungarians lived, up until the fifth century AD, in the expanses of Siberia, while the forefathers of the Turks came from Central Asia. In contrast with the inflecting languages of the Indo-European family (with their genitive, dative, accusative, vocative, instrumental and prepositional uses), the aforementioned Asiatic languages are agglutinating; for instance, the preposition becomes a 'post-position', placed at the end of the noun: 'out of the port of Helsinki' becomes 'Helsinki-the port-out-of'. We are, in other words, dealing with languages which operate quite differently from the Indo-European group. In Finnish, a verb expresses negation and the interrogative is formed using an interrogative particle suffixed to the first word in the interrogative clause. Yet these languages function as efficiently and effectively, with the same degree of logicality – or illogicality – as the Indo-European idioms.

English – a mixed language

In the list given above, English is classified as a Germanic language. Nonetheless, it is often referred to as a mixed language, since it contains a large proportion of French and Latin words. Highly formal written language even contains whole constructions modelled on Latin, e.g. 'The minister having declared the motorway open, traffic was allowed onto the new road' is reminiscent of a certain *ablative absolute* construction in Latin. Modern linguistic analysis of the forms of modern English confirms, however, that English is fundamentally a Germanic idiom: in its vocabulary, its facility for compound formation, its everyday sentence structure and its very way of categorizing the world. Speakers of both Germanic and Romance languages have equal ease of access to English (since it is mixed) and this is surely one of the reasons why it has become such an 'international' tongue. What is more, over its 2000-year history – thanks to close contact first with Viking dialects, then with Old French – it has managed to shed nearly all its inflected forms.

Language hierarchies and social dialects

So far we have looked at geographical and historical considerations of language but these alone do not do full justice to the variety of European language forms. There are social hierarchies within language, just as there are structural and other variants. Regional organization and social stratification sometimes go hand-in-hand: traditionally, the dialects spoken in the north of England are seen as socially inferior. Until well into the nineteenth century, there were no universities in northern England, the population consisting largely of farm and factory workers. The expansion of the universities into the North, starting with Durham and culminating in the Second University Extension of the 1960s and 1970s caused shifts in the hierarchy; as social – and hence educational – barriers came down, the English spoken in the north of the country climbed to the status of Modified Standard. The fact that 'Scottish English' has been more widely accepted through time than that spoken south of the Tweed is due to Scotland's having been an independent kingdom up until 1603. Even after that, it had its own parliament until 1707 and, right into this century, enjoyed a broader-based education system, with twice as many universities as England (St Andrews, Glasgow, Aberdeen, Edinburgh) and only one tenth of the population. From the middle of the 18th century, Edinburgh became renowned as a 'republic of erudition', which had positive repercussions on the social respectability of the Edinburgh accent.

Hierarchical factors come into play in practically all the European languages. Soviet linguists were particularly keen on the subject in the 1920s. The thesis being advanced then was that similarities within the speech of working-class people (regardless of language spoken) distinguished their utterances from those of the exploiting classes; the notion of international solidarity thus penetrated the realm of linguistic theory.

Language and culture

Historical perspectives

The newly born nation states of the sixteenth and seventeenth centuries, with England and France to the fore, were determined to see the dialects spoken in their particular capital cities promoted to the status of nationwide languages. National languages thus became symbols of sovereignty, cultivated so as to place them on a par with Latin and enable them to take over as the language of science, literature and the arts. The cultivation of language practised by the 'educators' (grammar school teachers and tutors to princes) in Tudor England, together with parallel efforts by the Pléiade poets in France (with Joachim du Bellay and his *Défense et illustration de la langue française* of 1549 at the fore) pointed the way ahead for other European states. At the same time, these new nation states, and in particular France, began to experience the need to promote their own national language abroad, using it as a vehicle for foreign and cultural policy, as well as for power politics. The Renaissance thus also marked the birth of language policy. Europe's most successful nation in this regard, France, managed to turn French into the international language of the eighteenth century, thus broadly supplanting Latin as the Euro-language.

Language and the people – language and the nation

The developments just outlined involve equating language and nation (or people – *Volk*[4]). In the Romantic period, when language and nation were seen as primal forces of human existence, this equation was invested with particular ideological emphasis. As the nineteenth and twentieth centuries moved on, this misguided language-nation parallel produced devastating results. In some instances, attempts were made to 'incorporate' foreign regions speaking the language of another nation state (the spurious rationale being: the people of Alsace and Lorraine speak German, therefore they are German, therefore the German Reich must be extended to take in Alsace and Lorraine; the Austrians speak German, hence Austria must be absorbed by the Reich). In other cases, entire ethnic communities, who happened not to speak the relevant national language, were resettled so as to create linguistically homogeneous areas; witness what happened in the Soviet Union under Stalin, or in Poland and Czechoslovakia after 1945, where the decision to expel ethnic Germans had its language policy component. Looking back at a statement made in France in 1972 by the then Prime Minister, Georges Pompidou, demonstrates how top political figures can still harbour outmoded ideas: *'Il n'y pas de place pour les langues minoritaires dans une France destinée à marquer l'Europe de son sceau'* ('There is no place for minority languages in a France whose destiny is to stamp its mark upon Europe'), he pronounced. Put bluntly, this meant that France still upheld visions of exercising cultural hegemony over Europe even though such a strategy would necessarily involve withholding from its own minority communities the fundamental right to speak their own language. The national language appears as an instrument in the power-politics of the nation-state. In France this line of thought has a long tradition.

This is not the place for sweeping anthropological assertions about culture. One thing is important, however, against the backcloth of their different ethnic origins, the nations of Europe have, over the past 500 years, consciously encouraged the growth of national traditions and cultures, which are autonomous variations of a European culture rooted in the Latin culture of the Christian Middle Ages, and therefore in the Greco-Roman cultures of antiquity. National cultural traditions bear the imprint of language; national languages are manifestations of national cultural traditions. Beneath this top layer of national values lie older regional cultures, themselves bearing the imprint of regional languages (e.g. Breton in France).

It does not really matter which definition of culture we use. Underpinning the cultural assumptions of the nineteenth and early twentieth centuries was the notion of the 'cultured bourgeoisie'[5] who would pay homage to literature and art and comply with an exacting moral canon. Today, however, we take a broader

---

[4] *Translator's note:* the cultural and political overtones of *Volk* cannot really be conveyed satisfactorily in English.

[5] *Translator's note:* the *Bildungsbürgertum*, a concept growing out of the Bismarck era, when 'education' became the watchword for the newly expanding middle class. The term in German has a slightly ironic edge – culture as ornament rather than true enlightenment.

view; culture spans the lives and works of all layers of society and if the definition includes a value judgement (in answer to the question What is Culture?), this will reflect the ideological background of the judgement. The term 'everyday culture' adequately subsumes this new modern notion. Language always mirrors the background culture of whoever is speaking; conversely, the thought-patterns of the speaker of any particular language are partly determined by the inherent concepts and symbols of that language. Consequently, linguistic variety is always an element of cultural enrichment.

Endangered species and endangered languages

Language and 'the people' (*Volk*) should not be equated with one another; still less should language and the nation. Language and culture areas are, however, congruent to a large extent. When a language dies, those who used to speak it find that their culture has lost its centre, becoming transmogrified as it moves into another language. Expressed in more extreme terms, when a language dies, then the culture which was expressed through it dies with it. These can, of course, be turned into museum pieces; we might even keep them in a state of artificial preservation but this, however, is no substitute for something living and growing.

There is plenty of talk nowadays about endangered species, yet languages and cultures can become endangered too. As we have seen before, there are a great many political, cultural and economic variables at play which have to be considered when assessing the vitality of a lesser-used language. It is therefore very difficult to say when a language has reached the critical threshold beyond which it is irrevocably launched along the path to extinction.

Unless the process is accelerated by wars or destructive intent, languages and cultures do not die overnight. Between the time when a tree begins to show signs of age – the first withered leaves – and the moment of its final demise, many years may pass; with languages, the process can take centuries. Over the last 200 years, quite a number of Europe's regional languages have become virtually extinct. Three examples spring to mind in the British Isles alone: Cornish (an idiom of Celtic origin, still widely spoken in the county as late as the eighteenth century), Manx (the Celtic dialect which was once the language of communication on the Isle of Man) and also Norn (the Old Norse/Viking language of the Orkneys and Shetlands, widely used into the eighteenth century). Manx is taken to have died out in the 1930s and early recordings of how it sounded can be obtained. British sources reckon there are some 1000 native speakers of Cornish alive today, although it would probably be more correct to refer to 'pseudo-native speakers', i.e. people who strongly empathize with the native culture of the region and have – in some ways artificially – acquired and 'revived' the Cornish language – it is more realistic to accept that Cornish became extinct in the nineteenth century. In Germany, the regional languages which have died out are: Elbe Slavonic (became extinct in the eighteenth century) and lower Sorb (most certainly died out in the nineteenth century, although the exact date is not known; attempts were made at revival in the Cottbus region between 1950 and 1990). The most noteworthy example from the Romance group is Dalmatian, which was last spoken by a Church dignitary who died in 1898.

A bilingual poster for the 'Autonomous Brittany' (Breton Autonomiste) movement, photographed in Rennes in 1973. Bretons are being urged to learn their language (credit: Roger Viollet, Paris).

Whether or not moribund languages should be given expensive life support – and, if so, for how long – is a matter for debate. Providing mother-tongue schooling for small groups of individuals whose numbers barely add up to a few thousand is extremely expensive, but then so is preserving endangered species. Maybe the world will just have to reconcile itself to paying the high cost of these things in future. Sustaining language and culture is part and parcel of an ecological approach towards society and it is doubtful whether life on earth can endure at a culturally acceptable standard without such a commitment.

From a medium-term perspective, many European languages lie well below the survival threshold, despite the sometimes desperate attempts to save them. Scottish Gaelic, Breton, Frisian, Upper Sorb and Alsatian are all cases in point. Numbers of Gaelic speakers are on the decrease, notwithstanding the rise of New Ethnicity in Scotland, especially in the Hebrides, and in spite of the fact that Gaelic is now regularly taught in the primary schools of the islands concerned. The fate of Breton hangs in the balance, bearing in mind the Pompidou proclamation alluded to above. Frisian is virtually confined to a small area in the north of Holland, plus a smattering among the island populations. Lower and Upper Sorb (see above) fitted nicely into the political agenda of the former GDR and were cosseted as the idioms of a fraternal Slavonic people, kept down by hundreds of years of centralized administration on the part of Prussia and the electors of Saxony. Time will tell whether things are set to change for the worse on that front with the new, post-1990 arrangements. (After all, the motto in Germany now is: the days of special status are over.) Alsatian, for its part, is overburdened by French and German. Very little is published in the languages we have been discussing; no specialist vocabularies exist; the idioms are hardly taught outside the areas where they are spoken; numbers of mother-tongue speakers are declining dramatically and there is by no means always a standard written form.

Perhaps we should look now at the major European languages and see how they are faring. Here, too, the first withered leaves – to stick with our metaphor – are beginning to show. Texts on microbiology, for example, are no longer published in Europe's second 'biggest' language, German; therefore a German technical vocabulary cannot possibly develop in this field. Likewise with 'computerese'; commands are always expressed in English. What, we may ask, of languages like Finnish and Danish? With more or less 5 million speakers each, they are further advanced along the road to perdition than other languages. All sorts of scientific material is no longer published in Finnish or Danish; films are hardly ever dubbed; specialist terminology either does not exist or is no longer employed and, understandably, few people learn the languages outside the areas where they are spoken. Finnish is particularly out on a limb because it is a Ural-Altaic language, with a reputation for being extraordinarily difficult to learn. When it comes to preserving the cultural heritage of Europe, however, its very rarity sets it apart as the epitome of a type of regional culture whose roots extend outside Europe.

Then we have Albanian, Lithuanian, Latvian, Estonian, Irish Gaelic (wishfully – and prematurely – branded 'Irish' as if it were *de facto* the first language of an Irish national state), Rhaeto-Romanic, Icelandic, Letzeburgesh. How are they going to make out? They do in fact form part of a set of 'minor' languages with enough life in them yet to survive a while without intensive care. There are sufficient native speakers for the creation of pressure groups at national level, which in turn means state subsidies. A prime example of this scenario is the case of Irish Gaelic. Until the first years of this century, the idiom was confined to a few linguistic pockets in the southwest of the Republic (known as Gaeltachts); in subsequent decades, however, a national renaissance took place and Gaelic became the focal point of national and cultural identification. Gaelic, referred to as 'Irish', began to figure as a subject on school and university curricula; a knowledge of Irish came to be a precondition for obtaining employment; pressure was brought to bear by the State (although the majority of the population were so caught up in the political fervour that they did not experience it as pressure). Observing the messianic spirit animating many a teacher of 'Irish' today, we cannot fail to be reminded of the appearance on the scene of Esperanto proponents. Although their enthusiasm may have bordered on the fanatical, it is understandable historically and in terms of cultural identity-building. The problem is that fanaticism is blind and state support programmes for national languages tend towards blindness too. The temptation is to elevate a particular language to the status of the absolute, which has a dampening effect on any international efforts to guarantee linguistic and cultural diversity.

An island location is undoubtedly an advantage when it comes to language conservation, whether we are talking about real islands in the middle of the ocean or those 'linguistic islands' with a sufficiently homogeneous population to hold them together. Icelandic and (to a lesser degree) Faroese thus enjoy comparatively good chances of survival. In the case of 'linguistic islands', the odds are at their highest where the local inhabitants rank their own culture above that of the surrounding area; maintaining their language is thereby equivalent to preserving their superiority. German-speaking communities in the Balkans, particularly in Yugoslavia and Romania, managed to hold out for centuries thanks to the fact that many of the original settlers had brought with them superior economic and technical know-how, which meant that their successors felt themselves to be invested with a cultural mission. Language and culture were also the only unbreakable links they preserved with German-speaking Central Europe, their lost homeland. Not to mention the fact that their native tongue was the one thing which held them together as a community, bearing in mind their very different social origins. These language islands developed their own insular linguistic forms, characterized by a certain archaic flavour.

Whereas island status can help to conserve a language, movements towards political unification generally lead to a reduction in the number of idioms used. The process of European integration, with the attendant threat of linguistic centralism (the motto being: English for all as *lingua franca*, with French thrown in as the language of culture), is not a unique phenomenon. Take the steps leading up to German unification and the creation of the German Reich in the nineteenth century; even here, linguistic impoverishment occurred, particularly in South Germany. The South German dialects, which in the multi-state era of the Holy Roman Empire had functioned virtually as state languages, gradually yielded up their status as written idioms. Having started out as self-sustaining dialects, they became downgraded to vernacular variants of the 'noble' tongue. Yet at the time of their demotion, the main southern German dialects could each claim several million speakers.

Into the black hole of language policy

One could raise the objection that almost all those European languages that can unquestionably be counted as 'big' from a world-wide perspective can and will survive very well, despite the doomladen predictions made here. Even if a language such as Finnish does not enjoy wide usage in scientific publications, there will always be sufficient native speakers who wish to read their daily paper in their native tongue; sufficient scientists anxious to chat with one another in Finnish when they are not bogged down in specialist terminology; enough poets for whom the language is their artistic medium and who will thus enhance and develop it. All well and good, but a note of scepticism should perhaps be sounded here; on the horizon lies something we might describe as the 'black hole' of language policy. The fewer the people who speak a language, the more expensive it is to publish in that language. Any book written in English, provided it is marketed properly, stands a chance of being sold around the world. Whereas 100,000 copies of an English book may be printed for the international market, barely more than 5000 would sell if a Finnish version were brought out. TV companies will dub American films into German, French or Italian, but not Finnish; that would be too expensive. Since books produced in the 'small' languages are costly, publishers in the relevant countries will inevitably ask themselves whether it would not be more expedient to publish right away in the 'international' tongue or one of the other 'big' languages. Once popular science and even teenage fiction start being published mainly in foreign languages, another stage in the downward spiral has been reached. The man and woman in the street, and members of the younger generation, are going to perceive their own language as of less practical use than those idioms which have supplanted it. The more people's native tongue declines in *de facto* worth, the larger the sums needed to be invested in teaching foreign languages (in the schools and elsewhere), since language-learning will have become a lifelong necessity. The corollary is that less time, resources and effort will be given to instilling in people a knowledge of their own mother tongue – originally their main source of cultural reference. The level of mother-tongue proficiency will thus sink still lower, the vicious circle will tighten and the poor language will to all intents and purposes be sucked into a black hole. National, or nationalistic, endeavours to salvage languages with subsidies (as with Irish Gaelic or Sorb) will counter the pull only as long as the money lasts or the political regime remains in place. The end result will inevitably be official transition to bilingualism (i.e. national language plus international language), where the dominant role of the international language is a foregone conclusion.

Yet there are no guarantees that speakers will attain anything like near-native proficiency in the new international tongue. The 'big' language countries have learnt how difficult it is for students to achieve proper command of their compulsory first foreign language (English in continental Europe, French in Britain); given that between four and nine years are spent in the classroom, teaching methods surely leave much to be desired. Even in those countries where English pervades all areas of life (from labels on packets to specialist periodicals to non-dubbed feature films on the TV screen in the evening), English evening classes and other adult education programmes tend, unwittingly, to act as social filters. Outreach to certain population groups (e.g. via distance learning) proves impossible because those concerned lack, or believe they lack, the necessary linguistic knowledge to take things further.

In this connection, it is worth taking a look at Table 3, which was drawn up in 1987 and details the proficiency of young Germans (in the Federal Republic as it was then) in English and French.

Table 3   Young Germans and language proficiency in 1987 (%)

| | English | | | French | | |
	Fluent	Can make myself understood	Do not speak	Fluent	Can make myself understood	Do not speak
14–16 yrs						
male	9	76	15	–	19	74
female	23	69	8	9	39	52
17–19 yrs						
male	27	65	8	7	34	57
female	31	57	12	9	44	43
20–22 yrs						
male	25	63	11	6	36	57
female	35	54	2	16	44	37
23–25 yrs						
male	22	66	9	5	28	63
female	21	70	8	5	37	55
26–28 yrs						
male	36	53	10	7	38	55
female	18	65	16	5	37	52

Source: Finkenstaedt and Schröder, 1990, p. 25.

The maximum figure in any group for fluency in English is 36 per cent of the respondents and, for fluency in French, 16 per cent. Most of the scores for English are below the 30 per cent mark and for French below 10 per cent. Gender-specificity is unmistakable: doubtless because they have less opportunity to practise their languages, women lose foreign-language competence faster than men, although their abilities are clearly more pronounced than those of their male peers at a younger age.

As we have seen earlier with immigrant workers and their second-generation offspring, the uncontrolled, mass cross-over of a cultural community from its native tongue to a new quasi-mother tongue is practically bound to lead to a loss of shared cultural understandings, of rootedness and common values, with people emerging semi-competent in two languages. Native culture is partially eclipsed, the cultural traditions of the host country often appear inaccessible and individuals acquire a kind of cultural tunnel vision. Their critical faculties are impaired and a subculture develops, bringing with it all sorts of social problems for those concerned and for society in general (social and literal ghettoization).

When we ask ourselves whether certain languages should be preserved, and if so to what extent, we are effectively opening up the whole issue of whether regional culture *per se* should be sustained; we are confronting the challenge of cultural diversity. Here there is a need for an overarching strategy, one that is able to cross language-based territorial boundaries. In my opinion international agreements are the only answer and the guiding principle must be that the right to one's own language is a fundamental human right; in the long-term, the groups affected will not usually countenance even a partial denial of that right. A look at the regional armed conflicts being fought out in Europe today illustrates abundantly that language deprivation is always one of the triggers for strife and, in some cases, is *the* trigger. Any support programmes set up to maintain 'small languages' need international underpinning; multilateral agreements would have to be signed to form a framework which would be available when it came to making bilateral arrangements or taking action within a particular country.

Language and identity

Human existence and human culture are only possible thanks to language, for it is language which enables us to pass on experience – and historical consciousness is vital when shaping the future. Humankind's activities, good and bad, are always intimately bound up with language. In order to survive and coexist in our societies, we have to speak the 'right' language; if we do not, we have no say. The Ancient Greeks called those who failed to speak the right idiom 'barbarians' (*barbaroi*), meaning 'stammerers', yet individuals are fairly powerless in the face of what constitutes the 'right' language (in the context of a social group, a profession, a religious creed or whatever). Language provides a point of identification, a bridge to the collective consciousness; getting it right means giving off the right scent and being welcomed into the fold. Language thereby becomes an element in the power game, an instrument for exercising authority and holding on to it. To deprive people of their language is one of the worst punishments there is, precisely because the ensuing withdrawal symptoms are so painful. These factors also explain why, if a particular system is to be brought down, the need is usually felt to target the language of that system, the 'right' language.

Language is learnt and language is taught

Everyone has an inborn capability, i.e. they can cope quite naturally with one or more specific language systems, with all the various sounds, forms, sentence structures and vocabularies. Human beings learn their first language at such an early age that later they cannot recall how it happened; it is only when they come to work on a foreign language that they become aware of the actual process of learning – the often agonizing task of repeating things over and over again, putting bits together, practising, grappling with half-understood rules. Across the world, and even in our proudly emancipated societies, the most important teacher an infant ever has remains his or her mother; mother tongue is thus a pertinent term. In acquiring their mother tongue, individuals learn proficiency in living and gain entry into the culture of their particular linguistic community, whose rules, conceptions and dreams they absorb along with the language. This communion of thought, feeling and action has often in the past been misinterpreted as an emanation of some kind of 'soul of the people' (*Volksseele*), or national spirit, laying the whole concept of language identity open to contempt – or to excessive idealization. Yet without this long process of assimilation into a linguistic community (which continues into professional life, although ways of articulating tend to become indelibly set at an early age) humans are at a disadvantage and sometimes even endangered. Generally speaking, because the process of learning our mother tongue leaves such a mark on us, we desperately resist renouncing our linguistic 'home territory'.

Foreign-language acquisition takes place against the backcloth of first-language apprenticeship. Nobody ever achieves one hundred per cent facility in a language, not even in their mother tongue. And today there is no one who knows the same number of foreign languages as he or she knows foreign nationals. Learning languages is determined by authority and authorities. In the first place it is usually the mother or other carer who represents the language authority, followed by the peer group, the school system, the media, the whole nation with its particular lifestyles. Even anti-authoritarian parents or schooling represent in this sense, not least in their linguistic component, authorities.

Language conflicts and barriers

Many of today's political conflicts are *also* language conflicts; or they are political conflicts *because* they are language conflicts. Let us look at some examples.

Speakers of Catalan mostly live in northern Spain and the Balearic Islands – although some are to be found in the French province of Roussillon – and their language ranked for centuries as a 'genuine' idiom, the vector of a self-supporting regional culture with a firmly enshrined literary life. The Catalan spoken in Roussillon fell victim to French centralism in the seventeenth century, yet even in Spain, those bigger Catalan-speaking areas eventually became sucked into the wake of the Spanish Crown's centralist thrust. In 1932, when Spain became a republic, Catalonia was granted autonomous-region status, but this was taken back after the Republic fell. The heavily centralist approach which marked the Franco era meant that sweeping measures were introduced against the Catalan language and Catalan culture. The idiom was forcibly downgraded to the level of a *patois* and its use in education and the media forbidden. This loss of autonomy, coupled with the language ban, led to the birth of a guerrilla movement and armed regional conflict. The situation was only resolved when, after Franco's death, the government gave Catalonia linguistic and cultural autonomy. The recent moves towards decentralization in Spain have helped to bring about reconciliation, involving as they have done language-policy decisions. This has been the case even in the Basque Provinces, where matters look somewhat different in that Basque, unlike Catalan, is not a member of the Romance family; it is effectively a foreign body, whose status as a language, moreover, is less secure than that of Catalan. Furthermore, Basque areas of settlement span the French-Spanish border (until Spain's accession to the EC, a heavily guarded border), thereby producing a divided culture – and there is, of course, no official acknowledgement on the French side of the Basques even having a culture.

It has to be said, however, that strange things do happen under the banner of Spanish decentralization. Aragonese, a dialect with but a few thousand speakers and virtually no political or literary tradition, has now been elevated to the rank of regional language; schoolchildren, just because they happen to live in Aragon, are obliged to learn the language, whether or not they want to and regardless of its no longer being their mother tongue. This sounds a bit like the story of the road-sweeper in Bolzano/Bozen, South Tyrol, who had to pass an exam in German before he was allowed to start sweeping. Thus it is that our new Europe's efforts at language and culture conservation can go awry – and new divisions certainly look set to arise.

The tug-of-war between Flemish and Walloon has brought down governments in Belgium. Yet these two languages, representing as they do two different cultures and traditions, will remain mutually hostile until the day when all Belgians are made to feel that they are getting equal treatment and a fair share of what the nation has to offer, whilst retaining cultural autonomy. A tall order which perhaps cannot be met on this earth.

Every tourist has come up against Belgium's bizarre language legislation, with the quasi-complete linguistic autonomy of the regions leaving its imprint on the signposts. Anyone driving through the Ardennes from Germany starts with Lüttich, then gets Liège, only to run into Luik. Ticket collectors on trains also rigorously respect the language boundaries when announcing the next station. Woe betide travellers who have left their trilingual dictionaries at home!

One can easily find further examples in western Europe of the close link between regional cultural identity and language. Let us not forget that bombs continued to rain down in South Tyrol in Italy until the province was granted autonomy as a bilingual entity. Peace in the region now hinges on the delicate balance between the two languages in question, German and Italian. Few echoes are heard in France of difficulties with Breton, Alsatian and Flemish, but this does not mean that there are no conflicts. As for the Irish problem, it might initially appear not to involve a language component, since there are virtually no native speakers of Irish Gaelic in Northern Ireland. We need to remember, however, that the pro-Catholic, pro-Irish side sees Irish Gaelic as its spiritual home – albeit a long-lost one, possibly more a political construct than anything else.

In the countries of eastern Europe, language is even more important as a point of identification than in western parts, particularly now that Communism has collapsed. Take the break-up of the former Soviet Union; new borders have coincided with language boundaries, since language is what holds people together. This applies in the case of the Moldavian Republic (regional language = Romanian; Latin script) and it applies in the case of the Baltic Republics (languages = Lithuanian, Latvian, Estonian; Roman script) and the rule even holds good for the Ukraine and Belorussia, although they in fact speak closely related Slavonic languages and use Cyrillic script. The crumbling of Yugoslavia is rooted to some extent in language conflicts which are also cultural conflicts. An integral part of the formation of a federation under Tito was the creation of a new compound language, Serbo-Croat, whose existence was denied by most Yugoslavs. The idea behind Serbo-Croat was that it should bridge old divides, which had widened still further just a few years before. Yet the enforced linguistic marriage of two closely related idioms, Serbian and Croatian, only served to sharpen the edge of existing hatred and foster the erection of artificial language barriers. Even before the recent civil war, people

Scenes such as this by Welsh language demonstrators outside a Magistrate's Court in 1971 were graphic demonstrations of their rejection of English language street signs (credit: Cymdeithas yr Iaith Gymraeg, Aberystwyth).

would maintain that they could barely understand one another, if at all. The point is that they did not want to understand each other. For both parties, the fact that Croatian had traditionally been written in Roman script, and Serbian in Cyrillic, was – and still is – a welcome and tangible signal of the total difference of one idiom from the other.

Language is always a social institution (though this fact was largely neglected by observers of language until well into the twentieth century). With regard to the construction of social identity it is a commonplace of individual and group psychology that belonging implies exclusion. The construction of a linguistic identity is always the construction of a group identity, which implies a degree of exclusion. The differences between languages can be emphasized to bring out this exclusive factor, thus possibly creating conflict and in turn increasing the emotive attachment to the home language. Such artificially emphasized language barriers may be regional in nature, designed to keep regions apart; we have seen the example of Serbian and Croatian. A language barrier can be deemed to exist wherever the inhabitants of one region claim not to understand their neighbours across the regional border, when just a little goodwill would certainly suffice to get half way there at least. This emerges with particular clarity in the case of the Slavonic languages, which are so akin to one another that those who really want to communicate could get their message across (albeit imperfectly). In the 1970s and 1980s the inhabitants of Poland and Czechoslovakia seemed to make particularly heavy weather of understanding the neighbouring Slavic language, Russian.

Language barriers, then, are put up in order to exclude people who speak differently, either because those people are disliked, or because they are perceived as a threat. Such barriers also have another function, however; they make it possible for certain cultural and economic advantages to be maintained and existing hierarchies to be cemented. Language barriers thus operate between the various social dialects (which can be regional dialects, as the northern English example reveals) of one and the same language, or between a patois and the standard idiom. In some European countries, moreover, anyone who speaks the standard language with a strong regional accent will be taken to be of lower social origin, and hence less educated, than speakers without an accent. This is why people with accents and speakers of dialects feature so prominently as ingenuous oddballs in the standard jokes repertoire.

Language problems due to migration of workers

A special kind of language conflict has been building up in Europe for a generation or so now, the extent and significance of which the political authorities have so far failed to grasp. This new conflict arises from the situation of immigrant workers and, in particular, that of the second and third generations of those workers. We are not dealing here with self-contained *minority* communities; hence there is less scope for furthering the development of linguistic and cultural enclaves; bicultural education is not an option either, since such immigrants and their descendants do not gather in specific communities. By maintaining the illusion that these people will either return home or apply for naturalization, European states pay lip service to liberal attitudes whilst at the same time contracting workers who are then treated as second-class citizens and whose children are often alienated as much from their parents' native culture as from that of the host country. Most of these children could safely be described as semi-lingual in two languages. The data that is available indicates both directly and indirectly that the latent and overt difficulties experienced by young people in the immigrant communities (unemployment, crime) correlate with their linguistic abilities and are thus brought about by those circumstances. Post-1992, with greater mobility within the EC, these problems will not be restricted to the 'lower classes' and, hence, will no longer be able to be kept at arm's length. With so many immigrant workers in Europe, we should perhaps be talking of mass migration (or *Völkerwanderung*) rather than mobile minorities; the Federal Republic of Germany alone has well over 4 million *Gastarbeiter* – equivalent to the population of Denmark; Switzerland has percentually more.

A precondition for sensible integration into a society that offers more than an opening as an ancillary worker with the risk of unemployment is obviously a thorough grounding in language, be it of the parents' culture or the new one. No matter how often politicians pay lip-service to it, a bicultural education is bound to remain the exception. People will only accept having to speak a foreign language in order to go about their daily business and pursue their lives if the personal disadvantage they suffer (e.g. fewer civil rights) is compensated for by economic bonuses. However, this only applies to first-generation immigrants and seasonal workers, not to their children and grandchildren. Since migrant workers settle in all sorts of different areas, either of the options alluded to will be expensive: on the one hand, a policy of acculturation (the goal being complete linguistic and cultural participation in the host country); on the other, a genuine minority community approach (the aim here being to maintain and cherish original language and culture, with the host country ensuring civil rights and decent remuneration). Pushing the whole problem to one side is, of course, much more straightforward and a lot cheaper.

It is easy to say (if we accept the fiction of a 'free' market) that workers should sell their labour and live their lives where the yields are highest. Yet to turn our back on the languages spoken by 8 per cent of the population (the figure for Germany) is tantamount to putting up a language barrier. To make the majority language (German, in our example) the only passport to what has become a multilingual and multicultural society ('If you cannot speak German, you do not belong') means enshrining a dominant language, whilst at the same time withholding it *de facto* from one segment of the population. At some point, conflict is bound to arise.

What happened in the Soviet Union is instructive; introducing Russian across the Republics as the language of the Socialist state was equivalent to privileging those who had Russian as their mother tongue and discriminating, in the long term, against the remaining national languages and cultures. It has only proved feasible to employ a foreign tongue as the language of state or official language if its use effectively means that all other languages are equally discriminated against. Witness some of the new African countries, where English is the language of state; or India where, contrary to the intention of the Constitution, English still serves as an official language. In nineteenth century Hungary, the use of Latin as the official parliamentary language actually made it possible to fend off many a conflict – at the linguistic level, anyway. Europe no longer has these options open to it. Neither Latin nor Esperanto will be there to take on the role of a pan-European language. The challenge therefore still lies ahead. It is up to us to bring down existing language barriers and stop new ones from springing up, for we can rest assured that, once in place, they will be harbingers of strife.

Human identity, rooted in the *patois*, the sociolect or regional dialect, i.e. in the mother tongue of the individual, is vulnerable to deliberate emotional attack. This is where dialect poets and folk singers find their target, as do – more recently – the deliberately regionally-oriented, grassroots mass media (especially the local radio and TV stations, but also certain kinds of newspapers). But, as indicated earlier, this is also an area where nationalist tendencies find an echo.

ĈAPITRO DUA

En Kiu

Pu Faras Viziton kaj
Iras en Striktan Lokon

Edvardo Urso, konata al siaj amikoj kiel Winnie-la-Pu,
aŭ (mallonge) Pu, promenis tra la arbaro unu tagon, fiere
zumante al si. Ĝuste tiun matenon li verkis etan zumon,
dum li faris siajn Dikecajn Ekzercojn antaŭ la spegulo:
Tra-la-la, tra-la-la, dum li streĉis sin tiel alten, kiel li povis,

kaj poste *Tra-la-la, tra-la—ho, helpon!—la*, dum li klopodis
tuŝi siajn piedojn. Post la matenmanĝo li ripete diris ĝin al
si mem, ĝis li ellernis ĝin parkere, kaj nun li zumadis la
tuton ĝis la fino. Ĝi sonis jene:

18

Tra-la-la, tra-la-la,
Tra-la-la, tra-la-la,
Ram-tam-tidi-lam-tam
Tidi-lidi, tidi-lidi
Tidi-lidi, tidi-lidi
Ram-tam-tam-tidi-tam.

A familiar text – but an unfamiliar language for most of us. Despite the enthusiastic support it still retains among its adherents, Esperanto has never achieved universal support (Credit: E.P. Dutton Children's Books).

With the advent of ever bigger partnerships between nations and the general internationalization of our lives, it is easy to understand how New Ethnicity movements have grown up in Europe and around the world. People are striving to retain a sense of regional and social belonging so as not to disappear into the amorphous spaces all about them. The conscious rediscovery throughout Europe of regional language forms and dialects and the revival of idioms which were practically extinct (even if only as 'working museums' in the shape of street names and fixed expressions such as '*Prost*' or '*Auf Wiedersehen*') are all examples of human efforts to counter the overall trend. As the twentieth century draws to a close, the striving for regional-based cultural and linguistic supports is certainly stronger in Europe than it was at the onset, when the idea of the nation state was the cultural paradigm and people placed their faith in standard languages as the vectors of (narrowly middle-class) cultural values – and when some were dreaming the internationalist dream of socialism.

The problems that arise from individual identification with different languages, and therefore also from the manifold contacts between languages and from the varied and multi-faceted misunderstandings between them, must also be considered from the perspective of national and international law. A glance at the available literature reveals an ambiguous picture. Those who write on law acknowledge that language is now a major player and point to the problems necessarily arising where two or more languages coexist. The overwhelming sentiment, however, seems to be that the difficulties can be overcome (if they have not already been so). Pursuant to human rights undertakings, foreigners enjoy protection before the law, as does their language. During a trial, it is an official requirement that an interpreter be present. Protection of the language and culture of minorities is secured, provided they are minorities within the meaning of the law, i.e. nationals. The impression is in fact given that there are less legal problems with minorities than was once the case since there are fewer of them – partly as a result of forced resettlement and the manipulation of statistics. In other words, the language and social problems stemming from the fact that Germany has millions of non-German-speaking *Gastarbeiter* (who are entitled to remain in the country, but do not in practice apply for naturalization) can quite simply be ignored from the standpoint of the law. Yet, in tomorrow's Europe, 'guest worker' status looks set to be the most likely one.

Freedom of movement in Europe does not automatically mean that people will cross the boundaries and become virtual 'nationals' of their particular host country. The idea of European citizenship, protecting each individual as a member of a national minority within the common European home, is unlikely to become a reality. The only option, then, is to make peaceful co-existence easier by changing our attitudes towards speakers of other languages. Fostering language *rapprochement* will entail more intensive teaching of a wider variety of languages – combined in several European countries with more and better mother-tongue education for a number of minority groups. Given the current legal framework, this is the only way of attenuating, if not resolving, the problems facing us. Looking beyond those problems, we should remember that a bilingual second-generation is an amazing asset for any workforce.

More intensive teaching of a wider variety of language does not necessarily mean using up any more chunks of curriculum time than is now generally the case in Central European schools; getting more language subjects on the timetable should not be the goal we set ourselves. What is required is a qualitative improvement in foreign-language teaching, as will be seen later. Language-learning, moreover, needs to become a life long enterprise, pursued in and out of the classroom. We must move away from the notion that learning languages is a miserable business; the whole process should be viewed with excitement, as a means of satisfying our curiosity about other cultures and how they operate. No fear should be attached to language-learning; on the contrary, we need to open wide the doors to different ways of doing things.

Language and politics

The historical perspective

Since ancient times, the practice of granting and withdrawing language rights has proved its worth as a method of waging politics. Trade and home affairs policy, foreign policy, power politics – all have their language component, as we have just demonstrated. Let us now take a look at the interaction of language and politics as it has actually taken place in Europe over the last 600 years.

As we have seen, language serves as a reference point for people's ethnic and cultural sense of belonging, at the same time mirroring the progression (by no means always smooth and linear) of their culture through the ages. So it is no wonder that political authorities seize on languages and even commandeer them for their own purposes. The following section deals with the purposeful exercise of influence, first on the native idiom of the country concerned, then on 'foreign' tongues.

Politics and mother tongue

Political influence on language has ranged from the subtle renaming of unpopular agenda items (not 'atomic waste plant' but 'recycling park') to the deliberate prohibition of foreign words (for instance, in French advertising), from the insistence on 100 per cent competence in the dominant language for entry to the Civil Service to a complete ban on speaking a particular minority language. The following section deals with the deliberate exercise of influence on the mother tongue of a country. An interest group, party or government can try to use language to support desirable political developments or they can make it serve the ruling system.

As Orwell demonstrated in *1984* with 'Newspeak', totalitarian states can pursue their goals with ruthless consistency. The German of the Third Reich had a series of newly coined terms added to it, specifically designed to reflect Nazi ideology and alter the population's patterns of thought. A particularly striking example is the expression 'to commit race defilement' (*Rassenschande*), meaning *to have sexual relations with non-Aryans, especially Jews or non-whites*. The word *Rassenschande* is a racialist neologism, but in many cases new words of that kind are not necessary; the semantics of existing words can be changed according to the ruling ideology. The word *völkisch* in German grew out of the Romantic period and signified: originating in the people/nation (in the sense of basic political entity). Under the Third Reich, however, the term was reinterpreted to mean: originating in the National Socialist Movement. The Party gazette was called the *Völkischer Anzeiger*. In the Socialist 'Newspeak' of 1968 and thereafter, 'progressive and democratic forces' (*fortschrittlich-demokratische Kräfte*) meant those forces which were further along the road to the classless society of Marxism than any others – and which toed the Party line. This insidious 'ideologization' of language also creates language barriers. Texts from humanities disciplines written in the former GDR are most liable to misinterpretation by West Germans when they seem, on the surface, to be written in the mainstream German tradition. But words such as 'progress', or 'democracy' (as in German *Democratic* Republic) had been given quite different connotations.

In the European context, however, this type of language-influencing process is of secondary importance; more pertinent is the second variety, where fledgling national states and autonomous regions are determined that their language shall stand as an honourable symbol of their sovereignty, able to hold its own with other recognized languages. A prime illustration is offered by the newly emerging nation states of the sixteenth and seventeenth centuries, with France at the spearhead. In 1635, modelling itself on Italy, France created the *Académie française*, devoted primarily to the nurture of the French language. As we saw earlier, sixteenth century language theorists, together with the poets of the *Pléaide*, had already laid the groundwork. Backed by considerable amounts of state funding, French was promoted as the most mellifluous (so they said) and logical language of them all. From a French vantage point, these resources were undoubtedly well-placed; in the eighteenth century, French acquired a hegemonic position as *the* international language of Europe. France has in fact never ceased deliberate promotion of the language from the highest echelons of politics, witness the setting up of the *Haut-comité de la langue française* and the legislation passed in the 1970s to stop the language being flooded with foreign expressions. France's political attitude towards French-speaking Quebec similarly illustrates its commitment to active and cost-intensive language support.

Great Britain has always taken a more liberal stance on these matters; hence, there is no equivalent institution to the French *Académie* and this idea of language legislation is unthinkable. Nevertheless, it is only possible to understand that Shakespeare produced work like his with all its linguistic power and verbal richness (huge vocabulary, a wealth of metaphors and new coinages) against the background of the astute and sensitive approach to language study and promotion taken by the 'educators', those grammar school teachers and tutors to princes who flourished in the Tudor era. In subsequent years, it was the sermons of the theologians, the grandeur of the King James version of the Bible, the well-honed speech of parliamentary orators and the eloquence of legal men which made English the literary language of the Augustan Age (early eighteenth century), as well as of early Romanticism (post-1765, after the Seven Years' War) and Romanticism proper, thereby paving the way for its world-wide expansion in the nineteenth century.

In Germany too there have been few politically-inspired attempts at deliberate language cultivation. In the Baroque era, however, there were efforts to purify the idiom and rid it of various foreign terms and especially of French influences, a trend which went hand-in-hand with the pedantic Germanizing practised by state officialdom at the time.

In the nineteenth century there were again attempts to rid the language of influences from the arch-enemy France. Until quite recently, the official word for telephone was not the word everybody uses – *Telefon* – but the German coinage, *Fernsprecher*. Similarly, everybody in Germany drives an *Auto*, but the authorities still define it as a *Personenkraftwagen*, thankfully shortened to *PKW*. German publishing houses generally bow to the authority of the Duden dictionaries (which give admitted variations for Swiss German and Austrian usage), which are prepared by the Bibliographic Institute in Mannheim 'on the basis of the official orthographic rules'. These were laid down at a conference in 1901 and are presently under discussion again. Although the Duden – like any standard dictionary – exercises a conservative influence by giving orientation on accepted standards, it also observes changes in usage and incorporates these in its regular publications. It does not attempt to stop people using words like T-shirt or Tiramisu, only to show them how to use and spell them in the generally accepted German way.

Although the process whereby those in control seek to influence their country's language is first and foremost a cultural issue and thus a matter of domestic policy, a foreign-policy thrust does on occasions develop. The French example is again instructive. One reason why the Münster negotiations (1640s) at the end of the Thirty Years' War dragged on so long was that the French proved so doggedly determined not to compromise on the language question, insisting that all documents be translated into French, whilst the Imperial negotiators, i.e. the Germans, were committed to Latin, the language of diplomacy and the official tongue of the Holy Roman Empire. Of course the French negotiators understood Latin, and the German delegation understood French, but a principle was at stake. The French were claiming hegemony in Europe; therefore the language of diplomacy had to be French. The Imperial negotiators' insistence on Latin was tantamount to a refusal of French hegemony and, at the same time, they were laying claim on behalf of the Emperor to a hegemonic position he no longer in reality enjoyed. Particularly noteworthy is the fact that nowhere is there any reference to German: this did not become the national language until the nineteenth century. French in fact developed into the international language of diplomacy in the second half of the seventeenth century, a role which it held on to until the Treaty of Versailles in 1919 (the text of which appeared in both French and English, each equally authentic).

Since the nineteenth century, European powers have used their languages in the battle for political influence – Britain, France, Prussia and Russia have imposed their languages in or outside Europe. The tug-of-war over the areas on the German–French border may serve as a case in point. After the French Revolution, in the Napoleonic era, the Rhine's western bank passed into French hands and the Departments concerned were officially declared bilingual, a move which failed because of inadequate schools provision and disgruntlement on the part of the German population. Then, in 1871, Alsace and Lorraine fell to the newly formed Second Reich and together they became a *Reichsland*; a rigorous process of Germanization was begun. One of the pretexts advanced for this annexation was that the dialects of Alsace and Lorraine were offshoots of the High German language branch. The whole merry-go-round started up again in 1918, although in the opposite direction; the Saarland, too, came into the bargain at this point, having become split off from the Reich. 1939 and 1945 marked further political and linguistic shifts. From 1945 until 1957, the people of the Saarland had passports with 'République française, nationalité sarroise' printed on them. French began to be taught as the first foreign language in schools throughout the French zone

(Rhineland-Palatinate, Württemberg, Baden), as well as in the Saarland. The retention of French as first foreign language was one of the stipulations of the 1956 Saar Statute. Can it really be a coincidence that all the administrative centres of the European Communities are located in French-speaking areas (Brussels, Luxembourg, Strasbourg)?

The penetration of Spanish into Catalan-speaking regions and the concomitant suppression of the Catalan language has already been discussed. In the case of Italy, despite Mussolini's being in cahoots with Germany and the fact that the two countries were brothers-in-arms, a determined policy of Italianization was pursued in South Tyrol, which until 1918 had belonged to Austria. The short-term compulsory Germanization of the protectorates of Bohemia and Moravia and the general government of the East during the Second World War had a very clear speech component, which you can see, for example, in the 'Germanization' of place names (though it is not always possible to track down older German names in every case).

Russian obviously became the first foreign language in the Soviet-occupied zone of Germany after the war, as it did in the old Warsaw pact and COMECON states. Once the Soviet Union under Gorbachev ceased its hegemonic claims, Russian began to lose its key position in eastern Europe; in schools, regrettably perhaps, Russian is yielding to English. Faced with the likelihood that French will suffer in the wake of the restructuring process in eastern Europe and the former GDR, France has leapt in with its own language-policy measures, focusing particularly on the traditional Paris-Warsaw axis: promoting the teaching of the French language, opening up cultural institutes, offering fellowships etc. This is of course perfectly legitimate; several European states have their own cultural foundations, responsible for cultivating their national language abroad (Goethe Institute, British Council, Alliance française, Dante Alighieri Society). These basically carry out educational liaison work and occasionally hold language competitions. States which do not have their own foundations organize similar activities through their cultural attachés. Language competitions and similar activities which are part and parcel of a country's foreign policy, pursued to foster their own language and culture abroad, are nowadays called 'remote-controlled competitions'. Domestic competitions, in contrast, cover many languages, geared to the language needs (on the grounds of geopolitical position, trading partners, etc.) of the home market (e.g. the yearly German Foreign Languages Competition (FRG) or the Language Festival and Young Linguists Awards (UK)). The best example of a remote-controlled contest is the Russian Olympiad, held throughout the world with the prize awarded in Moscow. Activities of this kind are, of course, means whereby a country can foster its national language on the international political stage, yet they have their legitimacy and are acceptable provided they do not violate the laws and traditions of the countries hosting them.

Foreign languages and politics

In parallel to efforts designed to foster the image of a country's own national language at home and abroad, a trend has emerged lately whereby influence is exerted over 'alien' tongues in the hope of channelling them and keeping them under some control. There is in fact nothing new in this; the practice has been around ever since Babel.

A country's political thrust may centre on alien influences from outside or on minority languages within its borders (see the earlier sections on language conflict and language barriers). Another approach is positively to promote one or more non-native languages.

The chequered saga of acceptance and rejection of foreign tongues can best be illustrated using (yet again) the example of French, specifically the French spoken in Germany. By the end of the seventeenth century, despite their cultivation of French, the nationally-minded educated classes in Germany perceived the risk that French political and linguistic influence might spread too far. August Bohse, who had been full of praise for French in 1703, subsequently lamented that: 'these days, even our political men [are required to speak French], now that Germany has more dealings with its ambitious neighbour than makes for comfort' (Schröder, 1982, p. 14). A milder approach to the cultural significance of French was taken by Christoph Schwab who, in his prize-winning Academy treatise of 1785 entitled: *On the Origins of the Ubiquity of the French Language and the Probable Duration of its Supremacy*, drew attention to the rising popularity of English literature. He did however add the rider that the French language's potential rivals were too lacking in 'ascendancy and purpose' to be able to take on any role as general instruments of broad communication. He then proceeded to make an assertion which was probably included simply in order to round off the argument, but in fact prefigured future events remarkably accurately:

> There is indeed one way only in which another [language] might dethrone French, namely if it were to come about that the French language, or the culture of the French nation, or the political grandeur of that nation became in some fashion undermined; and presupposing that some other nation were to acquire such selfsame attributes in equal measure. Yet who would make so bold as to foretell such things, unless he be a prophet?
>
> *(Schröder, 1985, Vol. 4, p. 163)*

The outbreak of the French Revolution five years later set the wheels in motion, from the point of view of both language policy and power politics. By the summer of 1813, as the Napoleonic era drew to a close, French had become the language of the enemy. It was also the tongue spoken during the *Ancien Régime*, a system of rule which had not been vanquished; the very idiom transmitted antiquated modes of thought. At this stage, however, French was still able to retain its established foothold in Germany and it was to endure as the authorized second language in the Departments west of the Rhine; yet decisive breaches of its position were soon to occur. It was amidst all these national stirrings that, just before the famous *Völkerschlacht* ('Battle of the Nations') outside Leipzig, a professor from the University of Griefswald, Ernst Moritz Arndt, also a writer on political affairs, produced his dissertation entitled: *On the Hatred of Other Nations* [Volkshaß] *and the Use of Foreign Tongues* (1813). As the following quotation demonstrates, the text constituted both a settling of accounts with history and a rousing moral call to arms; the grandiloquence of the agitator replaced rational argument:

> I invoke hatred, that firm and steadfast German hatred of Frenchmen and their whole essence, for I despise this pitiful process of bastardization and ridicule whereby our Glory is denatured and emasculated, and our Power tossed as booty to the Foreign intruder; yea, I invoke hatred, fiery and bloody hatred, because the Foreign impostors are crying out that they stand, by right, as victorious over us, as our masters, and we must not tolerate this …

> I invoke hatred of the French, not just while this War lasts; I demand that it endure for a long, long time, I demand that it endure for evermore. Germany's borders will then be secure without need for man-made defenses … It will come as no great loss to us if the gaggle of French language tutors, dance-masters, Abbés, valets, cooks and quacks, together with the maids and governesses who infest our daughters' chambers and our brothels, prefer in future to shun these coarse, Alemanic lands, rendered so dreadful and unbearable to them.
>
> *(Schröder, 1989, p. 6)*

Special mention is made here of the language tutors: 'Native speakers go home' would be how we would phrase it today. And they went home, the upshot being that between 1820 and 1880 three generations of German schoolboys, university students, professors and modern language scholars grew up speaking the kind of French so fittingly mocked in the 1880s by the progressive language teacher Wilhelm Viëtor and his fellow reformers.

> Sprecht ihr aber doch Französisch
> solls nicht lauten wie Chinesisch;
> Träng, Detalch und Reglemang
> ist ein sonderbare Klang.

> ('If you are going to speak French it should not sound like Chinese;
> Treng (F. *train*), Detalch (F. *détail*), and Reglemang (F. *règlement*)
> sound strange indeed.')
>
> *(Viëtor, 1882 in Schröder, 1989, p. 62)*

French was taken off the curriculum in Prussian senior schools in 1816. When it was reintroduced at the beginning of the 1830s, the Rector of the *Gymnasium*[6] in Zwittau, a certain Herr Lindemann pronounced:

> We would be much better advised in future to prepare to meet the French with canons and bayonets rather than with open arms as our vanquishers, which is what will be the case if we insist on teaching our schoolboys and our daughters the French language … Even if they never acquire the art of speaking through their nose, our young people will none the less develop into capable citizens, learned men and good housewives.
>
> *(Schröder, 1989, p. 64)*

---

[6] *Translator's note:* roughly equivalent to British grammar school.

Napoleon was meanwhile doing all in his power to ban the teaching of English and, under his pressure, all native-English language tutors in Frankfurt am Main were expelled in the course of the first decade of the nineteenth century. In German-speaking Europe, however, illustrious *démarches* had already been taken against the English language a while back. When Vienna University sought to bring in a Reader in English in 1778, Empress Maria Theresa decreed:

> Let no English Reader ever be employed in any University of ours;
> better teach the tongues currently spoken within the Empire than a
> language which could not but imperil our religious and moral life.
>
> *(Schröder, 1985, Vol. 4, p. 85)*

Maria Theresa would have had three factors in mind here. In the states making up the Danube Monarchy, nationalist feeling was on the rise and native-Germans with a knowledge of the various languages and cultures of those states were now required. Secondly, English had by then virtually become the dominant language of Protestantism and the Danube Monarchy wished to protect itself against infiltration. Thirdly, there was a risk that libertine and subversive ideas from France might enter Austria in English translation (English press censorship being relatively lax).

The English language's fortunes in central Europe were nevertheless set to rise in response to the decline in influence of French. The merits of studying English were described in the following terms in 1840 by Otto Behnsch, a secondary school teacher and an English-language tutor at Breslau (Wrocław) University:

> The English idiom spans land and sea, it is the primary language of the
> merchants and could soon become that of politics and the salons; more
> importantly, it has many affinities with our own tongue and possesses,
> almost beyond comparison, such a rich and peculiarly spirited literature
> that it is worthier even than French of introduction into our school as an
> instrument of general education – something which is in part already the
> case, or soon will be.
>
> *(Schröder, 1969, p. 112)*

Behnsch belonged to the pro-English lobby in the battle between French and English, a lobby which was to gain strength as the nineteenth century progressed, so that in 1923 the first states of the Second Reich switched from French to English as their first foreign language. Throughout the whole process, in line with ideological concerns growing out of Romanticism, the English idiom's Germanic roots had been adduced in its favour and the true import of this in historical terms emerges if we move ahead in time and look at measures taken under the Third Reich. In 1937, the ministerial decree laying down 'transitional measures for harmonizing secondary education' made English the compulsory first foreign language, a move not without its Germanizing thrust. As a contemporary critic said: 'We are witnessing a uniform shift in German cultural thinking towards a German National (*völkisch*) world-view' (Aehle, 1938, p. 32). Back in the nineteenth century, however, during the revolutionary period around 1848–49, another element was included in the traditional catalogue of virtues of English (pre-eminence of its literature and its affinities with German), namely that the English political system stood out as a model to be imitated.

Ever since the early years of the nineteenth century, most European countries have had a state education system, or at least a system over which the state has exercised influence. Language-policy decisions taken in respect of schools (first foreign language, order in which languages are learnt, language-weighting) therefore inevitably reflect political priorities regarding foreign languages and act as a potent means of exerting leverage; hence all the domestic and foreign pressure groups fighting it out in any particular country (politically-motivated parent associations, federations of teachers of specific subjects, lobbyists acting on behalf of foreign powers). Most European languages have sadly been pushed into the wings as a result of the language policies implemented in Europe's schools. Over the period 1820-1980, the number of pupils in schools multiplied many times over, yet the choice of languages on offer became very limited (in alphabetical order: English, French, German, Russian and Spanish). Surveys were carried out during the late 1970s and into the 1980s to establish how university students from five European countries in the early stages of their first-degree courses felt about the range and quality of the foreign-language teaching they had been offered. They were then asked which languages they believed they needed to know and what their attitudes were towards a multilingual Europe. The results revealed that young Europeans barely thought beyond the bounds of the five languages listed above (plus Italian and, of course, their mother tongue).

The kind of political influence exercised on language policy described in this section has, with regard to today's Europe, one basic flaw: it is based on the notion of the isolated, individual state. Apart from this, the policies adopted followed contemporary concepts of the nature and aesthetics of language no longer acceptable to modern linguists, or even blatant nationalistic interests.

Nobody will dispute that Europe is on the way to becoming an economic superpower; equally clear is that no-one wants to see a new version of an imperial structure, entirely centrally-administered, using a single language – whether imposed, enforced or simply accepted – as a power symbol. Such structures have proved to be politically unstable in the past and run counter to the European ideals of freedom, tolerance and democracy, which, though political decisions obviously often fall short of these, form the often-invoked keystone of the whole process of social and political *rapprochement*. One of the vital building blocks in the new Europe should therefore be a common policy on the language question, supported and participated in by all states and regions in the area.

Foreign-language policy

The nurturing of regional culture is a precondition for political stability, as we saw earlier. Today's regional conflicts demonstrate that where entire regions suffer economic deprivation those affected often view themselves as culturally deprived as well; if economic deprivation is linked to linguistic and cultural deprivation, civil war is on the horizon. There may well be no more wars as we have known them in the past between European nations, but this need only mean that the next conflicts will be internal, i.e. civil wars. A Europe without proper policies to foster linguistic balance is a Europe ripe for just such civil strife.

European initiatives

Since the mid-1950s, European bodies have admittedly been calling – in statement after statement, declaration of intent after declaration of intent – for a multilingual Europe to which they pledge their full support, suggesting *inter alia* a broader approach to foreign-language teaching. Article 2 of the 1954 European Cultural Convention reads:

> Considering that the aim of the Council of Europe is to achieve a greater unity between its members for the purpose, among others, of safeguarding and realizing the ideals and principles which are their common heritage; considering that the achievement of this aim would be furthered by a greater understanding of one another among the peoples of Europe ...
>
> Each Contracting Party shall, insofar as may be possible,
>
> (a) encourage the study by its own nationals of the languages, history and civilization of the other Contracting Parties and grant facilities to the nationals of those Parties to pursue such studies in its territory ...
>
> *(Christ and Liebe, 1981, p. 12)*

Resolution 2 of 25.01.69, passed by the Personal Representatives of the Member States of the European Communities, is more specific:

> – that if full understanding is to be achieved among the countries of Europe, the language barriers between them must be removed,
>
> – that linguistic diversity is part of the European cultural heritage and that it should, through a study of modern languages, provide a source of intellectual enrichment rather than be an obstacle to unity,
>
> – that only if the study of modern European languages becomes general will full mutual understanding and co-operation be possible in Europe,
>
> – that a better knowledge of modern European languages will lead to the strengthening of links and the increase in international exchanges on which economic and social progress in Europe increasingly depends,
>
> – that a knowledge of a modern language should no longer be regarded as a luxury reserved for an élite, but an instrument of information and culture which should be available to all.
>
> *(Christ and Liebe, 1981, p. 36)*

The Council of Europe's Recommendation 814 'On modern languages in Europe', adopted on 5 October 1977, refers in its very Preamble to the intimate link between language and culture, focusing in particular on the need to protect language minorities:

> The Assembly,
>
> 1. considering that a knowledge of languages is not only essential for communication and exchanges between Europeans, but also leads to the mutual understanding of cultural values;
>
> 2. being of the opinion that cultural diversity is an irreplaceable asset, and that this justifies the active maintenance of language minorities in Europe;

3.   emphasizing the importance of ensuring that everyone should learn at least one widely used language, but at the same time encouraging the diversification of teaching in this area; ...

9.   Recommends that the Committee of ministers:

a.   call on the governments of the member states of the Council of Europe to develop the teaching of modern languages, taking account of:

I.   the particular needs of less privileged groups, particularly migrants;

II.   the need to diversify the languages taught;

III.   the cultural advantages of maintaining language minorities in Europe;

IV.   the pedagogical aspects of language learning; ...

(Christ and Liebe, 1981, p. 22)

Language maintenance as a means of preserving culture and promoting peace had already been dealt with as an issue in the Final Act of the Conference on Security and Cooperation in Europe (Helsinki Conference). The Contracting Parties agreed:

to encourage the study of foreign languages and civilizations as an important means of expanding communication among peoples for their better acquaintance with the culture of each country, as well as for the strengthening of international cooperation; to this end, to stimulate within their competence the further development and improvement of foreign-language teaching and the diversification of choice of languages taught at various levels, paying due attention to less widely-spread or studied languages.

(Christ and Liebe, 1981, p. 6)

Many similar positions have been adopted since 1978 and there seems to be unanimous agreement that the 'dominant language' model should be rejected. The European Parliament came out unequivocally in favour of a multilingual, multicultural Europe, arguing that it would not be expedient to make Esperanto, or one particular modern language, Europe's compulsory first foreign language.

The declarations by European bodies may sound extremely encouraging, but in most European states they have had scant impact to date on the actual language-policy decisions implemented in schools. Little has been done to offer more languages, provide greater choice or vary the order of priority for learning particular languages; nor have adequate efforts been undertaken with any language to chart innovative teaching methods and educational strategies commensurate with the new challenges.

The demand for languages

The industrial nations of western Europe are export-driven. Take the example of Germany; in the old *Länder* (i.e. not including the new eastern *Länder*), every third Deutschmark – and in some sectors, every second – has to be earned from exports. Only if export activity is buoyant can prosperity be assured.

It is a commonplace in business circles that the right language to use is the language of the customer. Importing goods is easy enough regardless of whether we

THE ADVANTAGES OF TRAVEL, OR 'A LITTLE LEARNING IS A DANGEROUS THING'
Comment se porte mon ami? – Moi, I am jost from de England. – Aha, you vas jost come from de England! Den how you like de bif? Le bif roti is charmant à Londres! – Yase, dat is vrai, bote je prefare le rum-tek! – Le rum-tek! Vat is de rum-tek? – Voyes-vous, it is toujours de bif-tek, mais, bote, day call it rum-tek ba-cause day pote de rum *in de sauce (14 June 1824).*

George Cruikshank, who never actually visited Paris, had a very jaundiced view of the value of travel and learning foreign languages (credit: Wardroper, J. (1977) The Caricatures of George Cruikshank, *London, Gordon Fraser.*

speak our mother tongue or an international language, but exporting is another story. The fact that English is spoken around the globe is irrelevant, as the Anglo-Saxon countries have recently had to learn – much to their dismay.

Let us make a brief historical excursion. As already mentioned, merchants and traders have always known that it makes sense to clinch deals in the language of the buyer. The merchants of the Hanseatic League – the medieval association of North German towns – knew this; back in the thirteenth and fourteenth centuries, a knowledge of Russian was deemed a vital prerequisite for anyone hoping to do business in the Novgorod bureau. By the fifteenth century it had become established Hanseatic practice to dispatch young language scholars to Russia so that they might learn the Russian language (Raab, 1956/57, p. 343). In 1423 the Hansa Parliament meeting in Lübeck forbade members of the League from letting young Dutchmen 'in on the act', i.e. teaching them Russian. Throughout the fifteenth century the Hansa kept vigilant watch to ensure that no party – especially not the

Dutch – challenged what it saw as its exclusive right to knowledge of the Russian language. The first Italian-teaching material on record was designed for German merchants in Venice and, in the early years of the 15th century, the texts in question still had to be hand copied by scribes at their desks. In 1554, the new rules drawn up for the London Hansa bureau (the *Stahlhof*) stipulated that young Germans studying in London should appear before the Elders and furnish evidence that they had devoted a year to the acquisition of English; if they failed the test they would be sent to the country for a year to work with a Master Weaver.

Some exploratory studies have now been carried out in individual European countries on the demand for foreign languages, but no official statistics are available. Until recently, European education authorities have demonstrated only marginal interest when questioned on this, turning up their noses at the very thought; they were there to educate, not to provide the sort of practical training that any Berlitz School could deliver.

A proper study of the breakdown of import and export flows is a first step towards any analysis of foreign-language demand, although it must be complemented by detailed study of industrial structures and sectors. Further indications on which languages are required, and who wishes to learn them, can be ascertained by considering companies' in-house language-training schemes; Europeans generally tend to be unaware of the scale of such programmes (in Germany for example, BASF in Ludwigshafen provides tuition for about 1000 employees during working hours and a further 1000 at evening classes). Transfrontier movements (tourism as well as postal traffic and telephone calls) can equally prove a valuable source of information. The spectrum of practically-oriented language teaching on offer in, for example, adult education centres and colleges of further education is also illuminating and we might learn too from language tourism (where people take trips with the express purpose of enhancing language proficiency).

Where this dimension has been properly researched, the results have yielded an unexpectedly varied picture. Initial exploratory studies of language demand in industry in three major economic centres in Germany have revealed that around 80 per cent of companies need at least two foreign languages in order to operate, and 45 per cent three. Leaving English aside, since all firms need it (even if not necessarily in the first instance), the other major languages required are: French (85 per cent of companies), Spanish, Italian, Dutch, Portuguese and Russian. Obviously this does not tell us anything about the breakdown and spread within individual undertakings; cautious estimates based on a sample survey carried out in southern Germany suggest that the average ratio between employees with a knowledge of English and those with a knowledge of French is 25:1 – despite the fact that it is now sometimes argued that French has greater commercial potential since France is probably Germany's main trading partner. In any case there are companies, big ones included, where French is already the primary foreign language, just as there are firms where Spanish has pushed French very much to one side. Unsurprisingly, Russian has played no major role in West German industry, although it does figure on the language-required list; its fate was quite different in former East Germany of course, Russian being paramount on the export front (no statistics are available, however). No one yet knows how things will turn out in the eastern part of Germany (firms have collapsed, everything is being restructured, Soviet orders have been cancelled), but it can safely be predicted that the long-term attractiveness for Germany of the Russian market will ensure that Russian is accorded high priority as a major export language.

The number of foreign languages required does not appear to correlate with the size of firm, although big undertakings clearly tend to need three or more languages. Predominantly export-oriented companies appear to need only marginally more languages than mainly importing ones, although proportionally more employees in the export-oriented sector presumably speak foreign languages.

Research carried out so far into the language needs of industry, commerce and the administrative sector is methodologically far from satisfactory and we are a long way off having proper longitudinal studies – vital for any true forecast of future foreign-language demand.

The German results as far as they go have received confirmation from research in Britain by Stephen Hagen, who has published his results in the book *Languages in British Business. An Analysis of Current Needs* (Hagen, 1988). He also endorses certain language-teaching options, for example, encouraging 'receptive' skills whose worth is currently much underrated in schools, just as the value of oral proficiency is still underrated. For those operating at a certain level, 'good enough' command of a foreign language is often adequate; people are required to have communication skills (to understand the spoken and written language, to be able to talk to others in the idiom), but they do not need perfect grammar and spelling – a totally new concept in the schoolroom context.

If we take a look at German schools, we find that the spread of languages on offer in the state sector nowhere near matches the needs of the modern world (certainly not in quantitative terms). Across the board, in all types of school, the overriding impression is that no account whatsoever is taken of real demand; this is the case with regard to Spanish and Italian, but Russian (in the western Länder) is not adequately covered either, let alone the 'exotic' languages, yet attendance figures at the *Volkshochschulen*[7] demonstrate that there is a clearly felt need among ordinary people, particularly the young, to learn a foreign language and the statistics reveal that many students compensate for poor language coverage in the state-run schools by taking courses at the *Volkshochschule*.

Further evidence of the fact that a poor view is frequently taken of foreign-language provision in the schools, especially the grammar schools,[8] is that stu-

[7]   *Translator's note:* in Germany the *Volkshochschulen* ('people's colleges') were set up to allow everyone, regardless of background or formal qualifications, to pursue courses of study for their own personal fulfilment. Broadly speaking then, they are adult education centres, although school-age students may also attend classes if they want to learn, say, a particular language.

[8]   *Translator's note:* comprehensive schools are not the rule in Germany, where they instead have the *Gymnasium* (grammar school equivalent), the *Realschule* and the *Hauptschule* (both along secondary modern lines), plus various vocational schools.

dents and parents can be seen to opt in huge numbers for private courses at home and abroad.

Students are not in most cases seeking to learn 'unusual' languages; usually they are interested in English. Taking the German commercial language-teaching sector as a whole, it turns out that intensive English courses to prepare for the *Abitur* ('A' Level equivalent) are among the most highly attended and 85 per cent of language tours for school-pupils and adults are to English-speaking countries. Needless to say, private language schools at home, let alone abroad, are beyond the financial reach of the majority, so that the State's failure to deliver proper provision in its schools heralds a new form of social selection, based on access to foreign-language teaching.

The prevalence of in-house company schemes illustrates that top executives are not the only people who need to speak foreign languages; so do skilled workers travelling abroad 'on the job' and secretaries called upon to telephone outside the country.

Table 4   Foreign-language teaching in West German *Volkshochschulen* in 1987

Subject	Teaching hours		Numbers attending	
German as foreign lang.	635,598	16.2%	126,940	8.2%
English	1,330,146	33.9%	595,921	38.7%
French	717,975	18.3%	309,611	20.1%
Italian	359,976	9.2%	170,251	11.0%
Russian	57,411	1.5%	22,528	1.5%
Spanish	333,340	8.5%	150,743	9.8%
Arabic	12,616	0.3%	5,467	0.4%
Chinese	11,578	0.3%	4,738	0.3%
Danish	20,261	0.5%	9,295	0.6%
Finnish	2,929	0.1%	1,160	0.1%
Japanese	10,881	0.3%	4,631	0.3%
Latin	11,157	0.3%	4,192	0.3%
Modern Greek	38,285	1.0%	17,137	1.1%
Modern Hebrew	4,416	0.1%	1,848	0.1%
Dutch	20,151	0.5%	9,715	0.6%
Norwegian	6,783	0.2%	3,312	0.2%
Polish	10,026	0.3%	3,989	0.3%
Portuguese	18,214	0.5%	7,948	0.5%
Swedish	25,977	0.7%	12,300	0.8%
Serbo-Croat	9,966	0.3%	3,884	0.3%
Turkish	36,126	0.9%	14,705	1.0%
Other foreign langs.	27,792	0.7%	10,313	0.7%
German for Germans	223,401	5.7%	51,722	3.4%

Source: Statische Mitteilungen des Deutschen Volkshochschulverbandes, Arbeitsjahr 1987, zusammengestellt von der Pädagogischen Arbeitsstelle der DVV, Frankfurt am Main.

As this table demonstrates, adults form an important part of the language-learning population. What is more, adult education courses offer a broader spectrum of lan-

German	French	English	Italian
Im Gasthofe zum Krebs.	À l'auberge de l'écrevisse.	At the craw-fish hotel.	Alla locanda di gambero.
Haben Sie Päffe?	Avez-vous des passe-port?	Have you pass-ports?	Avete passaporti?
Da find fie.	Les voici.	Here they are.	Eccoli.
Sie können fie wieder auf dem Polizei-Bureau eine Stunde vor Ihrer Abreife abholen.	Vous pourrez les reprendre au bureau de la police, une heure avant votre départ.	You may fetch them at the police-office an hour before your departure.	Potranno riprenderli all' ufficio della polizia un' ora prima della loro partenza.
Wir wollen Ihnen eine Aufenthaltskarte geben.	Nous allons vous donner un carte de sûreté.	We will give you a card of acknowledgement.	Le daremo una carta di sicurezza.

In einem Gasthofe auf der Reife.	**Dans une auberge pendant le voyage.**	**At an inn during a journey.**	**In un albergo per viaggio.**
Ich möchte zwei Zimmer mit der Ausficht auf die Straße, auf's Meer haben.	Je voudrais avoir deux chambres donnant sur la rue, sur la mer.	I should like to have two rooms facing the street, the sea.	Vorrei avere due stanze colla vista sulla strada, sul mare.
Belieben Sie mir zu folgen.	Ayez la bonté de me suivre.	Please to follow me.	Favorisca di seguirmi.
Der zweite Stock ift etwas hoch.	Le second étage est un peu haut.	The second floor is some what high.	Il secondo piano è un poco alto.
Kellner, führet diefe Herren in Nr. 2, im zweiten Stock vorn heraus.	Garçon, menez ces messieurs No. 2 au second sur le devant.	Waiter, show these gentlemen up to number two, second story in front.	Cameriere, conducete questi Signori al No. 2, al secondo piano verso la strada.
Haben Sie nicht ein Zimmer für mich allein?	Ne pourriez-vous pas me donner une chambre pour moi seul?	Have you not a room for me alone?	Non avete una stanza per me solo?
Nein, fie find alle befetzt.	Non, monsieur, elles sont toutes occupées.	No, they are all engaged.	No, Signor, sono tutte occupate.
Das thut mir leid.	J'en suis fâché.	I am sorry for it.	Mene rincresce.
Wünschen Sie ein Zimmer mit zwei Betten?	Voulez-vous une chambre à deux lits?	Do you wish for a double bedded room?	Vorreb' ella una camera con due letti?
Raucht vielleicht diefer Kamin?	Cette cheminée fumerait – elle par hasard?	Does this chimney smoke?	Fuma forse questo cammino?
Nein, er raucht nicht.	Non, elle ne fume pas.	No, it does not.	No, non fuma.
Der Kamin raucht, man muß die Fenster öffnen.	La cheminée fume; il faut ouvrir les fenêtres.	The chimney smokes; we must open the windows.	Il cammino fuma; bisogna aprire le finestre.
Oeffnen Sie die Thüre.	Ouvrez la porte.	Open the door.	Aprite la porta.
Wo ift die Feuerzange und die Feuerschaufel?	Où sont les pincettes et la pelle à feu?	Where are the tongs and the shovel?	Dove sono le molle e la paletta?
Ich erfticke vor Rauch.	La fumée m'étouffe.	I am suffocaded with smoke.	Affogo dal fumo.
Der Rauch hat abgenommen.	La fumée s'est un peu dissipée.	The smoke has diminished.	Il fumo si e diminuto.

This four-language guide for tourists published in the nineteenth century is unlikely to have been of much use to the majority of travellers.

guages and, taking all subjects covered by the *Volkshochschulen*, foreign languages come out top. Clearly, then, any pan-European language-teaching strategy must take on board that adults can learn too. After all, we only spend a few years in school and the blanket assertion that we can no longer learn a new language 'properly' after a certain age has long ago been refuted. The annual rate of increase in the numbers of students attending courses currently on offer in the *Volkshochschulen* lies at around 15 per cent. During the 1980s, annual rises of 5–7 per cent were to be observed in the language tourism sector (school trips, language-learning tours for adults). In other words, whilst prices remained broadly unchanged, there was a doubling of turnover in the language industry in the course of ten years.

The need to learn languages

Rough statistics on the language requirements of trade and industry can usually be established, or else some good old-fashioned fieldwork can be done. However, another parameter is relevant in all this: the desire of individual human beings to learn languages. Apart from some research carried out by a team from Augsburg (±4000 interviews in 6 European countries), sadly no consideration at all has been given to this dimension. In that individuals often learn languages which will be of use to them in their jobs, there is admittedly a link between their needs and those of commerce and industry. Yet personal factors equally come to bear – holidays, reading books in the original – and people may also have purely emotional grounds for wishing to learn a specific language, either empathizing with a particular culture and civilization (or members thereof), or else quite simply admiring the beauty of the idiom.

One thing emerging from the Augsburg surveys was that, in the case of adults, conceptions of what is 'beautiful sounding' very much governed choice of which language to learn. People across Europe relate to the tonal qualities of languages, sometimes the opinion-profile was just typical for one nation, sometimes opinions converge across several nations. The resulting picture is pleasing or otherwise, depending on where one stands! The Finns are as convinced as the Irish, British or Germans of the unsurpassed beauties of French – only the Flemings are not so sure. Reactions tend to be neutral regarding the attractions of English; some nationalities are for, others against. From Helsinki to Galway, however, Russian goes down badly, unanimously viewed as an ugly-sounding language. German shares a similar fate – in Britain and The Netherlands at least. In fact the German language came out bottom of the league in all twelve European countries surveyed, thereby faring worse than Russian.

Stereotypes of the speakers involved clearly play a part when it comes to judging how aesthetic a language sounds. Russian is the language of Communism, aggression and overkill. For the Dutch, German signals the unpopular Big Brother to whom they are economically bound and without whom they can no longer get by; it is also, of course, the language of the Second World War aggressor. In Britain, too, ugly-German clichés abound, kept alive by war films and comics.

Teachers of foreign languages need to be aware of the students' aesthetic preconceptions about what they are being taught, for only then will it be possible to work through the clichés; a stereotyped vision stands in the way of true learning. Empathy for the foreign language in question needs to be fostered, often against considerable odds, particularly if students are not studying it voluntarily (e.g. it is a compulsory subject at school, or required by an employer).

People also have preconceived ideas about the level of difficulty of different languages; English is universally deemed to be 'easy', Russian and German extremely 'difficult'. There is certainly some truth in this, especially if English is compared directly with German or Russian. It is important, however, to put some perspective on things; students and the public at large would benefit from a more differentiated approach. In the final analysis, every language is easy in some ways and difficult in others; English could be ranked as one of the hardest of them all, as anyone who has endeavoured for years to achieve near-nativeness, knowing it to be ultimately a hopeless task, will have painfully discovered. English is difficult partly because it has relatively few traditional-style rules of grammar and, for the foreign-speaker, idiomatic usage can be obscure. Finnish, on the other hand, is difficult grammatically, but being a 'regular' language, its idiomatic patterns (and its prosody) are fairly straightforward. The 'easy'/'difficult' dichotomy, does, notwithstanding, tend to channel people's language-learning efforts.

Collective attitudes about the desirability of learning this or that language form a rich tapestry, which we would do well to look at very closely if we are serious about developing a decent language strategy for Europe. This more subjective side of things has been badly neglected and further research is urgently needed, focusing in particular on people's feelings towards a multilingual Europe and their views on the place of individual European languages. The results may well endorse some of the other conclusions reached by the Augsburg group, which broadly speaking were that:

- throughout Europe, women are more motivated and more successful language-learners than men, even though statistics show them falling behind in middle age in the absence of equivalent vocational experience.

- the desire to pursue languages learned at school and the keenness to acquire new ones are equally pronounced – providing the framework is right – in both sexes.

- in the case of adults too, a popular teacher is the key to fruitful learning.

- young Europeans pay no heed to 'minor' tongues; their requirements revolve around six languages: English, French, German, Spanish, Russian and Italian in that order.

A word on translation

This is not the place for expounding translation theory, but no one is going to deny that nowadays translation is on the agenda, considering the enormous appetite of the EC; around one third of the Community administration budget goes on translating and interpreting work. Twelve member States mean 120 language combinations; surely it is time the EC financial authorities began to press for a halt to such extravagance? And how much money will be spent once the 'common European home' is in place and we have regional languages as well (e.g. Slovenian).

What has been said thus far shows that there will be no viable alternative to multilingualism; languages are quite simply symbols of sovereignty and no nation as Europe develops is going to surrender on that. At ministerial level, at the very least, countries will insist on using their national tongue (a regional language from the European perspective). Reductions can only take place if particular working languages are agreed upon for particular circumstances; or if 'pivot' languages are used in interpreting (i.e. Danish, Norwegian and Dutch, say, would be interpreted into German and then from German into Portuguese, thereby avoiding the combinations Danish-Portuguese, Norwegian-Portuguese and Dutch-Portuguese). Interpretation using 'pivots', however, has the disadvantage of building in added potential for displacement of meaning; any act of translation or interpretation involves a shift (there are no perfect equivalents) and translation of a translation accentuates the process.

In summary

No ready-made model exists to guide Europe along its multilingual path. A centralized approach, based on a legally enshrined dominant language, is certainly not the answer. We cannot afford to finish up with a governing class of Eurocrats, at

This ultra-fashionable magazine aimed at young people goes so far as to translate 10 per cent of its content into Japanese, so as to appeal to young Japanese living in London. It is also on sale in mainland Europe and covers events there (credit: G Spot).

home in a language which sets them apart from everyone else. Neither would an invented language resolve the problems. Europe is set to become one big region, made up of minorities unfettered by a majority voice; hence there can be no 'majority' language. Even if more than one dominant language were introduced, its 'natural' mother-tongue speakers would be at a huge advantage, as if always playing on the 'home pitch' – and we all know you cannot organize a football league on that basis.

Post-1992, every EC worker will be a potential migrant or *Gastarbeiter*, even if he or she does not immediately get up and go. Moreover, a lot of people who have previously enjoyed relative security will be exposed to forms of competition never before experienced. The language difficulties of today's immigrant workers and their families presage the future for a Europe unable to formulate proper language strategies. We must be careful to avoid passing blanket-style legislation which ignores individual needs and circumstances.

Bilingualism and bicultural education no longer make sense where more than two languages and cultures coexist; neither is there an obvious 'culture gap' in Europe (at the most there are different levels of development), so one language and culture does not emerge as the obvious leader from an educational point of view. Language problems do not only occur in 'high places' and in government and administrative circles; professional interpreters and translators are not therefore enough. We shall only be able to solve future problems if mother-tongue competence is fostered and a strategy devised for promoting intensive learning of foreign languages from an early age. Europe needs the active participation of everyone, whatever language they speak. Germany has an additional problem – really an opportunity – in that it must keep the doors open to eastern Europe and beyond.

Statistics indicate that the Federal Republic, and most of the western European industrial states, have largely answered the call of the European Parliament and Commission for all citizens to speak at least one foreign language. That foreign language however tends always to be English, which is not good enough. It is regrettable also that so few students in secondary education learn more than one language; after all, they could be taught receptive or passive skills, enabling them to *understand* several languages. It is also unsatisfactory that, despite lip service being paid to diversification by one and all, nothing is being done to branch out beyond German, English, French, Russian and Spanish.

Consequences for education policy

On the unsuitability of the 'dominant language' model

Traditional foreign-language teaching aims to promote equal attainment in respect of productive (speaking, writing) and receptive, or passive, faculties (listening, reading). With the amount of time available, results often fall short of the goal. Receptive skills on their own, however, can be furthered relatively quickly and communication based on comprehension is already practised with a reasonable degree of success in many areas of the world.

The model of 'receptive' multilingualism means that more languages can be cultivated: those of countries and regions bordering on our own plus other idioms barely taught in schools at the moment. The labour market of the future will be an international one and receptive language teaching would facilitate cross-border and inter-regional understanding, which will without doubt be increasingly necessary. Simultaneously, our schools could rid themselves of the notion of 'major' and 'minor' languages; no neighbour should be more equal than another in tomorrow's Europe.

When speakers of two different languages find themselves communicating with one another via a third (international) language, they tend to feel hampered and awkward – unless they are brilliant linguists. Both sides have to transpose concepts into an alien system over which they are unlikely to have full mastery and their train of thought is interrupted by the need to grapple with grammar or the right turn of phrase; not to mention the problems of pronunciation. Precision goes to the wall, communication takes place on a monotone and content becomes over-simplified. What is more, listeners are treated to a very faulty, limited and unclear version of the 'real thing' as heard and studied in the classroom and their responses can prove unpredictable (fatigue, annoyance, even feelings of superiority or excessive self-confidence).

Cultural context, too, is broadly sacrificed when a language (in this case English) is used as an international tongue; yet the cultural rootedness of individual speakers is an important dimension of true communication, even in a technical environment (unless it is purely a matter of issuing instructions such as in air traffic control). Makeshift usage of an international language does not totally kill cultural overtones, but it does severely mask them. In addition it should not be forgotten that international languages always retain a nationally specific emphasis which means that they have their own idiosyncratic flavours.

As we have seen, the *lingua franca* model would involve around-the-world recourse to one international language: English. We have not quite reached that stage yet, although people in the most unlikely places are able to operate with 'minimal' English. However, minimalist communication is the problem world-wide, not the solution. Only if high-level command of English were to become the universal norm would it be possible to steer clear (in the main) of the inhibiting effects outlined above. The idea that resources will be mobilized to provide large numbers of people with top-level language teaching is, needless to say, economic and political 'pie in the sky' even in many European states. Take Germany, where English-language tuition is still not always given by qualified teachers of English in the *Hauptschulen* (secondary moderns); more than a third of lessons are taken by teachers of other subjects.

Another factor to bear in mind is that expanding English-teaching provision would lead to cuts in other areas, since school hours are not elastic. In poor countries, national-language education (and there is often more than one national language) would suffer too, the eventual outcome being cultural deprivation on a national scale. When a community as a whole experiences an erosion of its culture, collective panic ensues and the resulting mood can easily turn into neo-nationalism or religious fundamentalism, both of which are equally dangerous for international equilibrium. There has been no shortage of examples of this escalation in the course of the twentieth century.

The all-English model provides English-speaking countries with a twofold advantage; on the one hand, they finish up in the happy situation of a football club which plays only home games and, on the other, they are effectively the sole European states in a position to offer a broad foreign-language syllabus (comprising non-European languages too), since they do not have to invest time and money in the *lingua franca*. Whether or not the Anglo-Saxon nations would exploit such an opportunity is another matter.

Receptive multilingualism: a model for the future

An alternative to the scenario outlined above would be a model whereby as many Europeans as possible were able to speak their mother tongue and yet be understood by their opposite numbers. The inhibitions referred to earlier would be less widespread and people could at least speak and be heard, write and be read 'in the original', i.e. no more surrogate communication in the form of a *lingua franca*. Misunderstandings between cultures would also be reduced.

It is always easier to acquire receptive skills than to learn productive mastery of a language, particularly when sophisticated material is being dealt with; nor is there such a need for continuing training. Receptive language-learning can operate on the basis of the affinities between idioms – a method often leading into deep water at the productive, spoken level. Practice in adult education has revealed that receptive skills are still easier to acquire than active ones even where students have no knowledge (active or passive) of a related language. It is obviously useful to have had prior experience of learning a foreign language, although which one does not really matter. Germans with some knowledge of English will find it easier to develop receptive skills in French, Spanish or Italian than to attain active proficiency. What is more, the many historical and structural links between the European languages facilitate things; for example, the Latin component of English reappears in the Romance languages.

The receptive-learning model no longer works with rare or 'minor' languages, but a 'mixed' approach can be adopted instead. This involves allowing one side to speak its own language and the other will reply using the international *lingua franca*. The latter group will, as we have seen, feel somewhat restricted and hampered, but the others at least will be operating 'in the original', using their native tongue to fire back questions, check interpretations, put misunderstandings straight etc.

Unless the European nations can be made to coalesce on the basis of a proper strategy to promote receptive multilingualism, the position regarding language of today's immigrant workers will become the paradigm for tomorrow's communication. The use of ill-spoken international languages will spread, certainly at a regional level; witness what has happened in Germany as *Gastarbeiter-Deutsch* has developed into a *lingua franca* amongst Yugoslavs (of different ethnic origins) and Greeks as they travel by train between Zagreb and Salonika.

Our schools are where the journey towards a multilingual Europe might begin; languages should not be taught on the basis of some abstract notion of *educational* value. We live in a world where, as in the eighteenth century, encouragement is all around to learn many languages – and learn them faster and better. The educational dimension does not get short shrift just because emphasis is laid on receptive learning (reading, listening); after all, Europe's history and culture find their supreme expression in the standard written and spoken forms of its languages.

References

AEHLE, W. (1938) *Die Anfänge des Unterrichts in der englischen Sprache, besonders auf den Ritterakademien, Erziehungswissenschaftliche Studien 7*, Hamburg, Martin Riegel.

ARNDT, E. M. (1813) *Über Volkshaß und über den Gebrauch einer fremden Sprache*, Leipzig.

BEHNSCH, O. (1840) *English Made Easy. Praktischer Lehrgang zur leichten und schnellen Erlernung der englischen sprache. 1. Kurs*, Breslau.

CHRIST, H. and LIEBE, E. (1981) 'Fremdsprachenunterricht in amtlichen Verlautbarungen', *Augsburger 1 & 1 – Schriften 14*, Augsburg University.

DECSY, G. (1986) *Statistical Report on the Languages of the World as of 1985*, (Bibliotheca Nostratica Ser Vol. 6:1), Bloomington, Eurolingua.

FINKENSTAEDT, T. and SCHRÖDER, K. (1990) 'Sprachenschranken statt Zollschranken? Grundlegung einer Fremdsprachenpolitik für das Europa von Morgen', in *Materialien zur Bildungspolitik II*, Essen, Stifterverband für Deutsche Wissenschaft.

HAARMANN, H. (1975), *Soziologie und Politik der Sprachen Europas*, München, Deutscher Taschenbuch Verlag.

HAARMAN, H. (1983) *Elemente einer Soziologie der kleinen Sprachen Europas, Band 1: Materialien zur Sprachökologie*, Hamburg, Helmut Buske Verlag.

HAGEN, S. (1988), *Languages in British Business. An Analysis of Current Needs*, Newcastle-upon-Tyne, Newcastle-upon-Tyne Polytechnic Products in association with Centre for Information on Language Teaching and Research.

RAAB, H. (1956/57), 'Germanoslawisches im Ostseeraum an der Wende vom Mittelalter zur Neuzeit', *Wissenschaftliche Zeitschrift der Ernst Moritz Arndt-Universität Greifswald. Gesellschafts- und Sprachwissenschaftliche Reihe 6*, pp. 57–60.

SCHRÖDER, K. (1969) *Die Entwicklung des englischen Unterrichts an den deutschsprachigen Universitäten bis zum Jahre 1850*, Ratingen.

SCHRÖDER, K. (1982), *Linguarum Recentium Annales. Der Unterricht in den modernen europäischen Sprachen im deutschsprachigen Raum. Volume 2: 1701-1740, Augsburger 1 & 1 – Schriften 18*, Augsburg University.

SCHRÖDER, K. (1985), *Linguarum Recentium Annales. Der Unterricht in den modernen europäischen Sprachen im deutschsprachigen Raum. Volume 4: 1771-1800, Augsburger 1 & 1 – Schriften 33*, Augsburg University.

SCHRÖDER, K. (1989), 'Über Volkshaß und über den Gebrauch einer fremden Sprache. Zur historischen Dimension des Schulsprachenstreites Englisch-Französisch, unter besonderer Berücksichtigung der nach-napoleonischer Zeit', in KLEINSSCHMIDT, E., *Fremdsprachenunterricht zwischen Sprachenpolitik und Praxis*, Festschrift in honour of Herbert Christ on his 60th birthday, Tübingen, Gunter Narr, pp. 58–70.

SCHWAB, J. CHR. (1785) *Von den Ursachen der Allgemeinheit der französischen Sprache und der wahrscheinlichen Dauer ihrer Herrschaft*, Tübingen.

VIËTOR, W. (1882) *Der Sprachunterricht muß umkehren!* Heilbronn.

Essay 2
Education

Prepared for the Course Team by Bob Moon
Professor of Education, The Open University

> It's bad enough not being able to learn for the whole of life. Our
> forefathers set great store by the teaching which they received in their
> youth: but nowadays we have to relearn everything every five years so
> as not to get completely out of date.
>
> *Goethe: Wahlverwandtschaften I*

Introduction

This introduction sets out some of the issues that have characterized debate in
European countries over the past few decades; the democratization and opening up
of schooling, the reform of curriculum and the evolving patterns of control in different education systems. Three short vignettes provide examples of students and
institutions in three countries (France, Poland, England), illustrating where reforms are focused in the early 1990s and pointing to what will be discussed in the
rest of the essay.

The cartoons on pp. 66–7, two from France and one each from Britain and
Germany, provide an insight into some of the common understandings, the shared
problems and the subtle differences that characterize education systems in Europe.
You will probably recognize the tensions satirized here as factors within your own
education system. Common debates and controversies have dominated discussion
in many European countries. The placard in the German cartoon is saying 'Down
with ALEF'. Long-haired sixties youths are seen demonstrating against one of the
most famous modern maths schemes then being introduced into many German
schools. The 'New Maths' movement, an educational phenomenon that still survives strongly in public folklore, touched the policy and practice of every
European country. It became embroiled in the heady political unrest of the sixties.
In France one professor was moved to comment:

> Pornography, drugs, the disintegration of the French language, upheavals
> in mathematics education all relate to the same process, attacking the
> central parts of the liberal society.
>
> *(L'Express, 6 February 1972)*

to which his antagonist replied:

> Do we wish to sacrifice democracy and make two types of citizen? On
> the one side specialists, an élite monopolizing knowledge because they
> have access to scientific understanding, and on the other side a crowd of
> idiots content to be submissive because they cannot speak the language
> of the living world.
>
> *(ibid.)*

Education, like so many other social institutions, both forms and responds to culture and context. The British cartoon, also from the 1960s, a period when secondary school democratization was a dominant feature of educational reform. The raising of school leaving ages, the dismantling of centuries-old divisions between academic, élite schools and technical or general education became the focus of intense political debate. The move to a common secondary education in comprehensive schools gained the ascendancy. Even the ideological fervour of Margaret Thatcher, holding her first senior ministerial post in education at the beginning of the 1970s, failed to stem the tide. Ironically she presided, in a much quoted statistic, over the closure of more academic 'grammar schools' than any other minister before or since. The new comprehensive schools, however, were to provoke controversy across the political spectrum. From the right these new institutions were portrayed as grey, uniform and soulless, more akin to a car factory than the cosy memories of the small, intimate schools of yesteryear. The cartoonists exploited the critique. And then in the 1970s the failure of the new schools to increase social mobility, to raise working-class participation in higher education was to provoke more muted but equally polemical attacks from the left.

The democratization of institutional structures at secondary level was one of several issues in the post-war era common to many countries. Sweden, after extensive debate and research, was one of the first countries to effect wholesale national reform. In Germany and the Netherlands, despite national debate and controversy, the forces and interest groups opposing institutional reform retained the initiative. A few ex-

(cartoon credits: A Hundred of the Best Times Eductional Supplement Cartoons, Penguin Books, 1968, D. Lamb; Plantu, Wolfgang, tu feras informatique!, Gallimard, 1988.)

perimental schools were established in the Netherlands. In Germany only Hesse, one of the then eleven German '*Länder*', introduced common secondary schools and this development has been one of continued controversy. The debate found new fuel after the merger of the former Federal German and German Democratic republics in 1990 since the latter had a comprehensive system up to age 16. In France a more piecemeal approach (inconsistent perhaps with the notion of central planning but acknowledging political reality) brought about the college structure up to the age of 15 with the traditional *lycées* taking on the role of 'tertiary' institutions predominantly concerned with the teaching of the *baccalaureate*.

Even as Minister of Education, Margaret Thatcher may have been impotent to halt the implementation of comprehensive systems of schooling, but by the mid-1980s a new climate of reform was established. As Prime Minister, she presided over one of the most wholesale changes in British education since the establishment of a national system of education in 1872, bringing in new laws to move control to the centre. And yet, as a British Conservative government was concentrating power in the hands of central government, in Sweden, strong central control of policy and curriculum organization was devolving to local communities in a rapid and quite astonishing decentralization of responsibilities.

Educational viewpoints and positions cannot easily be attributed to political stances either within or between countries. In France in the early 1980s Jean-Claude Chevènement, the second education minister in the recently elected Socialist government, was making speeches and introducing reforms in schools that were not so dissimilar to those being advocated by Margaret Thatcher's most right wing colleague, Education Minister Keith Joseph. Within the German Federal Republic in the 1970s the reform of school mathematics, 'New Maths', was advocated and opposed by right and left wing parties in each of the *Länder*. In *Länder* such as North Rhine-Westphalia it was the conservative Christian Democrats who saw political advantage in opposing the reforms. In Baden-Württemberg the left-of-centre Social Democrats fought the proposals advocated by the right. In Hesse, where the influential ALEF project originated, local authorities controlled by the left rebelled against implementing it in their schools. We can see then that, over the last decade, reform has extended beyond institutional structures to the style and content of the curriculum. This debate has echoed through European history; it discusses the nature of knowledge, the purpose of schooling and our perception of the potentialities of human growth and understanding. Do schools exist to allocate places within the social order or to re-form the social order? Is the historical function of schooling to determine place-ments on a scale appropriate to the latter half of the twentieth century? Should the tearful child in the French cartoon with a below average IQ continue to be castigated? Was the basis upon which society acknowledged educational worth appropriate? Should we change our understanding of human potential or the criteria by which such potential is judged, or both? How can schools respond to social and demographic changes (the immigration of workers from Turkey and North African countries into Germany, France and other countries, for example)? Can schools be expected to educate children to be 'better' citizens than the exam-ples they find outside school (see last cartoon example)?

Educational reform has become a highly politicized process and debate about where the focus of power and control should reside has become equally significant and controversial. Most significantly, the role of central government as opposed to the decentralized autonomy of regions or local areas – what one French writer (Gremion, 1976) called '*le pouvoir périphérique*' – has been a source of ongoing debate throughout Europe, especially in the restructuring associated with the reforms in east European education systems. Controlling, democratizing and modernizing education are three themes, easily identified in the social and political history of all European countries, that this essay will address. First, however, let me briefly sketch out three biographies of students studying in the 1990s in France, Poland and England, which may illustrate those points at the chalk-face.

Nadia is a 20-year-old student at the Lycée Pierre et Marie Curie situated in one of France's most central towns, Châteauroux, at the heart of the old Berry region, today the *département* of the Indre. The town, known today as the birthplace and home for a few unhappy years of the actor Gérard Dépardieu and famous throughout France for a high security prison, boasts four *lycées* each with a distinct character reflecting the various reform phases of the 1970s and 1980s. The Lycée Pierre et Marie Curie offers five of the eight baccalaureate 'sections' available in France. Nadia's parents were born in Algeria and moved to France and Châteauroux in the early 1960s. Nadia, born in France, remains an Algerian citizen. Both she and her parents are practising Muslims. Nadia is one of the many young people who have responded to the French government's attempts to give 80 per cent of all French students access to the high status *baccalaureate* examination. Her choice was the linguistic Bac 'A' and last year she failed to gain the necessary grades to qualify for the award. This year '*elle a redoublé sa terminal*' (has taken her final year again). She aims to gain a University place reading law for which her *baccalaureate* is essential. Nadia's examination comprises six sections as the subjects and weightings in the table below illustrate:

Table 1   Bac. A. 2

A2: Literature and Languages	Duration	Weighting
Tests from the first group		
Written		
• Philosophy	4 h	5
• History–geography	3 h 30 m	3
• 1 modern language	3 h	4
• 2 or 3 modern languages, or 1 classical language	3 h	3
Oral		
• 1, 2 or 3 modern languages, or 1 classical language	20 mn	3
• Mathematics	20 mn	2

Source: Documentation Lycée Pierre et Marie Curie.

The Lycée Pierre et Marie Curie, originally a girls *lycée* in the town, has expanded to over 1500 students and has been chosen as the *département*'s specialist school for musicians. The rapid expansion of numbers has led to classes of over thirty-five and the building programme has failed to keep pace with the growth. In the early 1990s, students from Pierre et Marie Curie joined in nationwide demonstrations against their working conditions.

Zuzanna, 15-years-old, is just about to enter the *Liceum III* school in Wroclaw, Poland. She chose to attend the school, some distance from her home, and not the closest *Liceum* because it specializes in mathematics. Like Nadia in Châteauroux she has had experience of demonstrations. Under martial law the headteacher of her previous school banned the singing of carols in school. The students, in response to this, formed a large choir and proceeded to sing a selection of the most famous Polish carols right under the windows of the headteacher's office. Zuzanna, just before leaving the school, was able to witness the reception of a local priest into the school, the first time the church had access since the end of the Second World War. Unlike Nadia, whose classes occur any time between 8 o'clock in the morning to 5 o'clock in the afternoon, Zuzanna's classes finish at 2.30 p.m. She is studying for the *Matura* examination and in addition to her specialist classes in mathematics (taught by a teacher in the school and a lecturer from the university) has to study and be examined in ten subjects: Polish; geography; biology; history; physics; chemistry; art, music and two modern languages.

Zuzanna's parents are university lecturers; her father, a leading figure in the Solidarity movement in the early 1980s, was imprisoned for two years during the martial law period. Zuzanna is one of the 15 per cent who gain access to the *Liceum* style of schooling and she hopes to be one of the 10 per cent who proceed to university. She studied Russian and German at her previous school, and has now elected to take English for the first time. In the afternoons she attends a special music school where, as a talented violinist, she is making exceptional progress.

Thirty miles along the Thames from central London is the riverside town of Henley-on-Thames, famous for a rowing regatta which ranks alongside the annual tennis tournament at Wimbledon, a Lords cricket Test match, or 'Ladies Day' at the Ascot Races, in the English social calendar. James is studying for three Advanced level examinations in history, mathematics and chemistry at Henley College, a new tertiary (post compulsory) college created from the formerly separate St. James College, a sixth form centre specializing in academic Advanced level subjects and Henley College of Further Education. Each subject is studied separately and good grade passes in three (only a very small number of students study more than three subjects) are required for entrance to university. James came to Henley College from a nearby comprehensive school. Both he and his parents liked the atmosphere of the new college and in the evenings James is studying Italian, a subject that was not available at his previous school. James has many friends who are studying vocational courses within the College, although the courses and classes for these are taught separately. He has no idea about future jobs. His choice of Advanced level subjects means that he will not be able to go on to study certain subjects at university (medicine, for example) and he has already had a session with a careers counsellor about the different courses that are available. His predicted grades are not high and, therefore, his choice is more limited. The distinction between universities and polytechnics has now ended and

James is looking at courses at several of the 'new' universities. The government's reform of higher education has been matched by proposed changes in the structure of post-compulsory education. One major aim is to increase the current (in European terms low) percentage staying on into full-time education after the compulsory period of school. Increasing the staying on rate will also, it is hoped, have an impact on the percentage qualifying for and obtaining places in higher education (currently, again, low in European terms, about 14–15 per cent of the qualifying age group).

All three students are being taught within institutions that have undergone, and are undergoing, radical reforms. Each story illustrates the way the urge to democratize and open up education has moved to the older post compulsory years. In France the slogan of the '*80% Bac*' has created both political and educational debate. In England the sharp separation of academic A-level subjects and more vocationally oriented courses is seen as a deterrent to higher staying on rates and an inducement to subject specialization at too early an age. Numerous pressure groups have been advocating the adoption of a *baccalaureate* type solution with, as in France, a variety of vocational as well as academic options. In Poland the dismantling of the communist system of control has necessitated a re-evaluation of the purposes of the élite lyceum type school. Some small changes have taken place, such as the reintroduction of religious classes into schooling. The debate about reform, however, is heavily circumscribed by the constraints associated with the restructuring of the national economy.

There are differences, but also many parallels in the three contexts described above. This essay will examine these and related issues under four major headings. The first section deals with the origins of Europe's education systems, looking at their historical and political background. Particular attention is given to the way the control of education has evolved in different systems. The second part, on processes of democratization in education systems across Europe, considers the founding of national state systems of education, the extension of secondary education to all, the debate about the form that the expansion of secondary education should take and the opening out of the post-compulsory and higher education sectors. In a third section, the growing involvement of European and other international agencies in reviewing and reforming education systems is discussed; particular attention is given to the widespread concern about equality of opportunity in the education of girls and women throughout Europe.

The conclusion looks to the future, particularly in terms of the sort of education provision represented by this course, part-time learning and new forms of technology.

The historical and political origins of Europe's education systems

This section first describes how interest in the comparative study of education systems stretches back to the beginning of the nineteenth century. You will then be invited to consider the differences and the significant similarities you can observe in examining the characteristics of different systems. Four major traditions are described (Essentialism, Encyclopaedism, Polytechnicalism and Pragmatism) a combination of which contributes to the structure and content of education provision as we see it in Europe today. You will then be introduced to a discussion of the early years of national state education systems by looking at the nineteenth century concept of the 'common school' through the work and ideas of François Guizot in France and Hofstede de Groot in the Netherlands. Finally, the different ways that national systems have developed contrasting structures for controlling education are reviewed, and the question of how permanent such structures are is raised.

Comparative perspectives

Economic and political realignments in Europe have provoked an increased interest in comparative information across a range of institutional structures. Education is no exception. Interest in the relationship between economic performance and education provision is likely to ensure that this will be a recurring and controversial feature of academic and public debate. In many disciplines specialist branches of comparative enquiry and a theoretical and methodological literature have been established. It is interesting to note how far back the comparative traditions in education stretch. In Europe the first educationist to adopt a comparative approach was Marc-Antoine Julien de Paris who published in 1817 his *L'Esquisse et Vues Préliminaires d'un Ouvrage sur L'Education Comparée*. He proposed an analytical study of education in all countries with a view to perfecting national systems with modifications and changes which would be appropriate to local circumstances. In a passage which reflects the prevailing optimism about the emerging interest in science, he wrote:

> Education, as other sciences, is based on facts and observations, which
> should be ranged in analytical tables, easily compared, in order to
> deduce principles and definite rules. Education should become a positive
> science instead of being ruled by narrow and limited options, by whims
> and arbitrary decisions of administrators, to be turned away from the
> direct line which it should follow, either by the prejudice of a blind
> routine or by the spirit of some system and innovation.

Very soon after, in 1834, a professor of philosophy, Victor Cousin, published for the French government his *Report on the State of Public Instruction in Prussia*. This was to have an important influence, not only in France but also in neighbouring European countries. It established a tradition which continues to the present day, although nowadays perhaps the Japanese rather than any European country have become the object of curiosity, description, comparison and, for some, emulation.

Matthew Arnold writing, in England, in the second half of the nineteenth century, was another advocate of comparative study. In his inaugural lecture as professor of poetry at Oxford in 1857, for example, he insisted that 'connection is everywhere'; and that 'no literature can be adequately understood when isolated from other events and other literatures' (Rapple, 1989). Arnold attempted to imbue a more

Matthew Arnold (1822–1888), English poet, essayist and one of the most influential literary critics of the nineteenth century, Arnold served as inspector of schools from 1851 to 1886 (credit: courtesy of the Trustees of Dove Cottage).

cosmopolitan, a more European outlook in what he saw as his insular and provincial compatriots. Yet he was aware of the dangers of naive comparisons:

> It seems to me, then, that one may save one's self from much idle terror at names and shadows if one will be at pains to remember what different conditions the different character of two nations must necessarily impose on the operation of any principle. That which operates unwholesomely in one, may operate wholesomely in the other ...
>
> *(Arnold, 1861, quoted in Rapple, 1989)*

Arnold adhered to the view that the more that is learnt about other societies the greater the knowledge of one's own. Writing in 1868, he said that:

> Having long held that nothing was to be learned by us from the foreigners, we are at last beginning to see, that on a matter like the institution of schools, for instance, much light is thrown by a comparative study of their institution among other civilized states and nations. To treat this comparative study with proper respect, not to wrest

it to the requirements of our inclinations or prejudices, but to try simply and seriously to find what it teaches us, is perhaps the lesson which we have most need to inculcate upon ourselves at present.

(Arnold, 1868, quoted in Rapple, 1989)

In the twentieth century we have seen the growth of comparative education as a field of enquiry in its own right, with journals, designated professors in university departments and all the associated activities that accompany academic respectability and legitimacy.

In this essay I am not seeking to provide an analytical enquiry into the contemporary characteristics of different education systems, what *x* can learn from *y*, or to discuss the way in which prevailing trends can inform policy and practice within countries or across groups of countries. Rather, I hope to provide a basis for understanding the origins of education systems and a framework for thinking about systems today and the challenges and problems they face. Within such a framework the different kinds of education experienced by Nadia, Zuzanna and James have many common origins and many common challenges for the future.

First impressions

You may have had the experience, as an adult, of visiting schools, perhaps those your own children attend. You will have finely-tuned sensitivities in observing the way things have changed, or not, from your own school-days. Certain features are enduring. The grouping of pupils into classes, the titles of subjects, the lesson timing and timetables across the day, week or year. In other respects there are differences: the increased emphasis on information technology; less discernible, but no less important differences in the authority relationships between teachers and pupils and then, of course, styles and modes of dress.

When you visit schools in other countries and in different education systems you bring a particular range of criteria to bear in making judgements. Language and cultural barriers may make you less astute in analysing different characteristics of the situation you are observing. However, clues to the differences between systems are often to be found in the minutiae of daily school life. Last year, for example, in the space of a few weeks I spent days in rural English, French and Japanese primary schools. There was much to see but I remember particularly the different ways in which the midday meal was approached. In England the children ate quickly in a hall supervised by part-time non-teaching staff; in France the teachers presided over a much longer, three course meal; in Japan the children, divided into groups, had to take responsibility for serving and clearing away the chosen menu for the day. In England the lunchtime ritual seemed insignificant to the school's organization; in France it reflected a view of relationships, although in an implicit way, whereas in Japan the process was built into the purposes of the school. Within Europe there are always such differences: the English tradition of games and extra curricular activities; the midday end of classes in Germany; Saturday morning lessons in France, are three examples. There are other more significant differences. The starting age of schooling, for example. In France the majority of 4-year-olds now attend the *école maternelle*, whereas in Denmark formal schooling only begins at age 7. The Netherlands has four types of secondary school, the Swedes one. Swiss children learn two, often three, other languages whilst the British struggle to learn one.

These differences represent cultural and geographical factors. The English concern with games and other activities derives from the traditions of the prestigious private schools (confusingly termed '*public*' schools), which were boarding schools. The strict separation of church and state in France required freeing one weekly period (Wednesday afternoons) for voluntary religious instruction. The claims of various denominations have led to a variety of provision in the Netherlands with 80 per cent private schools (maintained, however, by the state). The sheer distances that children have to travel to school help explain the later school starting age for Danish children. Finally, the geographical location and political make-up of the Swiss nation explains much about the need and the motivation to learn languages. Education and schooling is, therefore, inextricably tied up with social and cultural norms.

There are, however, many basic similarities between our European education systems. Table 2 shows, for example, the weekly timetables of the lower secondary school in Italy.

Table 2   Subjects presented for the lower Italian secondary school

Subjects	Weekly timetable – No. of hours			Final Examination Tests
	I grade	**II grade**	**III grade**	
Religion	1	1	1	-
Italian	7	7	6	written; oral
History, civic education, geography	4	4	5	oral
Foreign language	3	3	3	written; oral
Mathematical, chemical, physical and natural sciences	6	6	6	written (math only); oral
Technical education	3	3	3	oral
Artistic education	2	2	2	oral
Musical education	2	2	2	oral
Physical education	2	2	2	oral
	30	30	30	

Source: Taken from the Description Papers of the International Seminar on *Core Curriculum in Western Societies,* SLO, Enschede, the Netherlands, November, 1985.

Anyone with any experience of secondary schooling in European countries would be familiar with the subjects. You would, of course, have to probe beneath the surface to see whether civic education would be comparable to that taught in Britain or Sweden. The same might be true of technical or what is termed artistic education. In other subjects there are likely to be many similarities. European education – western education – evolved from many common cultural and historical roots. Today we describe education systems in terms of national systems. Accounts of educational change are most commonly framed in national terms. Educationists and sociologists, like historians, have been drawn to the study of national institutions and to observing the attempts to resolve national problems. It is easier and more convenient, the material can be more readily collected and synthesized, it is politic and it has become a tradition. The nation is an important social unit and the most obvious one to study. People live in nation-states and possess national consciousness. Moreover as Shafer (1955, p. 265) suggests 'as practitioners of the scientific methods, scholars are bound to look for distinctions, for differences of kind, level and function; and nationality is the most significant contemporary group distinction'. This was not always the case. Across the course of European history the present pattern of nation states represents a very recent phenomenon. And in the Europe of the 1990s concepts of nationality and statehood are being tested in the aftermath of widespread political change.

Historical traditions

The periods, ideas and people that have provided the foundations for European education systems have been categorized in a multitude of ways. I want to take one of the most recent analyses produced by two comparativists well-known in Britain. Holmes and McClean (1989) identify four major strands that influence curriculum. They introduce their classification with the following statement:

> In Europe, and indeed throughout the world, changes in political theory have been more readily and widely accepted than the theories of knowledge on which curriculum theories depend. In so far as political and to a lesser extent psychological theory changes have influenced some aspects of national educational systems, here the retention of traditional epistemologies creates normative inconsistencies and curriculum lag in systems of education undergoing change.

The four strands are:

1   Essentialism

In the educational field this generally means concentration in the curriculum on what is defined as essential by those in authority. In *The Republic*, the Greek philosopher Plato envisaged a stable, hierarchical society, in which teachers were expected to perform a political public service. A just and stable society required a governing élite, including the philosopher kings, whilst others played a subservient supporting role, for which they should also be appropriately prepared. A man's position in society would depend on the intellectual ability he displayed. Plato's curriculum for the élite was a major influence on the development of European education. Some of the principles and their assumptions survive robustly to the present day. His curriculum was deliberately exemplary, not all-embracing. The subjects he saw as essential for developing intellectual rigour and for the demonstration of mental ability came to be strictly canonized by late antiquity. They are the seven liberal arts of the Romans. Plato's second stratum of society consisted of the warriors – followers and implementers of the more intellectually gifted leaders' orders – who were to receive a practical education. The strict differentiation between the prestigious study of ideas and the vocational studies thought suitable for the lowlier executives and administrators was born – and is still influencing thinking on education today. The 'essentials' for the élite became the subjects which dominated the content of education – almost exclusively in the hands of the Church – in the Middle Ages. The *quadrivium* – music, astronomy, geometry and arithmetic – provided content, and the *trivium* – grammar, rhetoric and philosophy or logic – developed the processes of personal enquiry or reasoning.

2   Encyclopaedism

From the 16th century onwards, scientific ideas and new modes of thought began to challenge the prevailing orthodoxy. The period of transition was replete with martyrs. The persecution of Galileo, for example, represented the meeting point of two conflicting approaches to knowledge and understanding. Perhaps the most powerful and effective advocate of a broader vision of education was Jan Amos Komensky, known commonly by his Latin name of Comenius, who was born in Moravia, part of present day Czechoslovakia, in 1592. In his lifetime Comenius, raised in the minority Protestant faith of the Unites Fratrum (Unity of the Brotherhood) was a refugee fleeing Catholic persecution in the wake of the Thirty Years' War. His odyssey took him to what are now Germany, Poland, England, Sweden, Hungary, Romania and the Netherlands. He believed in the underlying unity of all human experience and he saw education as the key to avoiding social and political disharmony. *Omnia sponte fluant absit violentia rebus* (were violence absent all things would flow spontaneously) was his personal motto. He firmly believed that knowledge needed to be encyclopaedic and available to everyone. In 1631 he published his own textbook, *Janua Linguarum Reserata (The Gate of Tongues Unlocked)*. This was a simple encyclopaedia with ninety-eight topics ranging from the organs of death to angels, and was an instant bestseller. The volume was translated into many languages. One edition had parallel columns in English, French, German and Italian. He advocated universal coeducation from the age of 7 and his curriculum for the primary stage included domestic economy and handicrafts. From the age of 13, the more intellectually gifted pupils would go on to the grammar (or Latin) school. Comenius emphasized a child-oriented approach, using practical examples for the child's environment, and the appeal to as many senses as possible. The more optimistic, egalitarian educational message of Comenius appealed to the French revolutionary governments at the end of the eighteenth century. They took his six-subject curricular proposal for the second school stage – grammar, dialectics, rhetoric, ethics, physics and mathematics – and developed a curriculum structure that spread throughout France and to most other European countries:

Mathematics;

Classics;

Physical and biological sciences;

Geography;

History;

Fine arts;

Mechanical drawing.

This pattern of subjects, similar to that now presented for the lower secondary school in Italy (see Table 2), has persisted over time. Consider the curriculum for the English secondary school (Table 3) as prescribed in 1904, 1935, and 1988:

Table 3   Subjects prescribed for the English secondary school

1904	*1935*	*1988*
English language	English language	English
English literature	English literature	
One language	One language	One language
Mathematics	Mathematics	Mathematics
Science	Science	Science
Geography	Geography	Geography
History	History	History
Drawing	Drawing	Technology
Due provision for manual work and physical exercises (Housewifery in girls' schools)	Physical exercises and organized games	PE
	Singing	Music
		Art
	[Manual instruction for boys, dramatic subjects for girls]	RE

This fusion of the essentialist and encyclopaedic traditions has done much to shape the schooling we see across Europe today. There are, however, two further traditions, more recent in origin, which have significantly affected thinking on the what, how and why of schools' curricula.

3   Polytechnicalism

Holmes and McClean have adopted this term to describe those theories, Marxist in origin, which see the major task of the curriculum as eliminating, in a post-revolutionary period, the false consciousness inherited from a capitalist society, whilst giving pupils an all-round introduction to the technical knowledge and insights into production and organizational methods they need to come to terms with work in a modern industrial society. In the history of ideas, this approach to education can be seen developing in the ideas of utopian thinkers, from Thomas More and Francis Bacon to the early socialist thinkers Claude-Henri Saint-Simon, Charles Fourier and Robert Owen. Marx knew of Owen's factory school and this doubtless acted as a model as he developed his ideas on education. Another strand in the development was provided by models of higher technical education such as the first *École Polytechnique* in Paris in 1794, which was soon copied throughout Europe, accompanied by the setting up of the first agricultural colleges. It was seen as a necessity to confront the young with the world of work – an increasingly technical and scientifically determined environment – whilst still at school. Pestalozzi, the Swiss educational reformer, was another influential pedagogue who advocated elementary education for industry. Giving children insight into productive techniques and understanding of the whole context of production was intended to have an emancipatory effect. Polytechnical education, for Marx and his followers, formed the central axis of their educational thinking, with a major role in the formation of well-rounded socialist personalities and with the aim of overcoming the inhumane effects of industrial production techniques. All children were to have wide-ranging technical-scientific training, which would enable them to take up the place of their choice to contribute fully to the industrial society. Ideally, schools were to have close links with production plants. This approach was not without its critics within the Soviet bloc, which has been as prone to fashions in education as any other society (one problem was the incompatibility of pedagogic planning and production schedules), but in the past two decades it has again had the upper hand, whilst it was well-recognized that general education must not be neglected either. In the German Democratic Republic, all comprehensive schools were called polytechnic schools and in certain grades children actually made parts which were later incorporated into the production process of some local factory. Major problems with the approach arose from the wish to produce youngsters with a good all-round technical and general knowledge whilst a system short of resources cried out for specialists, i.e. from the conflict between the ideal (utopian) long-term aim and the short-term economic necessity. From a Western perspective, obviously, the greater problem was the all-imbuing socialist ideology imparted in all subjects, which became inseparable from the polytechnic approach.

The social purposes of a curriculum are well illustrated by the Soviet concept of *vospitanie* or moral education which in the mid-1980s was made up of eleven components:

Socio-political awareness (to make citizens politically active and literate);

Morality and ethics;

Patriotism and internationalism (to encourage love of the socialist motherland and worldwide proletarian solidarity);

Military-patriotic education (to develop the desire to defend the motherland);

Labour education and professional orientation;

Mental development and the raising of general culture;

Atheism;

Knowledge of the law and the obligations of a citizen;

Economics;

Aesthetics;

Physical education.

Similar creeds were established in many eastern European countries. Agnieszka Wojciechowska (1990), a Polish educationist, has been particularly scathing of the impact that this type of orientation had on the curriculum in Poland. The remarkable political changes that swept across many countries in the 'revolution year' of 1989 have, of course, had important consequences for education, with whole systems in turmoil as curricula – and staff – at all levels are quickly 'recycled' to fit a new market-economy orientation.

When considering previous national policies for the curriculum in Poland (as typical of other Socialist states) we must look at two separate problems connected with two groups of school subjects. The first group contains those subjects with some ideological content, which can be used to indoctrinate pupils overtly (history, Polish literature, Russian and occasional special ideological subjects). In the second group are mathematics, sciences, music and sport, where the propaganda goals could be realized only incidentally and rather indirectly, albeit with a powerful 'hidden curriculum'.

Looking at the first group we can see that from the 1950s to the 1980s the main goal was the same: to educate the ideal member of the 'developed socialistic society'. The methods changed slightly over time, becoming more sophisticated and less repressive, but over the whole period the same three paths of indoctrination were used in schools. The first of these was reticence – persons, events, works not convenient for communist propaganda were simply doomed to non-existence in the lessons of history and literature. The second was simply lies – the facts to be taught were garbled or misrepresented, some persons were denigrated, while others were whitewashed. The third was an attempt to build the Marxist world outlook and a pro-communist and pro-Soviet attitude among the pupils.

This third group of educational efforts was completely unsuccessful, but the first two had some effect. The curricula and history textbooks mainly charted the events of Polish–Soviet relations, the history of the communist movement, with something of the history of pre-communist Poland. But even this earlier history misrepresented what had happened. (Germany, for example, was presented as the main enemy of Poland from the beginning and the long-term problem of relationships with Russia since the sixteenth century was consequently diminished. The Polish–Soviet war of 1920 and the Soviet attack on Poland on 17 September 1939 did not exist in the manuals of history. The history of Poland in the inter-war period was distorted, as well as the non-communist and anti-Nazi resistance. Many leaders of the Polish underground were called traitors and the – very small, in fact – communist guerrilla group had its importance greatly exaggerated.) Post-war Polish history was even more misrepresented. The teachers themselves were ignorant in these areas, as they had been educated in the same system, or they were perhaps afraid to teach pupils anything different from the textbooks.

Bias, of course, cannot be solely laid at the door of the polytechnical curriculum. The representation of most national histories is open to such accusation. However impartial the intentions of teachers, as textbooks often illustrate, differences of interpretation are bound to appear. The Georg Eckert Institute in Germany has been studying the books used in schools for a number of years. Table 4 shows how two parallel German history texts chose to highlight markedly different events in describing the origins and development of the Industrial Revolution in Europe.

Stripped of its propagandistic aims, the polytechnical approach remains a fruitful source of educational thinking. Painfully slowly it seems, western ideas on schooling are changing to allow pupils a peep at the technical and technological wonders of the modern world. With extreme scepsis, educationists are allowing industry into the classroom or placing youngsters in factories and firms for a taste of the world of work. Advocates of a good basic education in technical subjects still have a long way to go to gain acceptance. Many of the initiatives of the EC in the field of education are in fact in this area of studies.

4 Pragmatism

In a fourth category, Holmes and McClean see the work of the American philosopher and educationist, John Dewey, as having particular influence. Significant knowledge, for Dewey, was that which enabled pupils to deal with problems, preparing them for life in a democratic society. For him this entailed starting from the interests of the child and building up on them. The teacher was to be a guide and facilitator, providing opportunities for pupils not only to reflect but also to act. He was concerned to find a style of schooling which was in accord with the democratic principles of the United States. For him this could only mean a common school for all children:

> There must not be one system for the children of parents who have more leisure and another for the children of those who are wage-earners. The physical separation forced by such a scheme ... brings about a division of mental and moral habits, ideals and outlook ... A division of the public school system into one part which pursues traditional methods, with incidental improvements, and another which deals with those who are to go into manual labour means a plan of social predestination totally foreign to the spirit of democracy.

> The democracy which proclaims equality of opportunity as its ideal requires an education in which learning and social application, ideas and practice, work and the recognition of the meaning of what is done, are united from the beginning and for all.
>
> *(Dewey and Dewey, 1978)*

His practical work, in an experimental school, was carried out in Chicago in the early years of the twentieth century. His influence, however, quickly spread to Europe. Through the 1920s and 1930s new, progressive, experimental schools were established, commonly independent of the national state-funded school

Table 4   Comparative chronologies of the Industrial Revolution taken from two German textbooks

From	*Erinnern und Urteilen**	From	*Die Industrielle Revolution***
		1690	Dennis Papin builds first piston steam-pump in Marburg
1705	Thomas Newcomen develops piston steam pump used for draining mines		
1733	The weaver John Kay invents the flying shuttle, which doubles production on one loom		
1735	The iron manufacturer Abraham Darby makes coke from coal to replace charcoal		
1738	P. Lewis invents a mechanical procedure for cleaning cotton		
		1750	First rolling-mills founded in England and France
1766	First blast-furnace in England		
1767	Invention of the 'Spinning Jenny'' by weaver James Hargreaves to operate several spindles at one time		
1769	Precision tool-maker James Watt constructs an efficient steam-engine		
1771	Barber Richard Arkwright combines several spinning machines driven by water power to form a factory		
		1774/6	Claude Jossroy tries to use steam to drive ships on Seine and Doubs
1779	Samuel Crompton develops a machine for spinning very fine thread		
		c.1780	Invention of twisting machine in Wuppertal
1782	Watt supported by Matthew Boulton, develops a steam-engine that transmits the movement of the piston into a revolving movement		

From	*Erinnern und Urteilen**	From	*Die Industrielle Revolution***
		1784	J.-G. Brügelmann founds first mechanical spinning factory in Germany
1785	Steam-engine used to drive spinning machines	**1785**	First German steam-engine used in a mine
1786	Edmund Cartwright develops first practicable mechanical loom		
		1794/6	First German coke blast-furnace in Gleiwitz
		1797	First iron bridge on the Continent near Striegau
		1799	Königshütte (second German blast-furnace)
		1801	First German steam-operated factory
		1802	Foundation of Cockerill's in Liège
		1804	Experiments with a steam-streetcar by Evans in Philadelphia
1807	First steam-ship built in New York		
		1808	Invention of the Jacquard loom in Lyon
1810/14	Friedrich König and Andreas Bauer build steam-driven printing machines in Eisleben	**1810**	Foundation of Henschel's in Essen
		1812	Invention of ship-screw by Ressel
1814	Mining engineer George Stephenson builds first steam-locomotive		

*From *Erinnern und Urteilen III*, p. 65. Explanations slightly abridged.
**From W. Killmann, *Die Industrielle Revolution*, 6th edn, Stuttgart, 1982, p. 15ff.
Source: Georg Eckert Institute.

The first German coke blast furnace at Gleiwitz (credit: Deutsches Museum, Munich).

83

Denis Papin (1647–c.1712) French-born British physicist, who invented the pressure cooker and suggested the first cylinder and piston steam engine (credit: Bildarchiv Preussicher Kulturbesitz).

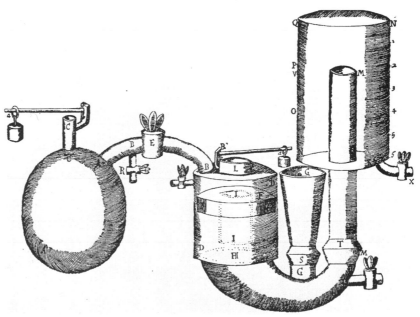

Papin's prototype steam pump, in a drawing dated 1706 (credit: Bildarchiv Preussicher Kulturbesitz).

system and espousing his child-centred, project-based methodologies. These ideas in time have come to have a significant influence on the content and methods used in primary schooling in many European countries and the principles of curriculum development that have underpinned many subject reforms at secondary level. Dewey's ideas can be linked to many of the philosophers of the post-Renaissance period and beyond. His optimistic vision of human potential, the ambitions for the rapidly populating USA and the new means of communicating ideas quickly across the Atlantic made his work especially influential. In Dewey we see one of the signs of the passage of ideas between Europe and America, a fruitful and continuing process that has come to be one of the most significant educational developments of the twentieth century.

Towards the end of his life he experienced many attacks on his basic tenets as critics alleged that this mode of schooling neglected essential core subjects and produced ill-disciplined students. This 'progressive v. back-to-basics' controversy continues today.

Holmes and McClean have selected their own personal categorization of traditions influencing education systems today. Other authors have chosen different labels. Religious traditions (Catholic, Anglican, Puritan) and secular ideas (socialism, nationalism) provide categories that would give different perspectives. Other great historical terms – Renaissance, Reformation, Enlightenment – have all provided the organizing structure for comparative and historical awareness. It is important to understand, whatever the perspective, that the education systems we now have are shaped in part by these earlier influences.

Political origins

In many countries the Platonic conception of curriculum fused with the encyclopaedic movement that was so significant in the late eighteenth and early nineteenth centuries in revolutionary France. Both influenced the way, through the latter part of the nineteenth century and the early years of this century, that all European countries established mass, compulsory, state-controlled education systems. In secondary education, for example, most countries in western Europe retained a separation of schools into those serving an academic élite and the majority that prepared young people for technical, manual or 'housebound' roles.

The theme of democratization goes back well into the last century and marked a first break in the dominant hold that the church had on school provision. In some countries (Italy, for example) the education system evolved in parallel with the nation state. In other countries (France) the nation state had been well-defined and the imperative was to extend access to schooling, both as part of the citizen's individual rights and in response to the rapidly evolving needs of the social and economic structures.

I want to briefly illustrate the process of establishing national education systems by reference to two countries, France and the Netherlands, and two reformers, François Guizot and Hofstede de Groot, for whom the common school, not necessarily in the form we see it today, was one of the principal means for establishing and promoting the ideology of modern democracy.

François Guizot in France

François Guizot in the mid-nineteenth century was a social reformer determined to establish a new social order. He was firm in his opposition to the restoration of feudal privileges and deeply suspicious of the role of the Catholic church in national affairs. For Guizot, government and society were inextricably fused with education and schooling occupying a critical place in the new World Order.

The task as he saw it was to: 'create a government by the action of society and society by the action of government' (Guizot, 1817). And so:

> The state obviously needs a great lay body, a great association deeply united to society, knowing it well, living at its heart, united also to the state, owing its power and direction to the state, such a corporation exercising on youth that shapes it to order, to rules.
>
> *(Rosanvallon, 1985, pp. 232–3)*

For Guizot a national system of education was an issue of control as well as rights. He wanted 'a teaching corps belonging to the state, fed by the state … It is essential to establish and strengthen the ties of the teaching corps to the state' (Guizot, 1860). In 1832 Guizot became Minister of Public Instruction and immediately set about extending popular education and significantly endeavouring,

François Guizot (1787–1874) French political figure and historian. He was minister of education from 1832 to 37 and was responsible for the so-called Guizot law, which established the principle that secular primary education should be accessible to all (credit: Paul Nadar/ c Arch. Phot. Paris/S.P.A.D.E.M.).

as he said in his memoirs, 'to penetrate even to the soul of popular teachers', (Guizot, 1860, pp. 71–2).

In terms of provision he achieved a great deal. Between 1834 and 1848 the number of boys' elementary schools increased from 22,641 to 32,964. The number of pupils in school rose from 1,935,624 in 1831 to 3,240,436 in 1846. Guizot heralded the rise of a national system of closely inspected elementary schools. It is important to note the fervour with which the state became independent of the church:

> Formerly, the church alone possessed the control of minds ... All this is over. Intelligence and science have become expanded and secularized ... But precisely because they are now more laical, more powerful and more free than formerly, intelligence and science could never remain beyond the government of society ... the government should not remain careless or ignorant of the moral development of succeeding generations and ... as they appear upon the scene, it should study to establish intimate ties between them and the state.
>
> *(Guizot, 1860, pp. 14–16)*

Guizot's assertions about the moral duties of government and the extent of the control of government reverberate down through the nineteenth and twentieth centuries. In its extreme form, however, some manifestations of his sense of duty might seem excessive to societies moving into the twenty-first century. In one of his most famous initiatives he sent a letter to 39,000 teachers, each of whom had to both acknowledge receipt and indicate what impression it had left with them. I quote from the letter:

> liberty can neither be assured nor regular, except with a people sufficiently enlightened to listen, under all circumstances, to the voice of reason. Universal elementary education will become henceforward a guarantee for order and social stability ... Faith in Providence, the sanctity of duty, submission to parental authority, respect to the laws, to the sovereign, and to the common rights of all – such are the sentiments which the teacher must labour to develop ... The peace and concord he will maintain in his school ought, if possible, to prepare the tranquillity and union of future generations.
>
> *(ibid., pp. 327, 330–31)*

Hofstede de Groot in the Netherlands

In the Netherlands an academic protestant theologian, Petrus Hofstede de Groot, was advocating a similar moral purpose for the common school. Attitudes and values for de Groot were as important, if not more so, than skills of literacy and numeracy. Unlike Guizot, whose career ran in parallel, de Groot was primarily an academic who performed a part-time role in school inspection and the in-service training of teachers.

The Dutch embraced the concept of the common school in the early years of the nineteenth century with laws in 1801, 1803 and 1806. These achieved notable results and attracted the interest of French reformers such as Guizot. As in many

Petrus Hofstede de Groot (1802–1886) was professor of theology at the University of Groningen from 1829–1872. In 1833 he accepted an appointment to the part-time position of school inspector, visiting each school in his district annually, and holding 'in-service' training sessions for teachers several times a year (credit: Rijksmuseum, Amsterdam).

countries the extension of schooling in the eighteenth century had been a haphazard affair with church and charities playing a major role. Central control of the Netherlands, however, was much weaker with the balance of power both between religious traditions and between church and state much more evenly balanced. The Dutch word *verzuiling*, a derivative of *zuil* meaning pillar, is used to express the concept of pluralism or separate development. The division of Dutch society into such pillars (sometimes taken as a reference to the various schools of advice offered by the followers of St. Simeon Stylites, hermits who squatted out their lives at the top of pillars) has long historical roots dating back to the break between the Protestants of the United Provinces and the Catholics of the Spanish Netherlands in the sixteenth century. By the early nineteenth century Dutch society had absorbed a greater degree of tolerance towards religion and religious difference than in countries such as Catholic France to the south. The rising middle classes who advocated *volksverlichting*, or the enlightenment of the common people, had what Siep Sturman has called a very watered-down Christianity, a modernism which was 'essentially a faith in the improvement of the world and the educability of mankind through rational interventions' (Stuurman, 1983, p. 107).

The Dutch attempted to graft on to church schooling liberal and secular purposes within the concept of a common school. Through different laws, and in response to changing political influences, the relative importance of church and state fluctuated across the early years of the nineteenth century. These fluctuations were often associated with impassioned public debate. De Groot, unlike Guizot, was a fierce champion of the role of religion in the formation of national character:

This led to an emphasis upon the instrumental, subjective side of
religion, its role in the progressive development of the human
personality, coupled with a disregard for the Orthodox Protestant and
Catholic teaching that such 'sanctification' is a stage subsequent to and
dependent upon an objective act of Redemption by God in history.

(Glenn, 1988, p. 55)

In 1844 De Groot published a book with the title *Are Separate Schools for the
Various Church Fellowships Necessary or Desirable?* a question to which he
gives a clear answer, no! But schooling would still, in contrast to Guizot's secular-
ism, be based on generalized Christian principles. The debate in the Netherlands
was to remain undecided. Advocates, however, of strong central government
control were constrained by religious interests, which to the present time separate
secular, Protestant and Catholic types of schooling existing in a decentralized
structure of educational responsibilities.

Guizot and De Groot were both advocates of the common school and the
democratization of education through the provision of elementary schools. A
century on, this same process, as we discussed in the introduction, was to be
extended to secondary schooling. The lifetimes' work of both these nineteenth
century educationists was dominated by the relation of church and state. This
relationship and the way it was reflected in the newly emerging education systems affected school structures and curriculum. It was also to have a major
influence on the forms of educational control that developed through the nineteenth and twentieth centuries and is, therefore, of major importance in understanding the way in which different countries make decisions about educational
issues. The issues raised are of great significance if any future plans for
European unity have implications for the nature of authority and control within
national education systems.

The control of education

In popular imagination there are some sharply contrasting conceptions about the
way education is controlled. Traditionally the French, *par excellence*, are seen as
having a highly centralized, sophisticated and bureaucratic means of directing policy, even day-to-day events, from Paris. How many times do we hear a repeat of
the oft-quoted but mistaken portrayal by Hippolyte Taine of the Education
Minister who could look at his watch and observe at a certain hour 'in a certain
class all pupils are interpreting a certain page of Virgil' (Ambler, 1987). Until the
advent of Margaret Thatcher and the Education Reform Bill of 1988, the system in
England and Wales was often juxtaposed as the antithesis of French centralization,
with control devolved to very localized regional authorities and often – concerning
staff appointments and the curriculum, for example – to the school and headteacher. This has changed significantly, although the process of change has been
controversial with a prolonged struggle for power between local and national
agencies and departments. The opposite direction towards decentralization and
regionalization has already been cited in the case of Sweden, and since the 1960s
France has been attempting to move in the same direction. The referendum upon

which General de Gaulle staked and lost his political future was in part about regional policy. Numerous articles, books and reports from European educationists have examined the issue of control.

A report by the Organisation for Economic Co-operation and Development, for example, says that the contrast between centralized and decentralized systems is 'an obvious indicator of style, both with regard to education in general and curriculum development in particular' (OECD, 1972, p. 36) – a view reflected in a wide range of books and reports (see Moon, 1986).

These concerns provide a starting point for analysing the extent to which these models and categories are borne out when we observe the way different parts of the education systems work in practice.

I indicated briefly that the existing format structures for control date back to the different ways in which national education systems were established independent of, or related to, the Church. One of the most frequently cited authorities in this area is Margaret Archer who in 1979 produced a lengthy analysis of the social origins of educational systems (Archer, 1979). In the context of the social and political changes taking place in Europe it is significant to consider the extent to which systems do exercise control in different ways and, where there are differences, just how meaningful these are. Archer set herself the ambitious task of answering the question: 'how do education systems develop and how do they change?' (ibid., p. 1).

Using a macro-sociological approach illustrated and supported by evidence from France, Russia, Denmark, England and Wales, she advances a theoretical model which explores both the origins and development of education systems as well as proposing possible ways in which they may change over time. The church, in its different forms, is identified as the common historical factor in each of the systems. Varieties of structure, centralized and decentralized, are seen to have arisen from the different ways in which successive groups became liberated from religious constraint. Centralized systems developed where freedom from the old orthodoxy was achieved through political action and the restriction of the activities of the church by law (Guizot and other French republicans). Decentralized systems were more likely to originate where financially powerful groups, disadvantaged by religious control, established educational institutions outside the influence of church or state (the Dutch merchant classes and the ecumenical influence of De Groot). The emergence of the state system, however structured, represents the second cycle in the model.

Within the second cycle more varied forms of interaction appear, relating to centralized or decentralized systems. The distinction is a central feature of the theoretical framework. Two different styles of interaction are proposed. In centralized systems:

> political manipulation is the main process through which educational
> change is pursued and produced ... the study of interaction, is,
> therefore, the study of educational politics *stricto sensu*.

(ibid., p. 271)

On the basis of this overarching theory it is suggested that two further variables exert a crucial influence and explain, therefore, why countries with centralized systems may proceed along a distinctive path. The first is the structure of political decision making (an aspect of the political structure) and the second the structure of educational interest groups (an aspect of the social structure). Both interrelate within an arena which is distinctly 'political' and where issues, decisions and processes occur (ibid., p. 277).

In decentralized systems, however, different conditions obtain. Archer stresses the greater complexity of interaction:

> Instead of the simple convection current pattern of the centralized system (in which grievances were cumulated, passed upwards to the political centre, negotiated there through political interaction, before being transmitted downwards to educational institutions as policy directed changes), a more complicated pattern of cross currents characterizes interaction and change in the decentralized system.
>
> *(ibid., p. 393)*

This greater complexity is seen as manifest in a threefold rather than a single political mode of interaction. Internal initiation, external transactions and political manipulation are seen as of equal importance in the analysis. The first describes the process whereby increased autonomy enables professional educators to play a part in determining the rate of exchange between resources received and services supplied (ibid., p. 239).

The second indicates:

> ... relations between internal and external interest groups. It is usually instigated from outside educational boundaries by groups seeking new or additional services ... the profession is one of the groups involved in these negotiations, but the other party opts into the transaction of its own accord.
>
> *(ibid., p. 240)*

Whereas in internal initiation the parties engaging in negotiations are given, and their interaction inescapable, in external initiation the parties vary and their interaction with professional groups is voluntary. Thirdly, political manipulation is the final resort for those who have no other means of gaining satisfaction for their educational demands.

> This form of negotiation arises because education now receives most of its funds from public sources. In time a whole series of groups (depending on the nature of the regime) acquire formal influence over the shaping of public educational policy.
>
> *(ibid., p. 242)*

Power, therefore, must be seen in terms of the availability of various kinds of resources. The extent and location of such resources will change over time. Archer acknowledges the complex interrelationships of these three forms of negotiation and infers more than once that they give rise to greater complexity in decentralized systems.

In the final part of the analysis, centralized systems in a phase of structural elaboration are seen as characterized by a 'stop-go' pattern because:

> policy-directed changes are usually slow and cumbersome to bring about ... they represent a punctuation of educational stasis, for education can change very little between such bouts of legislative intervention. Patterns of change, therefore, follow a jerky sequence in which long periods of stability (i.e. changelessness), are intermittently interrupted by policy-directed measures. This has been termed the *Stop-Go* pattern.
>
> *(ibid., p. 617)*

For Archer, however, the very different characteristics of the two systems suggest that:

> the prospects for change are that future educational interaction will continue to be patterned in dissimilar fashions in the two systems and that the products of change will reproduce the main features of centralization or decentralization.
>
> *(ibid., p. 790)*.

This is only a very brief account of a very detailed argument. Inevitably for a major work it has attracted significant critical comment, for instance, that anyone knowing how a system is manipulated at a local level must be sceptical as to whether the different controls foreseen are visibly operative in the institutions themselves. Some see the French system (her choice for an example of centralization), as a case in point, or argue that the evidence fails to justify the degree of decentralization accorded to the English system.

Researchers in other fields have grappled with the same issue. Douglas Ashford, for example, in looking at local and national planning policies has cautioned against the dangers of allowing traditional and formal procedures to obscure our understanding of the way systems work in practice. In a comparative study of French and English bureaucracies he argues:

> that central–local relations, viewed through the multidimensional components of the subnational system, are paradoxically more formal and rigid in Britain, a country often admired for its pragmatic politics. In France [however] the subnational system is more important to the political system and the formalities of administrative and political behaviour can easily cloak the more flexible and diverse ways that political action has devised to influence each other.
>
> *(Ashford, 1982, p. 367)*

An oversimplistic categorization of national systems also begs the question of scale and geography. In Germany, for example, a number of the sixteen *Länder* are larger than some of the existing nation-states of Europe. Control of education is devolved to the *Länder*, which are exceedingly wary of any moves by Brussels to gain a foothold in the control of any educational decision-making.

My own research into the ways in which the formal structures for controlling the school curriculum worked in practice raised many questions around the theoretical model advanced by Archer (Moon, 1986). I looked at the introduction of new modern mathematics into the systems of Denmark, England, France, the Netherlands and what was at that time West Germany. My conclusion was that formal systems of control represented just one of a variety of variables that determine how events develop. In the 1960s other social forces steered by significant interest groups (reforming teachers, university mathematicians, textbook publishers) tended to bypass the existing authority structures or subvert them to their own ends. In the late 1960s, for example, hundreds of thousands of French elementary school children were studying new maths textbooks against the backdrop of curriculum regulations that had not altered since 1945! Similarly in the Netherlands the 'stylite' devolved form of control was circumnavigated by a successful and highly centralized national agency for mathematics based in Utrecht.

To understand the way that systems work and how change occurs you have to look, therefore, beyond the rhetoric of official and formal structures at local, regional and national level to the much more complex interplay of interest groups, social movements and, on occasions, the activities of key individuals. In recent years disillusion with the usefulness of macroanalysis has pushed many educational workers into a concern with the more tangible and important world of local developments, microanalysis of schools, studies of classroom interaction and so forth. Yet national systems, as we see daily in the media, do have an identity and meaning of their own. Linking the way policy is developed nationally to our increasing understanding about how schools work successfully is an ongoing challenge for educationists, a challenge made significant by the emerging debate about the internationalization of education. If the 1970s and 1980s have been concerned about central–regional relations within national systems, the 1990s and first decade of the next century are likely to add the supranational or European dimension, perhaps enhancing a new concept of regionalism. In coming to decisions about where control should reside, decisions informed by a plethora of historical traditions and contemporary value judgements, our understanding of the way systems work in practice will be crucial.

The democratizing of education across Europe

This section examines the ways education has been affected by the democratization of European societies. The structure of schooling that characterized the early period of national systems of education is considered and the influence of the progressive school movement of the 1920s – a movement that often saw itself as an alternative to state schooling – is discussed. The development of the common secondary school and the democratization of education at this level across Europe (with particular reference to Sweden) is reviewed. The uncertainties and doubts that became associated with state schooling in the 1970s and 1980s are explored, as are the questions that are now informing debate on the opening out of the postcompulsory and higher education sectors.

The different national forms of European education, so much determined by historical, political and social developments within the separate countries, show a striking homogeneity when viewed from a non-European perspective.

(Rowlinson, 1974, p. 29)

We concluded the first section by reflecting on where the control of education resided and whether this would change as the impetus towards the internationalization of national concerns developed across Europe. We also looked at the moves towards establishing common schools that began in the early years of the last century and gathered pace in the 1870s and 1880s in parallel with the social transformations that accompanied rapid industrialization. In this section I want to look at the process of opening out or democratizing schooling with specific references to the controversies surrounding secondary school reform in the 1960s and 1970s and the current interest in access to the post compulsory and higher education sector today. As we consider both it is interesting to reflect on the extent to which these are, and will remain, issues of merely national concern.

Guizot and de Groot's advocacy of the common school was to come to fruition in their own countries and across Europe towards the end of the century. A series of major education reform bills, often concerned with religious issues as well as educational exposure, are clustered around the 1870s and 1880s. Forster's 1870 Act in England and Wales, Ferry's 1881/2 Act in France, Kappeyne's school law in the Netherlands in 1874. In Prussia, where as early as 1841 literacy rates approached 90 per cent (Bowen, 1975, p. 322), an 1868 law extended the *Volksschule* curriculum to eight years with compulsory attendance.

The extension of both elementary and secondary education was still conceived within separatist and divided systems. Nowhere in western Europe was the American high school to be replicated until the latter part of the twentieth century. Educational expansion was largely confined to elementary education, especially for the rapidly expanding industrial working classes, and to secondary education for the newly emergent middle class. Figure 1 shows the growth but also the segmentation of Prussian secondary education in the period from 1870–1911.

Access to the élite *gymnasium* remained restricted over the same period. Between 1875–1899, for example, three quarters of those successfully obtaining the *Abitur* (the leaving examination providing access to higher education) had fathers from one of the established learned professions. Only 9 per cent had family origins in agriculture, 7 per cent in technical occupations and 4 per cent in commerce (Ringer, 1987). The social divisiveness of secondary schooling, such a major preoccupation in most national systems in the latter half of the twentieth century, was to impinge little on policy in the 1920s and 1930s.

In the nineteenth century the linkage of class and education was simply taken for granted. This permitted Lord Taunton's Commission in England, for example, to propose in 1868 a three grade system of schools to reflect the three grades of society, each with its own curriculum. First grade schools were to prepare children for Universities and their curriculum should be that of classics, elements of politi-

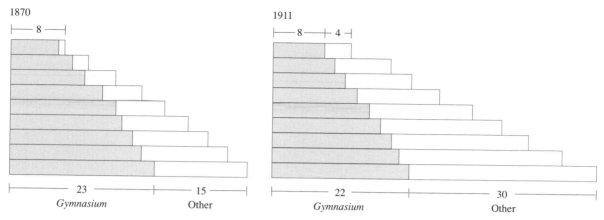

Figure 1 *Growth of Prussian secondary education, 1870–1911*
Source: Ringer, 1987.

cal economy, modern languages, maths and natural science. The Second grade schools were to prepare pupils for professions, business and the army and should have a curriculum of Latin, Maths, Science and a Modern Language. The Third grade schools were for those who would be artisans who should enjoy a curriculum of basic subjects plus inorganic chemistry, practical geometry and drawing.

This unquestioning acceptance may have been eroded by the political upheavals of the twentieth century and the implicit search for meritocratic forms of schooling, but the separation of schools – public–private; elementary–secondary; grammar–technical – was to prevail through most of the first half of the century. In some measure (how much is an issue of some debate) the different types of school reflecting the class structure of the nineteenth century was bolstered by scientific twentieth-century evidence from the newly emergent field of psychology. Across Europe, in part influenced by the works of people such as Thorndike in the USA, the belief in a single inherited type of intelligence that could be measured at a very early age took hold. In England, for example, a major national report on the education system drew heavily on the evidence of people such as Sir Cyril Burt, a dominant international figure in the determinist school of psychology, in arguing:

> Intellectual development during childhood appears to progress as if it were governed by a single central factor, usually known as 'general intelligence', which may broadly be described as innate all-round intellectual ability ... Our psychological witnesses assured us that it can be measured approximately by means of intelligence tests ... We were informed that, with few exceptions, it is possible at a very early age to predict with some degree of accuracy the ultimate level of a child's intellectual powers ...
>
> *(The Norwood Report, quoted in Moon et al., 1989, p. 93)*

This conviction about generalized intelligence was to deeply influence the structure of schooling. Those defined as above average, sometimes well above average, were allocated to the élite school – *gymnasium, lycée,* grammar school. A more general, sometimes technical education was presented for the remainder.

The issue remains a live one to this day, both in terms of the retention of separate schools, as in Italy, Germany or the Netherlands, for example, or in the debate about the internal organization of the unified comprehensive schools of Sweden and Britain and the *collège* in France. Before looking at this issue in rather more detail it is important to note one development that has had significant influence in most countries and achieved a much acclaimed institutional presence around the 1920s.

The foundations for the so often termed 'progressive' ideas of the 1960s, much maligned by some politicians, is to be found in the ripple of, often privately funded, progressive schools that were established half a century or more earlier in most countries. Each grew from a particular mix of influences and inspiration. Most (and here you can go back as far as Tolstoy's very personal school) were founded by evangelists for educational reform who led by example and through personal charisma. Rousseau, Dewey, and others provided the philosophical foundations and most were much discussed and in some small measure emulated within national education systems.

There are many examples: A. S. Neill at Summerhill in Suffolk, England; Kurt Hahn at Salem in Germany; and Kees Boeke's *Werkplaats* in the Netherlands. Most were founded in the aftermath of the 1914–18 war with high aspirations for creating a new type of education within the global, rather than the national, com-

A class of Prussian 17- and 18-year-olds photographed in the late nineteenth century (credit: Archiv für Kunst und Geschichte).

munity. Some espoused Christian principles, others adopted a deliberate humanistic perspective. At the *Werkplaats* (workshop) in Bilthoven near Utrecht the founding figure, Kees Boeke, who with his wife Beatrice Cadbury (the youngest daughter of the creator of the chocolate industry with that name in England) decided to educate their own children, and subsequently others, on the basis of principles that owed much to Quaker pacifist traditions. Having given away all their money Kees and Beatrice Boeke tried to build up a school to demonstrate that just as children love the direct and spontaneous, so they love order and method; and indeed that, without the latter, spontaneity breeds only disagreement and strife, leading in the end to a rejection of freedom. Thus the problem of school life was how to preserve the spontaneity that gives rise to strong personalities without losing the order and friendly co-operation that are essential to a harmonious community. Order can be preserved, for a time at least, by the imposition or threat of force. But the fears and tensions due to such methods put an end to all naturalness and spontaneity. Some way must therefore be discovered of securing order with as little compulsion as possible, so that children may grow naturally, without their character being warped by fears or frustrations.

This 1992 photograph of a class of German 17- and 18-year-olds makes an interesting contrast with the Prussian youths photographed a hundred years before; girls make up nearly half the class (credit: Buergel-Goodwin).

A. S. Neill's school at Summerhill. Neill (1883–1973) originally founded a community school at Hellerau, near Salzburg, which eventually settled at Leiston in Suffolk in 1927. Summerhill was described as a progressive school which 'began as an experiment and became a demonstration' (credit: John Walmsley).

The school was highly successful, with many of its offshoots surviving the war-time period and eventually achieving recognition as an experimental school type, partially funded by and linked to the national system of education.

Although much discussed, such schools in other countries rarely achieved the recognition afforded to the *Werkplaats*. The economic problems of the 1930s, the educational vacuum created by the war years from 1939–45 and the massive programme of reconstruction that followed, diverted attention away from the philosophical questions raised by these experimental schools.

Although the immediate post-war question centred on the physical provision of schools for the rapidly expanding school population, questions about the form of that provision were soon to be raised. Sweden was one of the first countries to question the traditionally separate forms of secondary schools and in the process attracted worldwide attention, both for the ideas pursued and for the process which eventually led up to the 1962 legislation that unified the secondary phase of schooling.

There is considerable evidence of the influence that the Swedish experience had on other national systems. Torsten Husén (1989) has indicated the links and visits to the British Labour Education Minister in the mid-1960s. A decade earlier the Permanent Conference of Ministers of Education in the Federal Republic of

Kurt Hahn (1886–1974) founded his school at Schloß Salem and was head from 1920 to 1933, when he was forced to flee from Nazi Germany to Great Britain. He founded Gordonstoun School in Morayshire in 1934. This is how Salem School looks today (credit: Schule Schloß Salem).

Germany appointed an *Ausschuß* (committee) with the task of co-ordinating school reform amongst the educationally autonomous *Länder*. The committee was to visit Sweden to look at the pilot programme of comprehensivization. In France, Jacques Delors revealed his interest in and awareness of the Swedish experience in a 'book long' interview called *Changes* which was published in 1975 (Delors, 1975).

Through the 1960s across Europe, the growth of secondary school pupil numbers, the expansion of economies and the widening of social aspirations, particularly amongst the middle class and skilled workers, was fuelling the debate about a more democratic, unified structure of secondary education. In England and Wales large numbers of local authorities moved towards a comprehensive system. Pressure from government ensured, as we saw above, that Margaret Thatcher, as Minister of Education in the Conservative government from 1970–74 following six years of Labour control, was to preside over the introduction of more comprehensive schools than any minister before or after. In her first 32 months as Secretary of State for Education she received 2,765 schemes for comprehensivization and rejected fewer than 5 per cent of these. It should also be noted that in her

thirteen years as Prime Minister, from 1977–1990, despite rumours and some rhetoric to the contrary, no school or area was changed back or allowed to exercise selection of any sort! Unlike England, where the process of comprehensivization was spread over a decade or more, other countries took, like Sweden, a more deliberate approach. In Denmark legislation, first developed in 1972 and passed in 1975, brought into effect the nine year comprehensive school in 1976. And in France René Haby first proposed a unified college structure in a report of 1975, a reform introduced systematically over a number of years.

Added to all this, in many countries there was growing strength of what has in some countries been termed the 'New Right' with a polemic, and sometimes a political power base, strictly opposed to comprehensive school reform. Arguably the polemic of the 'New Right' began defensively as a response to the myriad of ways in which tradition and authority, especially in education, had been challenged in the wake of the 1968 student rebellion. One example, achieving notoriety at the time, was the Danish *Little Red School Book* first published in 1969, translated a year later into German and achieving the distinction of being banned in Britain in 1971. The radical questioning of automatically assumed authority, especially in schools, the marked neutrality on sexual issues, and the advice on contraception, all provoked a storm of protest.

Controversy was rife and the forces of opposition in some countries proved sufficiently powerful to constrain the common secondary school to specific areas or to

The Danish Little Red School Book *was widely translated and used, particularly in the Scandinavian countries, around 1970 (credit: Kongelige Bibliothek, Copenhagen).*

DEN LILLE RØDE BOG FOR SKOLEELEVER

BO DAN ANDERSEN
SØREN HANSEN
JESPER JENSEN

HANS REITZEL
KØBENHAVN 1969

BO DAN ANDERSEN
SØREN HANSEN
JESPER JENSEN

KOULULAISEN PIENI PUNAINEN KIRJA

KUSTANNUSOSAKEYHTIÖ TAMMI
HELSINKI

the status of other long-running experimental schools. The debate in the Federal Republic of Germany was particularly strident. The controversy about the *Gesamtschulen* developed strongly after the publication in 1969 of a special study by the Federal co-ordinating body, the *Deutscher Bildungsrat* which looked at the setting up of comprehensive school experiments. The study illustrates the ideas and ideals associated with comprehensivization in the late 1960s:

> the starting point for all justifications for the need for *Gesamtschulen* lies in the demand for equality of opportunity. Furthermore it is nowadays becoming clear that educational reform in the cause of greater equality of opportunity can also lead to better schools for all pupils; it can enhance the achievement of the education system as a whole, contribute to a greater individualisation of learning, and come to terms with the fact that in our society all people are increasingly oriented towards an academic education.
>
> *(quoted in Mitter, 1991, p. 156)*

Reflecting the social as well as educational motives underpinning the proposed reform, the report suggested that:

> Common social experience in the *Gesamtschule* should not aim at accommodation to harmony in the community. The meeting of the various social classes in the common school can rather lead to the discovery and awareness of social differences. Social conflicts can be articulated and collectively discussed. The pupils come to understand

Das kleine rote schülerbuch

verlag neue kritik

BO DAN ANDERSEN   SOREN HANSEN
JESPER JENSEN

LE PETIT LIVRE ROUGE DES ÉCOLIERS ET LYCÉENS

Nouvelle édition revue et augmentée
par
SOREN HANSEN
JESPER JENSEN

Traduction et adaptation française :
Lonni et Etienne BOLO

101

that the forms of life that are taken for granted in the family are not in the nature of things unchangeable. The perspectives which can thus be gained *vis-à-vis* one's own social origin and the forms of life that have previously been taken for granted can operate in an individual's favour.

(quoted in Mitter, 1991, p. 156)

In the Federal Republic, as in the Netherlands as well as Mediterranean countries such as Spain and Italy, resistance to secondary school reform marginalized attempts at comprehensivization. Any discussions that attempted to move beyond structural issues to consider pedagogy, curriculum or dispassionate review of the evidence from experiments, have been dominated by ideological polarization not always on right–left party lines. Thus Spain, still under Franco's dictatorship, passed a law in 1970 that curtailed the tradition by which wealthier families were able to enter their children on the *bachillerato* route at the early age of 10. However, in legislation passed in 1990, after several years of socialist government, it was still maintaining a separation between technical and academic routes in the secondary school.

In the United Germany the debate continues, but in the *Länder* of the former GDR only Brandenburg, under the Social Democrats, is envisaging the comprehensive school as the normal means of providing secondary education. In the remaining *Länder* the comprehensive – up till now practically the only type of schooling up to age 16 – might be one of a number of types of school (for example in Mecklenburg-West Pomerania) or forming a type of pilot/experimental school (as in Thuringia). The debate remains unsettled and in different forms and contexts is likely to persist through the coming decade (Mitter, 1991). At present the percentage of children in unified, comprehensive schools has only fractionally increased in the 1980s and in many parts of the country has decreased (see Table 5).

Table 5   Share of pupils in integrated comprehensive schools in the total school population in Grades 7 to 9

	1980	1985	1989
Baden-Württemberg	1.8	2.2	0.8
Bavaria	0.5	0.6	0.5
Berlin (West)	25.2	28.2	27.3
Bremen	9.3	9.8	10.6
Hamburg	7.5	19.4	18.9
Hesse	16.8	15.7	15.6
Lower Saxony	2.6	2.6	2.9
North Rhine-Westphalia	3.0	4.7	8.1
Rhineland-Palatinate	0.7	1.4	1.7
Saar	2.1	3.6	8.9
Schleswig-Holstein	1.1	1.5	1.3
Federal Republic of Germany (West)	4.0	4.9	5.7

Source: Federal Ministry for Education and Science (ed.) (1990/1991) *Basic Structural Data. Education Statistics from the Federal Republic of Germany*, p. 36ff.

Advocates of comprehensivization had always advanced a mix of social and educational motives for their proposed reform. These motives included the evidence of the disproportionate representation of children from the middle classes in the academic secondary schools, the waste of talent and the inaccuracies occasioned by the processes of selection for different types of secondary school. Their opponents, supported by the weight of the status quo would refer to the dilution of standards, of forcing children into inappropriate forms of schooling. Of the three students described in the introduction, Nadia in France and James in England experienced a common secondary school. Across Europe, if figures were available they would in the 1990s be unlikely to represent the majority of children.

The issue was, and remains, a live one. The pace of institutional change, however, slowed in many countries through the mid-1970s. The reasons are complex, although three factors must have contributed to some degree. First there was the economic recession that followed the OPEC oil crisis of 1973. More than one commentator has pointed to the significance this had for the climate of innovation and expansion that many saw characterizing the 1960s (Papadopolous, 1980, Shipman, 1981). Second, there was the drop in the birthrate, a phenomenon across the industrialized world that in itself inevitably dented the mood of exposure and growth of the 1950s and 1960s. Third, there was the growing evidence that in terms of the social mobility that the comprehensive school was expected to promote, the outcomes were disappointing, in many instances reflecting patterns similar to those of the previously selective institutional arrangements.

The quote from the French professor at the opening of this essay illustrates how critically charged the debates could be. Secondary school reform, like the reform of the mathematics curriculum, became inextricably tied up with the politics of the day. In Britain a group of right wing educationists, writers and politicians achieved a very high level of media attention in publishing a series of what they termed 'Black Papers' on the direction and standards of education in that period. Reproduced below is an extract that shows how the move to democratize schooling was linked to the perceived decline in standards.

> 'You can have equality *or* equality of opportunity. You can't have both.' Equality of opportunity is totally different from the present cult of egalitarianism, which is indeed its chief enemy at the present time. The frightening aspect of egalitarianism is that while it costs far more to bring into effect than equality of opportunity, it disintegrates the standards and structures on which education depends. It is a levelling down process, actively unjust to brighter children, who become a new under-privileged class, and for this same reason dangerous for the nation as a whole. We *need* first-class surgeons, engineers, scientists, mathematicians, lawyers, scholars, and these can only show up through a system of élitist training and competitive exams. This has been called a 'fascist' viewpoint; but we should like to hear a progressivist arguing this one with a patient in need of complicated surgery, or with the Chancellor of the Exchequer in his more realistic moods.
>
> *(Black Paper Two, 1970, p. 16)*

These views came to have increasing significance across the 1970s and into the 1980s. Disappointment with the success of democratization in promoting greater social mobility, and in particular access to higher education, dented the evangelical zeal of the reformers. In this period discontent with the potential of education to make any difference to life chances had been fuelled by popular interpretations of a number of studies in the USA (the Coleman Report, for example) which appeared to show how socio-economic variables heavily outweighed any influence that schools or teachers could bring to bear.

The common, or comprehensive school concept, therefore, came under fire. If the polemic came from the right the defence was to come from those who had painstakingly argued the case and, in Sweden, for example, provided evidence from pilot projects to support the case for nation-wide legislation. Torsten Husén was a prime mover in this, not only for the empirical data he had collected in Sweden but also in his key role within the International Association for the Evaluation of Educational Achievement (IEA), a major longitudinal study of educational standards in some twenty countries across the world.

What we have seen, then, in most European systems is a move from institutional, structural issues to a focus on the outcomes of schools and the quality of the educational experience offered within them. The consequences of this shift, in political terms, tended to cross political distinctions when you consider country upon country comparisons. And so, in the mid-1980s, whilst the Conservative government of Margaret Thatcher was advocating and preparing for a major shift to the right within the school system, Jean-Pierre Chevènement in France, the socialist Minister of Education, was pursuing not dissimilar policies, particularly in terms of the structure of the school curriculum and teaching methodology.

Chevènement was particularly influenced by the ideas of one of his close advisers Jean-Claude Milner, a former Maoist who had published a comprehensive reform programme with populist appeal in his book *De l'école*, published in 1984. This reaffirmed the value of rigorous, orthodox study in basic subjects throughout primary and secondary school. Chevènement's group, his '*club de reflexion*', argued for 'republican élitism' which would promote the cause of working-class advancement through the extension of traditional programmes rather than the provision of alternative, inevitably lower status options. For Chevènement, and here, to be fair, he was picking up an idea of his predecessor Alain Savary, the aim was to extend the previously very restricted *baccalaureate* to 80 per cent of the student population.

French plans to extend the *baccalaureate* to most students illustrate perhaps the most significant and contemporary public policy issue for education. Access to, and the nature of, post-compulsory and higher education is now debated and discussed throughout Europe.

Changes in economic and industrial structures, rising aspirations of parents who have experienced an extended secondary education (confirmed by Andrew McPherson and his co-workers at the University of Edinburgh Institute for Educational Sociology) and greater awareness of the performance of neighbouring countries within and outside economic communities have all contributed to this new concern for the 1990s and beyond. This interest extends across the countries of east and west Europe. In east European countries the concern about the social equity of access to different forms of higher education is just as highly developed as in most west European countries. Hungary, for example, is looking at the process of admission into higher education over four decades where a variety of policies to promote access to higher education for working-class families were tried.

From 1972 to 1978, as a result of an egalitarian educational policy, the percentage of students having manual-worker parents increased at colleges and universities. However, after this time the numbers began to decline again.

This, of course, was by no means an accident. In 1978 the Hungarian Socialist Workers' Party announced a return to the principles of economic reform.

Subsequently, opinions stressing the importance of selection in the search for professional competence reappeared in the press. Thus there was pressure for selection to be based on the principle of attainment. Attacks were made on the previous lowering of secondary-school requirements and of higher education admission requirements, and also on instances of 'crude' political interference in educational processes, ostensibly for the sake of egalitarianism. Preparatory work began on altering the admissions system, resulting in new regulations coming into

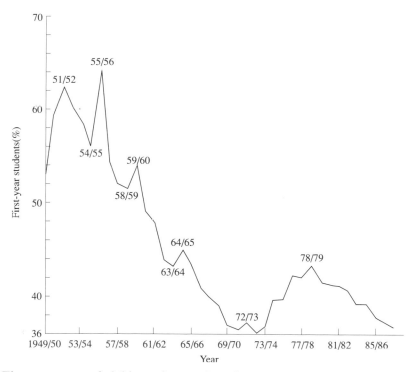

The percentage of children of manual workers among first-year students attending regular courses at institutions of higher education (%).

force from the early 1980s onwards. According to these, when assessing the students' secondary-school results, it was once again their secondary school average grade that was taken into account, though in a modified form. Several earlier rules designed to help applicants for higher education from semi-technical schools were revoked. Since then, there has been a succession of similar measures: for example, the statutory provision that obliged secondary schools to run free courses for the children of manual workers in addition to the regular lessons has been revoked. These free courses were intended to prepare such children for university. In 1987, for the first time in over 20 years, an important item was omitted from the ministerial directive regulating details of the admission procedure – namely, the one that prescribed that, given a choice between students with comparable achievements, manual workers' children should be treated preferentially.

It is not surprising in this situation that the percentage of children from disadvantaged social groups among those admitted to educational institutions continues to decline.

(Lukacs, 1989)

In the 1990s, whilst the debates about primary and secondary schooling continue, the focus of interest is almost inevitably shifting towards the post-compulsory sector, particularly with regard to young people between the ages of 16–19 and higher education generally.

Questions revolve around the problems of access and equality of opportunity, of value for tax-payers' money, of adequate use of and introduction to the new technologies, the relationship between vocational and academic education in this sector, the provision of life-long learning opportunities, and the status and concept of the university *vis-à-vis* other types of higher educational establishment. There is also debate on how much should be spent on educational research, where Europe lags far behind Japan and the USA.

All these questions are high on the agenda in most national systems. Each is generating an increasingly voluminous literature. And for this sector the will and the funding for co-operation across Europe appears to be growing. The democratization process which developed from Guizot and de Groot through Forster and Ferry and into the development of the common secondary school has now reached the tertiary and higher sectors of education. A multitude of ideas and models are appearing. How these develop over the next decade will be enormously significant for the structure of European education in the twenty-first century.

Internationalizing educational concerns

This section looks at issues across Europe. The first part includes an agenda for reform which characterizes thinking in many European countries. The second part discusses the role of European and other international agencies in promoting review and reform. The third part considers the way the international community is addressing one particular issue, namely the education of girls and women; this is illuminated by looking in some detail at a recently completed project by the Council of Europe.

In the first two sections of the essay I looked at the expansion and democratization of national education systems, a process that is continuing today as access to higher education becomes a realistic proposition to more and more people across all the countries of Europe. These developments reflect the complex interplay of philosophical (individual rights), social (individual and societal needs) and economic (national imperatives) factors. The relative significance of these factors has changed over time and attempts to weight the influences, historically as for the future, are fraught with methodological difficulties. I have shown how, despite some very real differences rooted in national styles and traditions, there are many common characteristics across European education systems. Common agendas are apparent to anyone who compares debates across national systems.

When translations are available there are few papers on educational policy, practice or research that cannot be understood across national systems. Specific subject areas may require specialist understanding but experts now move easily from one country to another and international communities of interest that are already strong are expanding, particularly in the myriad of links and exchanges being set up between west, central and eastern Europe.

In the second half of this century a number of international organizations have played a prominent role in this process. Four, in particular, assisted the process of co-operation and research within the wider economic community. UNESCO, in the 1950s, gave resource and backing to a range of activities, not necessarily constrained to the European scene but through the establishment of international networks directly giving a boost to European co-operation. Reform of the school mathematics curriculum is an example. It was UNESCO that provided the initial funding to bring experts to a now famous conference at Royaumont in France in 1956. Under the explosive title of *Euclid Must Go*, a doyen of university mathematicians, Jean Dieudonné, delivered a polemical address calling for reform. Subsequent meetings in Athens and other parts of Europe led to the founding of the International Committee for Mathematics Education which held a first meeting in Lyon in 1968 and has become a highly successful force for printing new ideas and research with attendance at the four-yearly conferences running into the thousands.

A second organization which has similarly had an international role but with a particular emphasis on European affairs is the Organisation for Economic Co-operation and Development (OECD). More widely known generally for the task of economic monitoring and forecasting, OECD, a grouping of all the major industrialized countries, has within the education sphere promoted numerous studies that bring together experts from across the world to consider specific issues. In the early 1970s, for example, they sponsored a major look at innovation in education exploring how the focus of control varied from school to regional to central government depending on national traditions and contemporary circumstances; a topic, as I have shown, which is currently of significant interest today. More recently they have looked at the evaluation of education and the range of performance indicators that can be used to make judgements of institutional quality. The French daily newspaper, *Le Monde*, devoted a special feature to this work. The Centre for Educational Research and Innovation (CERI) within OECD has co-ordinated a number of proposals, one of the most recent of which is looking at the way the curriculum is being rethought amongst the member countries of OECD.

The European Community (EC) is the third organization that is involved in educational issues as the significance of co-operation within the EC has become increasingly apparent. The original Treaty of Rome had no mention of education. This has been used by some member countries to veto debate of educational issues which they see as a national, rather than community, concern. Over the years, however, this stance where it existed has slowly been eroded. The close links between economic co-operation and vocational training, the issues of language acquisition and the need to harmonize a range of technical and professional occupations are areas where the EC has inevitably been drawn into educational issues. Major funding has been given to facilitating movement between EC countries for students as well as experts. (The ERASMUS project, for example, has been particularly influential.)

Recognizing the importance of language teaching as a factor in facilitating mobility of young workers in Europe and in contributing to understanding of European neighbours, the Commission set up the LINGUA programme in 1989 to promote foreign language competence in the Community. To encourage better education opportunities for handicapped people and their integration into the work force the HELIOS (economic and social integration of the handicapped) and HORIZON (improvement of job market opportunities for handicapped and other disadvantaged groups) programmes were created. A more recent EC initiative in higher education is the TEMPUS programme, set up in 1990 and aimed at linking academics within the member countries of the EC with colleagues in neighbouring eastern European countries.

On the distance education front, the EADTU (European Association of Distance Teaching Universities) – one of the few European associations with such an inelegant acronym – was formed a few years ago in western Europe. It was never confined to EC countries but has been successful in achieving recognition for distance education in the corridors of Brussels, so that this mode of education is in the meantime able to receive funding from general educational programmes or programmes with educational relevance such as ERASMUS, FORCE (action programme for the development of continuing education in the vocational sector in Europe), LINGUA, EUROFORM (programme to support new vocational qualifications and job skills and new job opportunities opened up by the post-1993 Common Market), NOW (programme to support updating/upgrading programmes for women, especially in remote regions), EUROTECNET (an action programme in the field of vocational training and new information technologies), HORIZON, COMETT (encouraging universities and industry to cooperate on education and training in technology), DELTA (Development of European Learning through Technological Advance) and SATURN etc. A meeting of high-level distance educators from EFTA, EC and eastern European countries under the aegis of the International Council for Distance Education, the EADTU and the EC

Commission led to the setting up of EDEN (European Distance Education Network) created in Prague in 1991 and facilitated by funding from the TEMPUS programme.

Finally, there is an increased tendency from the Commission in Brussels, often with ministerial support, to encourage a more federal approach to educational issues, not least those associated with European awareness. On 24 May 1988, for example, a resolution sought to increase the European dimension in education by asking ministers to set out the action they were taking to:

(a) strengthen a European identity, especially by reference to the principles of democracy, social justice and human rights;

(b) improve young people's knowledge of European culture;

(c) make young people aware of the opportunities and challenges presented by the Single Market.

This led to most ministries of education issuing memoranda to their curriculum planners or directly to education authorities to ensure the inclusion of a *European Dimension* across all subjects. In crowded modern curricula, however, if left to the discretion of teachers (rather than being a visibly examined subject), European studies as such are likely to remain peripheral and incidental.

On these and other EC initiatives information and documentation can, of course be had from EURIDICE, the European information centre on education.

The increased level of international co-operation and development to some degree creates its own momentum for reform. Changes in the mathematics curriculum within national systems in the 1960s were advocated by those who drew the legitimacy for their claims from the international pleas for reform. Other issues (vocational training, for example) may characterize developments in the 1990s.

Faster and cheaper means of travel, the revolution in communications generally, and the growing economic power of supernational organizations such as the EC, have all created a movement of ideas beyond the particular circumstances of the nation state. The implications for this are difficult to discern. It certainly changes the context of comparison from the rather anthropological forays of Matthew Arnold. The outcome of the EC meeting held at Maastricht in the Netherlands in December 1991 promises an even greater extension of social and educational co-operation. In a complex treaty negotiation, consensus from some countries on economic issues was gained at the price of a greater commitment to the social dimension.

Education is one of the concerns not even controlled at national level in several EC countries but devolved to regional or local authorities. It is not surprising, then, that this is an area where any 'interference' by Brussels raises hackles. Memoranda from the Commission in this field are hedged about with reassurances that the subsidiarity principle is not being eroded. The general EC agreement does not foresee any concrete measures being decided on at Commission level in the field of education; there can only be directives, resolutions, decisions, recommendations, guidelines or reports. The plethora of programmes in the educational field are nevertheless intended to have a broad effect on those in education – staff, students, administrators, theorists – and will inevitably influence the educational systems in time. Particularly in the field of vocational education – increasingly seen as including higher and continuing education – the Commission sees the urgent necessity for agreement on the equivalence (harmonization or equality are carefully avoided in the vocabulary!) of certificates and programmes of study and on mutual information policies which must reach the students concerned. How this evolves is likely to be a major influence on education in Europe in the 1990s.

In identifying issues and raising the status of concerns in different countries, international organizations can be seen as having a particularly valuable role. I want to conclude this section by looking at a fourth agency, the Council of Europe, and the specific theme it has recently addressed – the education of girls, an issue now high on the political agenda and providing an important further dimension to any discussion of democratization and access.

Below I have reproduced a short description of *International Policy and Equality of Educational Opportunity* that formed part of the final project report.

International Policy and Equality of Educational Opportunity

The right to receive an equal education has been a fundamental part of many human rights documents since the Second World War. This right has usually been expressed in terms of access to, rather than the content of, education, underpinned by the principle of non-discrimination. United Nations resolutions, such as the UN Declaration of Human Rights in 1948, the UN Declaration on the Rights of the Child in 1959 and the UNESCO Convention against Discrimination in Education in 1960, all upheld the principle of equality of opportunity in education. This was most clearly expressed in a 1967 resolution, subsequently incorporated into the 1979 UN Convention on the Elimination of all Forms of Discrimination against Women, to which all European countries were signatories. This stated that:

All appropriate measures shall be taken to ensure girls and women, married or unmarried, equal right with men in education at all levels, and in particular:

(a) equal conditions of access to and study in educational institutions of all types, including universities and vocational, technical and professional schools;

(b) the same choice of curricula, the same examination, teaching staff with qualifications of the same standard, and school premises and equipment of the same quality, whether the institutions are co-educational or not;

(c) equal opportunities to benefit from scholarships and other study grants;

(d) equal opportunities for access to programmes of continuing education, including adult literacy programmes, and

(e) access to educational information to help in ensuring the health and well-being of families.
(United Nations Resolution 2263, 1967, quoted in Wilson, 1991)

As this account illustrates, there has been a significant level of international interest in women in education mirrored by national debates of varying degrees of intensity. Like many contemporary issues of significance, there is a long history of concern stretching back hundreds of years and having expression in a variety of forms. (In 1831, for example, school children in Budapest were being asked to write essays in Latin to the following question:

> Potestne esse femina, quae dicitur heroina, materia Epopoeiae? (Can the totality of the Epic which embraces the world in unity and harmony and rises above every mere detail, admit a woman as protagonist?)
>
> *(Magris, 1986, p. 267)*

As Maggie Wilson illustrates, international debate has accelerated over recent years. The reasons for this represent that complex interplay between political, social and economic agendas. Universal suffrage, since the recent decisions in Switzerland common to all European countries, gave a boost to the cause of women's education. Changes in the male/female roles, particularly in occupational cultures, have created challenges to the traditionally divided curriculum which implicitly or explicitly provided different offerings and opportunities according to sex. Future demographic changes, a fall in workforce numbers as the downturn in the birthrate works through into the 20–40 age range, will create an economic imperative for rethinking the education and training of women and their roles in the workplace.

In most countries of Europe the provision of higher level education for women has significantly increased, in many countries catching up with the percentage male participation (see Table 6).

Table 6 Full-time students in higher education aged 19–24 as a percentage of the population in selected European countries, 1970–1986

	Belgium	Denmark	West Germany	Greece	Spain	France	Ireland	Italy	Luxembourg	Netherlands	Portugal	United Kingdom
Women												
1970–71	11	16	10	7	6	13	7	11	1	7	8	7
1975–76	15	25	16	11	12	18	8	16	1	11	9	9
1980–81	19	24	18	12	17	20	11	19	2	14	9	9
1981–82	20	24	19	13	18	22	11	18	2	15	9	9
1982–83	20	24	20	15	19	23	12	18	2	15	10	9
1983–84	21	25	20	17	20	22	12	18	2	16	11	9
1984–85	22	26	20	19	22	24	14	19	1	16	12	9
1985–86	25	26	21	–	24	25	14	19	–	17	–	9

Table 6 Full-time students in higher education aged 19–24 as a percentage of the population in selected European countries, 1970–1986 – continued

	Belgium	Denmark	West Germany	Greece	Spain	France	Ireland	Italy	Luxembourg	Netherlands	Portugal	United Kingdom
Men												
1970–71	18	22	18	15	17	17	13	17	3	18	9	11
1975–76	20	27	25	18	21	20	13	25	2	23	10	13
1980–81	23	24	24	16	21	20	14	24	3	25	11	12
1981–82	23	24	25	17	21	23	14	23	3	24	10	13
1982–83	23	24	26	17	21	23	14	22	3	24	10	12
1983–84	23	24	27	17	21	21	14	21	2	24	10	12
1984–85	24	27	27	19	23	24	16	21	2	24	11	12
1985–86	28	26	27	–	24	24	16	20	–	24	–	12

Source: Wilson, 1991.

However, despite such progress, as Maggie Wilson says:

> … marked disparities remain in enrolment in vocational education and training and in patterns of subject choice in upper secondary and higher education. Some areas of vocational education remain virtually single-sex, while engineering and technology in further and higher education remain male bastions in western European countries, despite progress in other areas such as law, administration and medicine. Indeed it has been suggested that gender-based subject divisions have become stronger, as more women have been recruited into higher education in both socialist and non-socialist countries (Sutherland, 1988). Where higher education is organized in different institutions of varying prestige, more male students are generally to be found in the higher status establishments. Indeed, there is some evidence to suggest that areas of study become devalued in employment terms once large numbers of female students are enrolled, a 'shifting of the goal posts', which has considerable implications for young women in the labour market (OECD, 1985). Within higher education, male postgraduate students still greatly outnumber female postgraduates, which in turn gives rise to a considerable under-representation of women in the academic workforce of universities and other institutions of higher education. At the lower levels of the education system teaching is becoming an increasingly feminized profession in many countries. As the OECD concluded in 1985, 'the removal of formal barriers of access to girls and women (in education) is by no means tantamount to realizing actual equality of opportunity and results' (OECD, 1985, p. 121).

(Wilson, 1991)

Wilson's claims are borne out by closer examination of enrolment figures in a number of countries. In French-speaking Belgium, for example, men significantly outnumber women on full degree courses, whereas the percentages are reversed to an even greater level of significance on short one- or two-year non-University courses in higher education (see Table 7).

Table 7   Distribution of male and female students in higher education in Belgium by sector, 1974–1975 and 1984–1985

	1974–1975		*1984–1985*	
% on	*Males*	*Females*	*Males*	*Females*
University courses	64.59	47.45	58.66	45.39
Non-university short[1] courses	19.20	47.14	24.12	45.88
Non-university long[2] courses	16.21	5.41	17.22	8.73
Total	100.00	100.00	100.00	100.00

Notes: [1]   Non-university short courses are one to two years of study.

[2]   Non-university long courses are three years of study in tertiary education.

Source: Wilson, 1991.

Looking at subject participation, again in higher education, Table 8 illustrates the situation in Ireland where technology and agriculture are still very much a male preserve, whereas in the humanities women outnumber men by nearly two to one.

Table 8   Distribution of all new entrants to higher education in Ireland by gender and representation of women within each field of study in 1986

	Males	*Females*	*Total*		*Representation of women*
	%	%	No. of Students	% of all Students	%
Humanities (including Arts)	10.9	21.2	2,720	15.9	63.9
Arts and design	2.4	5.7	683	4.0	67.9
Science	12.9	16.6	2,531	14.8	54.2
Agriculture	2.3	0.7	265	1.5	23.0
Technology	40.4	7.6	4,240	24.7	14.7
Medical sciences	3.2	4.1	626	3.7	53.8
Education	2.8	8.1	916	5.3	72.6
Law	1.4	1.8	273	1.6	53.5
Social science	1.8	5.9	639	3.7	75.0
Commerce	20.7	24.0	3,817	22.3	51.5
Hotel, catering and tourism	1.2	4.2	449	2.6	76.8
Total %	100.0	100.0	–	100.0	47.8
No.	8,964	8,195	17,159	–	–

Source: Clancy, 1989, Table 5.

In different parts of Europe, West Germany in the north and Greece in the south the differentials exist (see tables 9 and 10).

Table 9   Distribution of students in university education by sex and study area, 1990–91

Male choice of subject in rank order	Female choice of subject in rank order
1 Business studies	German language/literature
2 Mechanical engineering	Business studies
3 Electrical engineering	Medicine
4 Law	Law
5 Medicine	Biology
6 Economics	Economics
7 Information technology	Teacher education (pedagogics)
8 Physics	English language/literature
9 Chemistry	Psychology
10 Civil engineering	Architecture
11 Architecture	Mathematics
12 Mathematics	Sociology
13 Biology	Chemistry
14 Combined economics and engineering	Social education
15 German language/literature	History/science of art
16 Political economics	Geography
17 History	History
18 Philosophy	Sports/physical education
19 Political science/politics	Pharmacy
20 Teacher education (pedagogics)	Romance languages/literature

Source: (1992) *Statistical Yearbook for the Federal Republic of Germany*, p. 427, Federal Statistical Office, Wiesbaden, Germany.

Table 10   Representation of women in university teaching in Greece, 1986

Subject area	% women in upper grades	% women in middle grades	% women in lower grades
Humanities	15.45	33.77	58.79
The arts	8.33	21.42	50.00
Law	11.62	23.07	64.23
Social science	9.61	36.48	59.70
Economics	7.01	14.14	48.19
Science	4.48	18.45	27.33
Engineering	1.78	22.13	25.13
Health, medicine	13.07	27.49	37.70
Veterinary science	1.68	19.44	35.29
Education	33.33	19.60	0[1]
Total	8.20	24.16	38.55

Note: [1] No new staff have been appointed in these newly founded university departments since 1982, and so are not represented on the lower grades.

Source: Greek Ministry of Education, Directorate of Planning and Operations Research, Provisional Data, 1986.

Greece illustrates the situation of a number of countries. The school system is divided into four stages: pre-school, where attendance is voluntary; primary from $5\frac{1}{2}$ years to age 11; lower secondary (*gymnasia*) to age 15; and upper secondary where education is provided through different types of '*lycea*', as well as technical schools (which pupils attend from the age of $14\frac{1}{2}$). Georgia Kontogiannopoulou-Polydorides (1989) has looked at the empirical work which suggests that women are under-represented in academia, are paid less for equal work, and are to be found in the lower strata of the occupational hierarchy in the workforce (Psacharapoulos, 1980; Eliou, 1988a and b). In the Greek context, she argues, analysing data on a longitudinal basis, although women's participation in higher education reflects overall inequalities in the education system, it also represents a dynamic development towards equality between the sexes.

In looking at the background to this she argues that the following factors contributed to a growing awareness of gender in the 1970s:

1   The urgent agenda for reform that followed the period of military dictatorship between 1967–74.

2   Preparation for Greek entry into the EC and in particular the adoption of the *Directive on the Equality of Treatment Between Men and Women 1975*.

3   The dissemination of ideas about equality of opportunity amongst academics and politically active groups – international organizations are seen as having played an important role in this.

4   The implementation from the mid-1970s onwards of legislation to promote equal opportunities – for example the abolition of élite boys schools, the imposition of co-education on all schools, and the opening up of some formerly single sex post-secondary institutions to women students.

The issue of access and democratization, as well as affecting enrolment vertically from one phase of education to the next, also operates horizontally between groups within any sector. Here we are looking at gender. Access could also be developed around the issue of race or disability or, at the level of post-compulsory and higher education, age. In Greece there has been a significant rate of change which shows a clear trend towards a more equal representation of women in traditionally male dominated fields. Changes in the selection process to higher education, introduced in 1980, led to the reversal of sex differences in higher education and to an increased representation of women in terms of both the application and graduation rate. Importantly Kontogiannopoulou-Polydorides does, however, go on to point out that the increased rate of female participation in education does not reflect greater overall social equality but, on the contrary, has simply drawn into higher education new groups from the middle and lower classes. Higher participation rates have failed, she suggests, to remove other inequalities:

> The increased economic activity of women has been mainly limited to
> traditional areas, as indicated by their increasing participation in the
> public sector and the teaching profession. Although girls do better both
> in school as well as in such male-dominated fields of university study
> as science and engineering, their achievement patterns do not appear to
> increase their self-esteem and consequently their participation in
> economic life appears to relate to the decision of large numbers of

women to enter teaching, which partly reflects and reinforces the ideas prevalent in society about gender roles. The problems related to inequality in employment by gender are intertwined with the issue of women's unequal access to certain fields of study. The only likelihood of changing further women's perception of the function of education is by fostering an increase and wider dispersion in their participation in employment: for example, in the sectors of computer science and management studies.

The differences in the positions held by women and men in the labour market and the differences in pay for equal work show that there is strong discrimination by gender in Greek economic life ... Girls do better than boys at school, while boys do worse in the entrance examination for higher education. Girls do better than boys in (at least) the first year of university studies, even in male-dominated fields. These facts indicate strongly that the differences observed are not justified by the level of qualification. Research into relative earnings shows that they are not justified by productivity either, since the difference observed cannot be attributed to the measurable data normally explaining such differences. Furthermore, occupational sectors dominated numerically by women are dominated administratively by men, even in cases where there exists a standardized promotion policy, as is the case in the public sector and the school system.

At university level, women academics occupy lower staff positions and, although represented in proportion to their representation in university studies, they do not gain promotion at the same pace as men into higher staff positions.

If differences in qualifications and productivity cannot justify the observed differences in the hierarchical positions of men and women in the Greek division of labour, then discrimination becomes the alternative explanation. Such discrimination, be it direct or indirect, cannot be overcome by mere individual 'efforts' of qualified women to occupy 'male-dominated positions', despite the educational gains which women have achieved in higher education as part of a broader social dynamic. Women in Greece are, at the moment, supported in the ideological sphere by women's organizations and some state agencies. More specific employment policies are needed to give them the necessary 'push' in order to achieve more equality in the occupational division of labour. It is only specific labour policies and positive feedback from the labour market that will encourage women to compete for and achieve more desirable university fields of specialization leading to equal occupational choices.

(Kontogiannopoulou-Polydorides, 1989)

Conclusion

We have seen how formal education in Europe has rapidly expanded over the last hundred or so years. The development of elementary schools, the widening of participation in secondary education, the democratization of schooling for women, all have been important themes in every European country. The focus of this essay has been on schooling. It is an experience common now to us all and it provides visible evidence of the working through of these broad social movements that so significantly define communities and societies today. Inevitably much of the discussion has been historical. In this brief conclusion it is possible to speculate on the way in which the reforms and democratization of schooling will extend into the post compulsory and university sectors. In particular, will the traditional concept of 'student' change markedly as Europe moves into the twenty-first century? A number of trends are already contributing to this process. Higher education is expanding, in part because of the greater ambitions of an increasingly educated parent force but also because of the new demands of industry, commerce and the service occupations. In Britain a recent survey showed that employers expected to designate a whole host of new jobs as requiring graduate status employees in the future. Very few expected to redesignate any existing graduate occupation to a lower educational status. Higher education is also increasingly serving the needs of the expanding number of older people who in retirement or semi-retirement seek further learning opportunities. In this respect, the distance teaching universities across Europe and organizations like the *Université du Troisième Age* serve an important purpose. The new technologies, often associated with distance teaching, are transforming people's access to higher level learning and they are also changing the way the expansion of opportunity is listed and resourced.

At this stage, therefore, in the last decade of the twentieth century, a very significant transformation in the role of the student may be taking place (Tight, 1991). In Germany, for example, the most populous of the EC countries, with the largest higher education system in Europe:

> … Students no longer fit the classic picture of the young bachelor in his
> garret: in age at the start of their studies (well over 19) and at the end;
> in family status (marriage, partnerships equivalent to marriage,
> children), a feature that is even more marked in East Germany; in
> having their own flats far from the campus; and above all in being more
> or less gainfully employed, which can be seen as the unofficial German
> parallel to the part-time student in English-speaking countries and in
> Sweden.
>
> *(Huber, 1989, pp. 278–9)*

> Our universities, without knowing it or doing anything about it, are
> already teaching part-time students, and an increasing percentage of our
> students are working at the same time as they go to university …
> full-time students become the exception rather than the rule at least for
> most large city universities … Already today more than 60 per cent of
> the students are part-time students in our big city universities and up to
> 30 per cent hold a full-time job.
>
> *(Mitter, 1990, pp. 114, 119)*

In France, many students are, in practice, as in Germany, studying part-time and holding down part-time or often full-time jobs. Tight (1991) quotes the University of Paris VIII Vincennes which enrols a substantial number of adult students lacking standard entry qualifications and where 50 per cent of the French students work full-time. Cerych has also pointed out that:

> According to a recent survey covering six French and two Italian universities, nearly 60 per cent of students declared that during their last year of undergraduate studies, they had been full-time, part-time or occasionally employed. If only the first two of these three job categories are considered, about 37 per cent of the French students and 35 per cent of the Italian students had part-time or full-time work, and therefore, almost by definition, studied on a part-time basis. Fragmentary information suggests that this percentage is rapidly increasing.
>
> *(Cerych, 1990, p. 137)*

The experience of students taking '*What is Europe?*' is therefore becoming an increasingly common way of studying at the higher levels. Part-time study at each level of higher education is increasing in all European countries. One third to a half of all enrolments in the countries examined by Tight could be classified as such. And, he says, the characteristic of these students is also interesting. In most countries (except the UK) they are disproportionately women. They are, as we can guess, older and they tend towards the arts, humanities, social science or business studies, health education and law rather than engineering, science and medicine, where the more flexible opportunities for part-time study are less available and/or less demanded.

As Huber said: 'students no longer fit the classic pattern' either in age, in background, in purpose, in the place they are learning, in the technology available for that learning, or in the use to which that learning will be put.

This transformation of higher education is likely to become increasingly significant to the development of Europe, both within established unions (following Maastricht, for example) and as the agenda for Europe in the years that follow the revolution of 1989 becomes established.

References

AMBLER, J. S. (1987) 'Constraints on policy innovation in education: Thatcher's Britain and Mitterand's France', *Comparative Politics*, October, pp. 85–103.

ARCHER, M. S. (1979) *Social Origins of Educational Systems*, London and California, Sage Publications.

ASHFORD, D. (1982) *British Dogmatism and French Pragmatism*, London, Allen and Unwin.

ASSOCIATION OF UNIVERSITY TEACHERS (1991) *Investing in the Future: research and development in the universities*, London, AUT.

Black Paper Two (1970) London, Critical Quarterly Society.

BOWEN, J. (1975) *A History of Western Education*, London, Methuen.

CERYCH, L. (1990) 'Renewal of central European higher education: issues and challenges', *European Journal of Education*, **25**(4), pp. 351–9.

CLANCY, P. (1989) 'Gender differences in student participation at third level' in HUSSEY, C. (ed.) *Equal Opportunities for Women in Higher Education*, Dublin, University College of Dublin.

COUSIN, V. (1834) *Report on the State of Public Instruction in Prussia*, London, Effingham Wilson.

DELORS, J. (1975) *Changes*, Paris, Stock.

DE GROOT, H. (1844) *Are Separate Schools for the Various Church Fellowships Necessary or Desirable?*

DE PARIS, J. (1817) *L'Esquisse et vues Préliminaires d'un Ouvrage sur L'Education Comparée.*

DEWEY, J. and DEWEY, E. (1978) 'Schools of tomorrow' in FREEMAN BUTTS, R., *Public Education in the United States: from revolution to reform*, New York, Holt Rinehart and Winston, pp. 222–30.

ELIOU, M. (1988a) 'Women and education' in ELIOU, M. *Educational and Social Dynamic*, 2nd. ed., Athens, Poria, p. 224.

ELIOU, M. (1988b) 'Women in the academic professions: evolution or stagnation?', *Higher Education*, 17, pp. 505–34.

GLENN, C. L. (1988) *The Myth of the Common School*, Amherst, University of Massachusetts Press.

GREMION, P. (1976) *Le Pouvoir Périphérique*, Paris, Editions du Seuil.

GUIZOT, F. (1860) *Memoirs, 3*, London, Richard Bentley.

GUIZOT, F. (1817) *Archives philosophiques, politiques, et littéraires*, September/December.

HOLMES, B. and MCCLEAN, M. (1989) *The Curriculum: a comparative perspective*, London, Unwin Hyman.

HUBER, L. (1989) 'Teaching and learning – students and university teaching', *European Journal of Education*, **24**(3), pp. 271–88.

HUSÉN, T. (1989) 'The Swedish school reform – exemplary both ways', *Comparative Education*, **25**(3), pp. 345–51.

KONTOGIANNOPOULOU-POLYDORIDES, G. (1989) 'Achievement at university. Research in progress, partially published in "The main characteristics of the entrance examination"', in KONTOGIANNOPOULOU-POLYDORIDES, G., *The Transition from Secondary to Tertiary Education*, Athens, Vervakion Alumni Association.

LUKACS, P. (1989) 'Changes in selection policy in Hungary: the case of the admission system in higher education', *Comparative Education*, **25** (2), p. 226.

MAGRIS, C. (1986) *Denube*, London, Collins.

MILNER, J. C. (1984) *De l'école*, Paris, Seinal.

MITTER, W. (1990) 'Education reform in west and East Germany', *Oxford Review of Education*, **16**(3), pp. 333–41.

MITTER, W. (1991) 'Comprehensive schools in Germany: concepts, developments and issues', *European Journal of Education*, **26**(2), pp. 155–65.

MOON, B. (1986) *The New Maths Curriculum Controversy: an International Story*, Lewes, Falmer Press.

MOON, B. (ed.) (1989) *Policies for the Curriculum*, London, Hodder and Stoughton.

OECD (1972) *Styles of Curriculum Development*, Paris, OECD.

OECD (1985) *The Integration of Women into the Economy,* Paris, OECD.

PAPADOPOLOUS, G. S. (1980) 'Educational reform trends in the western world: the current debate', *Prospects*, **10**(2), pp. 159–68.

PSACHARAPOULOS, G. (1980) *Sex Discrimination in the Labour Market,* paper presented at the Modern Greek Studies Symposium, Philadelphia, Pennsylvania, November14–16.

RAPPLE, B. (1989) 'Mathew Arnold and comparative education', *British Journal of Education Studies,* **37**(1), pp. 54–71.

RINGER, F. (1987) 'On segmentation in modern European educational systems: the case of French secondary education, 1865–1920', in MULLER, D. K., RINGER, F.

ROSANVALLON, P. (1985) *Le Moment Guizot*, Paris, Gallimard.

ROWLINSON, E. (1974) 'German education in a European context' in COOK, T. G. (ed.) *The History of Education in Europe*, London, Methuen.

SHAFER, B. (1955) *Nationalism: myth and reality*, London, Gollancz.

SHIPMAN, M. (1981) 'The school curriculum in England, 1970–1980', *Compare*, **11**(1), pp. 21–32.

STUURMAN, S. (1983) *Verzuiling, Kapitalisme, en Patriarchaat,* Nimegen, Socialistiere vitgeverij.

SUTHERLAND, M. (1988) 'Women in higher education: effects of crisis and change', *Higher Education,* **17**(5).

TIGHT, M. (1991) 'Part-time higher education in western developed countries', *European Journal of Education,* **26**(1), pp. 63–85.

WILSON, M. (ed.) (1991) *Girls and Young Women in Education: a European perspective*, Oxford, Pergamon.

WOJCIECHOWSKA, A. (1990) 'Poland: education at a turning point', *The Curriculum Journal*, **1**(3) pp. 265–74.

Essay 3
The mass media

Prepared for the Course Team by Hans J. Kleinsteuber, Professor of Political Science, University of Hamburg; Torsten Rossmann and Volkert Wiesner, University of Hamburg. Translated by David Leighton

> These newspapers will, we hope, contribute to a general world literature of the most potent kind as they gain an ever-increasing readership. But we must reiterate that we cannot talk here about nations becoming of one mind, but rather that they should start to become aware of each other, that they should gain some understanding of each other so that, even if they don't come to love each other, they should at the very least learn to tolerate one another.
>
> *Goethe: Schriften zur Literatur*

Introduction

The first section of this essay looks at definitions and different forms of communication. It then takes an historical overview of the development of the mass media and attempts a definition of the current situation as far as the press, TV and radio are concerned (the cinema is not included here since, in Germany, it normally falls into a different genre). This part concludes by asking just how much effect the mass media have had on Europe, with a particular emphasis on the themes of stereotypes and prejudice.

The second part of this essay considers the make-up and nature of the giant European media market and how easy (or not) it will be to develop a truly European identity – as opposed to a national one. This section looks in detail at newspapers and magazines, radio and television and also the role of the news agencies.

What examples exist of pan-European newspapers and TV programmes? Do they *really* help to produce and disseminate specifically European images, news and views? The third part of the essay considers these controversial issues.

Finally, the last section of the essay considers the definition of a European cultural identity. The authors put forward evidence to suggest that cultural diversity is a better criterion than supranational identity and go on to discuss how the European mass media could contribute to that diversity.

Political and cultural roles of the European mass media

What does 'communication' really mean?

The word 'communication' derives from the Latin *communicare* (to share, unite) and signifies a relationship between communicators in which information is exchanged in a two-way process by means of language or other signs or symbols. Communication often leads to something like neighbourliness and understanding, and this too lies in the word's origin (Latin *communis* = in common), as when we speak of 'communal politics' (local politics). Today, however, communication is also possible over great distances, with the help of telecommunications (Greek *tele* = in the distance) in the form of telephones, fax machines, computer link-ups and communications satellites. Communication is thus possible both at the intimate local level and on a global scale. There are many forms and definitions of communication but here we shall take as our starting point the distinction between direct communication and mass communication.

Direct and mass communication

By *direct communication* we mean an exchange between individual human beings, or face-to-face communication, without the interposition of technology. Direct communication includes, for example, a conversation between two or more people, everyday exchanges, school teaching and political debate.

By *mass communication* we mean relationships set up by technical means, in particular, printed paper (the press) or, in the case of electronic media, electromagnetic waves (radio, television and computers). A wide public can be reached only with technical help. It is significant that the medium is directed at a target group which is not clearly delimited.

The carriers of mass communication are the *mass media*, 'medium' (another Latin word) being the means of forwarding information. Media are thus structures or products which are always technically created. Newspapers now come from gigantic rotary presses, television programmes from modern studios, transmitted from an aerial or carried by cable to the receiving equipment.

In contrast to other major parts of the world, Europe as a communications zone appears to possess some specific features which demand more exact analysis.

Europe as the birthplace of the mass media

There are many theories about what constitutes Europe, both from the chronological point of view, when it began, and geographically, where its frontiers lie, but we shall not be adding to those here. It seems reasonable to go along with Morin and place the beginning of an independent Europe in the modern sense between the 4th and 5th centuries AD: a period of mass migration across Europe, in retrospect, a gigantic process of exchange of people and shifting of cultures, and thus a gigantic communication event (Morin, 1988, p. 33ff).

We have the cultures of antiquity to thank for creating the essential foundations of our modern communication processes. Antiquity gave us our alphabet, the origins of which lie in the Near East, in the lands of the Assyrians and Phoenicians.

Communication in antiquity was, however, fundamentally oral, marked by conversation and debate, even though many important texts were already written down. Knowledge of the gods in the Greek and Roman pantheons was handed down principally by word of mouth. Christianity introduced more written communication; Holy Scripture was at the centre of all religious activity; constant fresh transcription of Bible texts became the most important activity of monks in the monasteries of the Middle Ages.

The Middle Ages, so often described as dark, showed a further fundamental difference of approach to communication from that of antiquity. In ancient times all the 'lowly' work was performed by slaves. If, for example, the latest news was required, a literate slave with a slate and a stylus was sent to a public place where the information was displayed.

By contrast, in the dominant strand of Christianity in the Middle Ages slavery was prohibited and so technical solutions were sought to facilitate routine work, which even today provoke admiration. Among the key inventions of this period is the

Two centuries after the development of printing by J. G. Gutenberg books were produced on a large scale in Europe. This engraving (1642), by Matthäus Merian, shows a contemporary book printing works (credit: Basler Papiermühle).

one that has greatest importance for our study: book printing. This truly epoch-making technique, originally begun in China, was developed so far by Johannes Gutenberg in Mainz that he was able to produce on his printing press whole pages of books using cast type. His 42-line Bible (otherwise known as the Mazarin or Gutenberg Bible) became famous, for it enabled him to rival the publication monopoly of the Catholic monasteries.

It was only a matter of time before the newly discovered reproduction technique of letterpress was also used to produce what we now call a newspaper. As far as current research shows, the first real newspapers were published in Europe in 1609 – the *Aviso* in Wolfenbüttel and the *Relation* in Strasbourg.

All inventions contain an element of adventure, and they can only succeed fully when the right technology becomes effective and economical. This is illustrated by the printed distribution of current news in Europe. At that time extensive long-distance trade routes were already in existence; the firms which managed them shared a common interest in what happened to their trading partners, such as whether natural catastrophes or political disturbances had occurred, or whether a ruler had gone bankrupt. Even before the introduction of newspaper printing there had been handwritten private letters, already known as 'news papers', which provided internal news exchange services. Newspaper printing enabled this work to be done better, faster and more accurately. Soon the newspapers themselves became an article of trade offered and sold along the length of the trade routes.

Europe was divided into many small political units and spoke many languages, so constant interchange was needed for trade to be possible. Europe operated as a kind of giant 'ideas market' (Morin, 1988), where peoples and cultures showed great interest in each other, and thus provided an ideal seedbed for the media to grow and prosper.

The combination of the technology which had been invented and the social conditions which necessitated and supported the development of the mass media meant that Europe was the only part of the world which was equipped for mass communication.

Freedom of the press

In early times all products of the press were authorised by the ruler of the region and subject to strict censorship. As the middle classes gradually grew stronger they defended themselves against this form of oppression and struggled for freedom of information, opinion and the press.

The start of this struggle for freedom of the press was marked in 1643 in Britain by John Milton's polemic *Areopagitica* (Figure 3). The declaration of human and citizens' rights at the start of the French Revolution laid down freedom of the press for France. The idea was also taken up in the constitution of the United States; in the first amendment (which came into force in 1791) the law is prohibited from limiting the freedom of the press. In the authoritarian lands of Germany the conflict over freedom of the press lasted much longer.

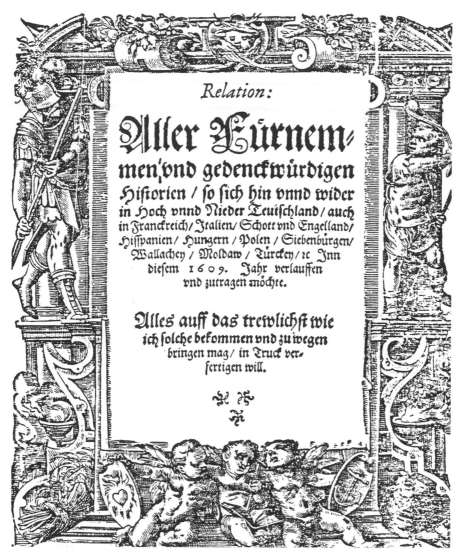

1609 front page of the Strasbourg Relation *which with the Wolfenbüttel* Aviso *of the same year was the oldest known European newspaper. By autumn 1608 Johannus Carolus, the editor and printer of* Relation *had begun to print weekly the newsletters he had been distributing regularly in handwritten form for 'quite a few years', because 'writing out was especially slow' (credit: Deutsches Zeitungsmuseum, Meersburg).*

Even today, the media and the people who work in them, particularly journalists, remain subject to the most varied economic and political pressures. But the concept of press freedom is highly valued; only a free press can guarantee public communication by informed citizens in a democracy. This argument is frequently used against threats to press freedom. The idea of the freedom of the press – like European-style media – has travelled round the world. This does not mean that freedom of the press is guaranteed everywhere, but rather that the idea of its necessity has become international, in the declarations of UNESCO, for example. In many UN member states the ideal still has to be laboriously fought for.

AREOPAGITICA;

A

SPEECH

OF

Mr. JOHN MILTON

For the Liberty of VNLICENC'D
PRINTING,

To the PARLAMENT of ENGLAND.

Τἠλδίθερον δ' ἐκεῖνο, εἴ τις θέλͻ πόλͻ
Χρησόν τι βύλδμ' εἰς μέσον φέρειν, ἔχͻ.
Καὶ ταῦθ' ὁ χρηζων, λαμπρͻς ἔσθ', ὁ μὴ θέλων,
Σιγᾷ, τί τὲτων ἐσιν ἰσαίτερον πόλͻ;

Euripid. Hicetid.

This is true Liberty when free born men
Having to advise the public may speak free,
Which he who can, and will, deserv's high praise,
Who neither can nor will, may hold his peace;
What can be juster in a State then this?

Euripid. Hicetid.

LONDON,
Printed in the Yeare, 1644.

The title page of John Milton's Areopagitica, *his plea for the freedom of the press (credit: British Library).*

What mass media are there?

This section takes a closer look at just what constitutes the mass media.

This is generally accepted to be:

- *Print media*, based on printing technology and conveyed in paper form, particularly newspapers and magazines;

- *Electronic media*, conveyed by electronic signals or by a conductor such as a cable, particularly radio and television.

The newspaper is the oldest mass news medium. In many countries it is locally focused and serves as a central source of information about the immediate area. Newspapers are traditionally published by entrepreneurial publishers and are financed from the proceeds of sales and advertising. In many parts of Europe the press is highly concentrated, i.e. many newspapers have disappeared due to purchases and mergers, while those remaining belong to big newspaper groups. In many towns there is often only one local newspaper which has a monopoly.

A magazine is generally designed to higher technical and graphic standards than a newspaper, with better quality paper and four-colour printing. They also appear periodically rather than daily. Many magazines address a universal public, though most today are aimed at specific target groups such as women, video enthusiasts or travellers.

Radio first achieved popularity after the First World War. By the thirties it was already the medium reaching the largest number of households. Hitler used it as his chief instrument of propaganda – reception of foreign broadcasts was prohibited. In Europe, programmes traditionally came from public service providers and used to consist of a mixed offering of news, education and entertainment. Once television had successfully taken over this role, radio switched increasingly to specialised provision for separate target groups. In particular, recent commercial providers are concentrating on specific types of music or sports coverage.

Television began to dominate European mass media in the fifties. Since then, it has without any doubt become the most significant medium; the average European spends several hours a day in front of the television set. Whereas public service providers strive for an integrated programme with various features, commercial providers concentrate on the entertainment sector. Television pictures are now not only sent to the receiver solely by terrestrial routes from the traditional transmitter aerials, but also via the so-called 'new media', cable, satellites and video-recorder.

The media used in Europe supplement each other and may frequently amplify one another, as when the first news reaches the interested public via the radio and television, while more in-depth reports and opinion-forming commentary are obtained from the newspaper. For local reporting, local newspapers and radio stations are unbeatable while larger geographical areas are covered by television and magazines.

Media may also compete for the consumers' attention and money. At present, the use of electronic media is increasing slightly, even above the existing high level of use, while interest in newspapers is tending to stagnate. Forecasts suggest that with the increasingly visual nature of our daily life and the growing consumption of images, the future will belong to the audiovisual and electronic media, particularly television.

Mass media and their operating areas

Media concentrate on certain geographical areas and thus contribute to the creation of communications areas. The simplest way to divide up these areas is to look at their sizes, on a scale beginning with global and ending with local.

Table 1   Communications areas, arranged by size

| | **Mass media (examples)** | |
	Print	**Electronic**
Global	News agencies (Reuters, AFP, dpa)	Communications satellites (Olympus, Astra) Global providers (CNN)
Continental	*The European*	European providers (Super Channel)
National	*Politiken, El País* *The Independent*	DR, BBC, Sat 1
Regional	*Bayernkurier* *The Scotsman*	NDR, BR, FFN, Yorkshire TV
Local	*Stuttgarter Zeitung* *Hamburger Abendblatt* *Wokingham News*	Kanal 2, Radio Oxford Radio Mercur (Copenhagen)
Sub-local	Advertisement papers Parish magazines	Local radio (Milton Keynes Radio)

Source: author's calculations.

In most parts of the world, newspapers are predominantly national; that is, they concentrate on serving the area of a national state. Even where papers advertise that they cover news from all over the world, as do *Le Monde* or *Die Welt*, their target readership remains national. However, it is these large, prestigious newspapers which are also read outside their country of origin, and are thus important intermediaries and lines of communication beyond their own areas. Moreover, the large news agencies (such as Reuters or Agence France Presse (AFP)) traditionally report from all corners of the globe and market their information world-wide. Whereas trans-world radio signals were only previously available on long-wave or, particularly, on short-wave radios and interested only a few enthusiasts, it is now possible with television satellites to transmit sound and pictures from one part of the world to another without any delay. So by using the most modern technology it is possible in theory to overcome both distance and time.

But does this work in practice? Many problems have impeded the development of a truly pan-European communication area and the most obvious is the lack of a common language; yet another is that it is not clear just where Europe's frontiers lie.

It has often been suggested that the process of European union be supported by fostering and guaranteeing pan-European media. The MEP Wilhelm Hahn explained as early as 1982: 'Information is a decisive, perhaps even the most decisive, question for European unification … a European consciousness will only arise if Europeans are suitably informed. Information via the mass media is currently decided nationally' (cited in Kommission der Europäischen Gemeinschaften, 1984, p. 2).

In its green paper *Television without Frontiers* (EC-Commission, 1984) the EC stressed in particular the need to create the economic conditions for Europe-wide television, more or less on the principle that a single internal market had to have high-performance information and advertising media. However, media which consciously target a pan-European public, and aim to make Europe their area of influence, are still the great exception today. Among these exceptions are *The European* (English-language) newspaper and a few satellite programmes from London, in particular Super Channel, Music Television and Screensport. There is more on these later in the essay.

A brief sketch of the multiple functions of the mass media follows. One particular part will be given prominence: communication across frontiers, as this will have the greatest significance for the future of Europe.

How important is the effect of the media?

Is it true to say that the security of Europe as a political and economic region will only be possible with the creation of a European communication area? Closely linked with this question is another: what effect do media at present have on Europe? Of course, that means the effect of national media, since to date hardly any European media exist. Some explanation should be given here of what we mean by 'effect' before we move on to a discussion of these questions.

The concept of media effect

The most heated discussions in communication science have traditionally concerned the effects of the media. It is relatively easy to produce data and to make moderately reliable statements about what media exist, about their contents, and their distribution. But to measure their effect is a very complex process. Discussion is not made any simpler because there is such a variety of interests involved in the debate about effectiveness. Yet another problem is that if we ask people whether media have any effect, we get an ambiguous answer: they accept an effect for people in general, but deny it in respect of themselves.

Much has also been said about the political effects of the media. But with political proselytising what is important is the previous attitude of the recipient: even the technically best advertising spot will not change a voter's mind if the party says nothing to him, the programme does not meet his expectations or the leading candidate seems untrustworthy.

Evaluations of the effects of media on the population have shown a range from the hardly perceptible to almost overpowering. At one end of the scale they show, at best, an intensifying effect, creating no opinions but strengthening existing ones; at the other, massive effects are claimed, for example, that television has an almost hypnotic influence on human beings. Much, however, remains as controversial as ever. The next section will outline how the media operate in an international, and hence inter-cultural context.

What the media tell us about others

Communication between cultures

In an area such as Europe where there are many languages, most of the communication takes place between people with a high level of common experience of life, socialization and expectations, that is, within their own culture.

However, cultures and nations also have to communicate with each other. The media act as a filter through which we gain our knowledge and understanding of other parts of the world. Table 2 demonstrates this very effectively. It lists what people perceived as the sources they drew on to form opinions about other parts of the world.

Table 2   Information about the USSR/USA

Obtained from	1988 (%)	1986 (%)
Television reports	91	85
Newspaper/magazine reports	80	79
Books about the country	20	23
Experience/reports from friends or acquaintances who have been there	16	29
Own experience	7	10
Conversations with Russians or Americans in the Federal Republic of Germany	6	23

Note: Double responses are possible.

Source: SINUS 1988, Table 18.

If what this table tells us is true – and the evidence seems convincing – then we need to consider how other cultures are represented to us by the media and how far they go in establishing and encouraging xenophobia, stereotypes and prejudices.

The origin of stereotypes

Do you believe that all Scotsmen are mean, Dutch people wear clogs and the Germans are efficient and humourless? The term 'stereotype' was introduced as long ago as 1922 by the American journalist and academic Walter Lippmann to designate these distorted images of other cultures (Lippmann, 1922, p. 79ff). Stereotypes are unavoidable; one could see them as a quick means of selecting certain elements from an overwhelmingly complex reality so as to try to explain it. Where our neighbours are concerned, this means that we always believe that the 'others', who are foreign to us, possess certain qualities, which may or may not have a basis in reality. These stereotypical opinions have been around throughout history; they are of decisive importance even today, and have often decided Europe's fate. They also provide an inexhaustible basis for humour: in heaven the comedians are British, the lovers French and the mechanics German. In hell, the comedians are German, the lovers British and the mechanics French (*Newsweek*, 14 May 1990, p. 40).

However, stereotypes often convey more than merely crude caricatures. They can degenerate into prejudices, into derogatory opinions about our neighbours formed without evidence, against which they are unable to defend themselves.

How do prejudices arise?

Prejudices tell us little about the 'pre-judged' person or thing, but rather more about those who make the judgement and often result in scapegoats being found for one's own problems: the fate of the jews in Germany remains the worst example of this.

It becomes dangerous when such prejudices are systematically stirred up and strengthened. Hostile images evolve, which drive human beings into warlike disputes. For hundreds of years French and German people hated each other for reasons which hardly seem comprehensible any more. These hostile images seem to be experiencing something of a renaissance in eastern Europe. Whereas in western European societies immigrants have always been subject to racial stereotyping and prejudice; this has been rationalized in part as fear of competition in a performance-oriented society.

The theme of stereotypes and prejudices is so important to this essay because the mass media are the chief means whereby stereotypes and prejudices are transmitted and perpetuated. Where else could we get our information about, say, the Mafia in the south of Italy? Very few people have seen the situation with their own eyes.

The mass media in intercultural communication

Will Europe-wide media have an integrating effect on inter-cultural communication or will problems of linguistic ethnocentricity increase? Many countries, like Belgium or Switzerland, are still divided by language differences, and it is not easy for them when foreign news reaches them via their nearest language neighbour – through France for the francophone Swiss, for example (Saxer, 1990).

Another problem is the way in which other cultures are reported. Mass communication, like the mass media, is created by journalists who are bombarded by so many news items that they have to select what seems worth reporting, according to certain criteria. Much is left out. Media research, which calls journalists 'communicators', describes this selective function as 'gatekeeping'. Figuratively speaking, the communicator opens or shuts the gate for the flow of information. He or she also, of course, has to follow certain institutional imperatives and instructions. So he is subject to 'agenda setting' or 'event management' by his employers, who are, in turn, subject to political, cultural and financial constraints. It is clear that media report far more about their own area, about local and regional events, because readers or viewers are much more interested in local events. The further away something happens, the less the information and the more clichéd it seems. Since, in general, we neither know exactly how things look on the spot, nor have a particular interest in events there, we are often only too ready to let ourselves be fed with standardized, even stereotyped news.

The media, and particularly the gutter press, always use banner headlines, attract the purchaser and provide a sensation-oriented view of the world in which oddities and absurdities are often reported, while the recurrent daily themes have no news value. These kind of media play on the customers' existing stereotypes and prejudices, strengthening rather than combating them.

A striking example of this was the reporting of the events at the end of 1989 in Romania – a country no more than a few hours' flying time away from any Western European airport. In December 1989 it was reported that the then dictator Ceaucescu's thugs had started a blood-bath in the town of Temesvar. Pictures of dead people in Temesvar went around the world. It was further reported that 4000, later 10,000 and finally 70,000 people had been barbarously butchered. Not until April 1990 did corrections follow (first published in the French magazine *Libération*): the massacre had without any doubt been invented; the gruesome pictures had been filmed in a hospital mortuary, the photographs were of people who had died natural deaths.

Internationally operating media look for pictures with which they can help us to understand the world. But they often create these pictures by their very presence: although some crimes are prevented because film cameras are running, unfortunately they are often committed for the same reason. In the case of Temesvar, the world knew that crimes of that kind were feasible. Accordingly, the media created the pictures to suit.

Does this mean that the further we are from the scene, the more difficult it is to evaluate media reports? The less we know about a region, the more we have to rely on the reports and comments of journalists. In this situation shorthand statements – stereotypes – are unavoidable; but *avoidable* false impressions, i.e. prejudices, also get reinforced.

Shorthand stereotypes and defamatory prejudices get in the way of common understanding in an area as large as Europe. The media have the power both to create and correct damaging stereotypes. This demonstrates how central are the communication media to an understanding of Europe and also how great their responsibility is.

Mass media in Europe

The European media scene

Europe is currently on the way to becoming the largest and most important media market in the world. The basic figures alone are impressive enough: 350 million Europeans in 22 countries own 210 million radio sets and 120 million television sets; they buy 90 million newspapers each day and take an enormous interest in magazines and films. If this were not so, over 1300 daily newspapers, roughly 3000 weeklies, 6000 general-interest and 18,000 specialist magazines would not be able to survive. Forty-four public and 47 private television transmitters provide 135 million households with almost 400,000 hours of programmes yearly; in addition, several thousand radio stations are broadcasting throughout Europe.

In 1993 the twelve EC countries, with their 322 million consumers and 118 million households, will constitute the largest single market in the world. Frontiers and restrictions on trade which have existed hitherto will disappear, which experts believe can only have a positive effect on the European economy. However, the concept of a unified European single market will be harder to implement in the media sector than in other areas of the economy. For despite its impressive size, the European media scene is more fragmented than any other in the world. Characterized by the most varied national developments, specific economic conditions and, not least, individual linguistic and cultural regions, the constituent national media differ substantially from one another. Efforts towards unification will encounter distinct linguistic and cultural barriers.

The significance of mass media for individual linguistic and cultural areas can not be precisely calculated. It is undisputed, however, that they play a double cultural role, first in the production of media content, and second in its distribution. Furthermore, they function on the one hand as classic 'producers of culture', and on the other, while propagating this content, they act to stabilize or to change social standards and attitudes. For this reason, the media in the projected EC single market can expect a significant role in the formation of a (politically desired) common European cultural identity.

In the long term, linguistic and cultural fragmentation must be expected to impede any supranational media expansion and therewith also a European identity. Nevertheless, developments in the media sector do show some similar features in almost all western European countries. The following may be mentioned here:

- the undeniable saturation of the market for print media;
- the shift of consumer demand from print to electronic media;
- the disappearance of public monopoly in radio;
- the consequent increased range of programmes offered;
- increased advertising revenue.

In this light, the internationalization of the electronic media market in particular seems inevitable, especially as new distribution methods such as cable and satellite are making it easier for private commercial companies to open up transnational markets. At the same time, economic and political pressure is increasing for the deregulation of national broadcasting systems, which for a long time have been not so much governed by market forces as considered a 'public good' and accordingly held within a state framework.

In the rest of this section, the current structures of print media, electronic media and news agencies in Europe will be considered.

Print media

Daily newspapers

The multiplicity of languages and cultures in Europe is reflected in its print media. Nowhere else in the world are there so many daily, general-interest and specialist publications. For example, in the EC there are 1051 daily newspapers with a total circulation of over 70 million copies. Equally striking is the clear division into local, regional and national newspaper markets.

As Table 3 indicates, the United Kingdom, Denmark and the German Federal Republic (not yet including the new states in the east) have the greatest density of daily newspaper coverage. Noticeably less well supplied are the newspaper markets in Spain and Portugal.

Table 3   The EC daily newspaper market, 1990

	Number of papers	Daily circulation	Copies per 1000 inhabitants
Belgium	35	1,726,000	175
Denmark	45	1,823,000[3]	355
France[1]	103	7,105,000	127
German Federal Republic[2]	356	20,960,000	343
Greece	132	1,175,000	118
Ireland	8	668,000	189
Italy[3]	82	6,764,000	118
Luxembourg	4	120,000	320
Netherlands	47	4,635,000	313
Portugal	24	400,000	39
Spain	110	3,000,000	77
United Kingdom	105	22,419,000	393
EC overall	1051	70,795,000	221

Notes:

1   1988 figures.

2   Without 5 new states.

3   1989 figures.

Sources: Fédération Internationale des Editeurs des Journaux, 1991; author's calculations.

As Wedell and Luyken reported in 1986, this is due not only to differences in prosperity, but, more directly, to the different market developments in the north and the south of Europe. It is generally true that the more prosperous and highly industralized countries in northern and western Europe possess much more differentiated and developed print media markets than do Mediterranean countries. Without wishing to analyse the causes of this further, we can conclude that the future development potential of these markets will also differ.

The number and circulations of daily newspapers in Europe do not necessarily indicate editorial and economic diversity. Since the 1950s, hundreds of small publishers have been taken over by large groups. Particularly in well-developed newspaper markets such as those, say, in the Federal Republic or Scandinavia, from early on small publishers were unable to meet the challenge of competition. They normally lacked the resources to cope with rises in production and distribution costs. Only the financially strong larger enterprises were in a position to create cost advantages and increase their market shares by introducing new methods and consequent rationalization. Numerous mergers, take-overs and bankruptcies resulted. Concentration processes such as these have characterized most of the national newspaper markets in Europe. The following overall trends can be seen in the European daily press:

- concentration, reducing the number of titles;

- stagnant print-run sizes, with density (copies per thousand inhabitants) only changing slightly;

- small and medium-sized newspapers maintaining themselves only with difficulty in the face of the mass press (such as *The Sun*, *Bild*, etc.), particularly as the proportion of advertising in print media is tending to decline in favour of electronic media;

- hardly any new daily papers being founded, the market presenting high barriers to entry.

In southern European countries, however, (as in eastern Europe since the major upheavals of 1989–90) considerable growth potential exists, and with growing prosperity this can be exploited. Over the next few years, developments there should move in the direction of the northern and mid-European print markets.

At present, there are few indications of any 'Europeanization' of the daily press. Newspapers remain nationally or regionally linked to linguistic or cultural areas, which, furthermore, possess very different political and public-opinion criteria as to what and how a newspaper reports. Some co-operation and national convergence worth mentioning is, however, occurring through new agencies, closer editorial collaboration between large dailies, and, to a smaller extent, through financial integration.

General interest magazines

For magazines, the north–south differences in numbers of titles and circulation figures are even more extreme than for daily newspapers. As Table 4 indicates, the German Federal Republic, the United Kingdom and France, as market leaders, have more titles than the 13 other European countries put together. The dominance of these three countries is also reflected in the total circulation figures. Federal Germany with 94.5 million copies is clearly at the top. Smaller countries like Denmark (with 3 million) and Ireland (with only 300,000) attain much smaller total print-runs. Next to the Federal Republic, the United Kingdom and France, the largest number of copies per inhabitant in relation to the population is found in Belgium, Finland, Norway, the Netherlands and Sweden. These are thus the countries with the greatest degree of market penetration.

Table 4   The west European magazine market, 1985

	Number of magazines	**Circulation in millions**	**Copies per 1000 inhabitants**
Austria	19	2.1	276
Belgium	129	11.6	1183
Denmark	31	3.0	588
Finland	56	6.5	1360
France	900	35.3	1018
German Federal Republic	1200	94.5	1539
Greece	50	1.5	154
Ireland	60	0.3	97
Italy	59	20.3	361
Netherlands	96	15.1	1055
Norway	35	4.0	975
Portugal	200	1.9	135
Spain	200	8.2	218
Sweden	49	9.0	1084
Switzerland	58	4.3	673
United Kingdom	1150	54.0	966
Western Europe	4292	271.4	768
EC	4075	245.5	785

Source: Luyken, 1989, p. 172.

In countries with the highest magazine density, the market must be considered saturated. For some time the consequence has been extremely bitter competition between magazines, illustrated publications and programme listing magazines, that has been further sharpened by the publication of more and more special-interest titles.

The Europe-wide trends in this sector are fairly steady, the most important being:

- the decline in traditional illustrated magazines as a result of competition from television, generally the dominant medium;

- fierce competition between the cheap mass publications, which are not merely stagnating but losing market share to special-interest magazines;

- the limited ability of the market to accommodate new titles and the efforts of supervisory bodies to prevent further concentration.

The greater the pressure in the national markets, the greater the attempt by large publishers such as Bertelsmann, Burda, Bauer or Springer to sell their products elsewhere in Europe. In the case of fashion, 'life-style' and travel magazines this has succeeded to some extent. 'The heart of this kind of expansion strategy is in every case the transfer of a nationally successful title idea which can be set up and adapted in a foreign-language market' (Luyken, 1989, p. 172).

Despite a certain degree of saturation in the daily press market and fierce competition among magazines, the print media sector continues to prosper. The limited growth potential of the market, in combination with the relatively healthy capitalization of most publishing firms, is bringing about two significant lines of development in Europe, although in view of the associated vertical and horizontal media concentration they are very problematic:

- Large enterprises and publishers are becoming more active in new parts of Europe by means of capital investment, take-overs, collaboration or transfer of titles.

- They are increasingly taking part in the audio-visual media which offer opportunities for investment and profit, particularly in the private broadcasting stations which have been set up recently in many countries.

The electronic media: television and radio

Hardly any branch of the media has altered so fundamentally in a few years as radio and television did in the 1980s. The general trend towards the internationalization and commercialization of broadcasting can not be overlooked. There are two basic reasons for this trend: first, the explosive development of technology, especially in the field of the so-called 'new media' such as videotext, cable and satellite television, and above all in new techniques for distributing programmes. Secondly, this development has coincided with the deregulation of electronic media, which has ended the decades-long monopoly of public broadcasting. Under increasing political and economic pressure, private transmitters have opened up alongside public ones throughout Europe. Closely connected with deregulation – in essence, the ending of state broadcasting monopolies – are two developments:

- The range of programmes offered has increased rapidly, due to the licensing of private commercial broadcasting stations.

- The growing use of cable and satellite has made reception of foreign programmes possible.

Commercialization: the trend towards the market model

For over half a century, broadcasting in Europe remained under public monopolies. At its inception in the 1920s, radio broadcasting was nearly always launched through private initiatives. Shortly afterwards, however, public monopolies were set up in most European countries. A variety of reasons were given from country to country to explain such monopolies, including the desire to regulate broadcasting (which eventually came to include television as well as radio), to exercise political influence over it, and to ensure provision of programmes for the whole population.

During the course of European broadcasting history, more or less binding principles of public broadcasting have grown up, and it has come to be seen as a public service, following the same ideals as the British BBC. Public providers arise, normally financed wholly or partly by fees, as non-profit-making organizations; the state is not the proprietor, and such organizations are under obligation only to the public, independent of party political or economic interests. There follows from this a comprehensive range of programmes which, even though differences exist, generally follow three principles:

- a substantial part of the programming must be produced nationally;

- programming must contribute to the formation of democratic opinion;

- programming must foster a cultural identity.

Only since the 1970s and 1980s have private stations started broadcasting again in Europe, stations which are not subject to the programming obligations of public broadcasting and which have no comparable organizational structures. Private commercial broadcasting shows the 'essential characteristics of a market economy arrangement' (McQuail, 1986, p. 633). By contrast with the public service, these stations represent entrepreneurial ventures which have to sell a service, namely their programmes, under competitive conditions. Apart from Pay-TV, they normally finance themselves by advertising. The larger the audience their advertising message reaches, the greater their profit. The maximization of profit can thus be achieved by optimizing audience size while minimizing costs. The consequences of this strategy are economical programmes which, 'in presentation and in content', find 'the lowest common denominator' of the largest possible public (Hoffmann-Riem, 1985, p. 185). In general, entertainment, sport and news programmes count as most attractive to the masses in this sense.

The European broadcasting system today is dualistic: public broadcasting, which dominated western Europe until the beginning of the 1980s now finds itself increasingly competing against commercial providers. Competition of this kind occurs under unequal conditions: whereas public broadcasting must continue to fulfil its public programming remit, its competitors can, without hindrance, broadcast programmes which, being cheap or attractive to the masses, or indeed both at the same time, serve exclusively to maximize profits. In these circumstances, the trustee image of public broadcasting is beginning to retreat before the market model of commercial broadcasting (see Hoffmann-Riem, 1985, p. 187). This process is called 'commercialization'.

The danger in this process for public broadcasting arises primarily from technical development, and is greater for television, as an expensive and more effective medium, than for radio. The possible consequences for public broadcasting of continuing commercialization have been spelled out in the following order by McQuail (1986):

- Public providers' programmes undergo popularization; the wishes of the majority of listeners and viewers are increasingly catered for.

- Public broadcasting behaves in a more market-oriented manner. Cost-consciousness and the spirit of enterprise increase.

- The principle of even-handed provision for all loses significance. In place of this, additional programmes based on economic considerations and individual payment are introduced.

- Commercial income becomes increasingly important.

- Privately organized providers appear, which restrict the scope and importance of public broadcasting.

- The telecommunications industry is privatized.

- Public broadcasting is partly or wholly privatized.

The question remains open as to whether this series of steps contains its own dynamic, which sooner or later is bound to lead to the privatization of public broadcasting. It may be that the legitimacy that public broadcasting derives from public willingness to finance it from fees will be called into question if numerous viewers and listeners switch over to private providers (cf. Sepstrup, 1989, p. 33). Fees which, due to lack of political support, are too low to keep up with rising costs harm programme provision just as surely as does a secure budget which relies mainly on advertising. In both cases the quality of programmes deteriorates.

It is clear that the commercialization of broadcasting in western Europe is following a general tendency to subject public communication to the control of market forces. As markets open up it is observed almost everywhere in Europe that broadcasting frequencies are increasing in number (cf. Hoffmann-Riem, 1989, p. 219). This implies more than the loss of the public monopolies. A range of problematic social consequences arises, which may be summarized as follows:

- Firstly, market forces lead to concentration and monopolies in the electronic sector as well as the print sector. This is especially promoted by the economic properties of a broadcast programme as 'merchandise': it can not be used up, and remains available for re-use without additional costs. When programmes are reused production costs do not increase and distribution costs increase only slightly; this also improves the chances of profitability according to the size of the market covered.

- Secondly, the 'sum total of individual preferences' generated by a purely market-oriented communication system is, 'from the socio-political point of view, not a suitable means of guiding production' (Hunziker, 1988, p. 129).

- Thirdly, a commercial broadcasting system is not in a position to provide equitable service, of which an essential part is accessibility to 'the entire population under the same – and favourable – conditions' (Hunziker, 1988, p. 129).

Internationalization: the trend to the international market

If commercialization means that broadcasting programmes are treated like economic goods, then internationalization offers the most profitable way to exploit them. For, as already indicated, the relative production cost of a programme lessens as its range increases. The more viewers or listeners a programme reaches, the greater the profit which its production and distribution achieve. For this reason, commercial providers intensively seek to enlarge their share of this market, where concentration pays better than in almost any other. The consequences of this are both a tendency for monopolies to form and a trend towards transnational markets.

From the economic point of view, radio and especially television programmes are still a scarce commodity. High production costs and the personal limits to creativity are mainly responsible for this. Hoffmann-Riem points out:

> In the market for broadcasting programmes, the companies which start with an advantage are those which not only have a powerful capital base but also have easy access to *creative staff* and experience in the production of media software. These are enterprises which are also active in other media branches, perhaps in films, press or records. The worldwide communication market is the *natural* market for multi-media enterprises with multi-national fields of activity. There are not many of these, and they are not distributed evenly among the countries in the world.
>
> *(Hoffmann-Riem, 1985, pp. 183–4)*

The box below gives information on the major media enterprises in Europe and illustrates the high levels both of concentration in the media sector and of single companies' holdings in both print and electronic media.

Media enterprises in Europe

Information is given in the following sequence:

Size ranking/name/country/total turnover for 1988 and 1989 in millions of deutschmarks/number of staff/main business activities/

1   Bertelsmann AG/Germany/11,370–12,438/43,000/books, records, printing, TV, radio, print media (100 per cent of Gruner & Jahr, Gruner & Jahr 100 per cent of Prisma/France).

2   Fininvest/Italy/9,180–12,225/25,000/largest TV group in Europe, shares in publishers, property, banks, insurance, foodstuffs.

3   News Corporation/Aus-USA/7,621–11,195/32,000/newspapers, magazines, books, printing, TV network (FOX), film studio (20th Century Fox); + News International UK/2,137–2,426/6,780/(European subsidiary of News Corporation, with 20 per cent of turnover) Newspapers (*Sun*), TV (BSkyB).

4   Hachette/France/7,198–?/28,500/France's third largest newspaper publisher, has 40 per cent of book market, newspapers, books, TV.

5   ARD/Germany/6,589–?/20,000/public TV and radio, income 60 per cent from fees, 20 per cent advertising, 20 per cent sales of programmes.

6   Reed International/UK/6,273–4,850/17, 500/largest print firm in UK, newspapers, magazines, books.

7   Havas/France/4,660–?/9,400/advertising, print, TV, privatized in 1967, holds 25 per cent of Canal Plus and 16 per cent of CLT, 90 per cent of turnover in France.

8   Granada Group/UK/4,580–5,117/27,900/very diversified leisure, share in ITV.

/continued...

---

9   Esselte/Switzerland/?–4,341/20,000/miscellaneous (technical office equipment, information systems, media) media accounts for about 16 per cent of the business (print, entertainment, publishing)

+ Esselte Media/Switzerland/?–704/2,697/.

10   RAI (Radiotelevisione Italiana)/Italy/4,038–?/13,800/public institution financed 60 per cent fees, 35 per cent advertising, 3 TV channels, 6 radio frequencies.

11   Pearson/UK/3,727–4,555/27,915/dominates European financial press, diversified in oil, china, press.

12   Maxwell Communications/UK/3,471–?/20,375/controls about 27 per cent of British press, newspapers, magazines, TV, turnover quintupled since 1984 by purchases.

13   BBC (British Broadcasting Corporation)/UK/3,307–?/28,000/public provider, financed by license fees and commercial enterprises.

14   Reuters/UK/3,130–3,703/10,071/news agency.

15   Springer AG/Germany/2,843–3,008/11,690/largest magazine publisher in Europe, newspapers (BILD group), TV (Satellite), share in radio.

16   Mondadori/Italy/2,500–3,400/7000/controls 30 per cent of print advertising in Italy, print (books and magazines), film company.

17   Hersant (Socpresse)/France/2,360–?/10,000/owns 30 per cent of French press (e.g. *Le Figaro*), share in private TV (la Cinq) and many local radio stations.

18   United Newspapers/UK/2,352–2,501/13,100/newspapers, magazines, free newspapers, information services in UK and USA.

19   VNU/Netherlands/2,216–2,312/12,000/largest Dutch newspaper and magazine publisher, share in two private TV channels.

20   RTVE (Radiotelevisión Espanola)/Spain/2,066–2,464/11,000/public provider, financed 30 per cent fees, two TV channels and local radio.

Note: Currency conversions were made at the average rates for 1988–9. In general, companies are ranked according to their total turnover for 1988, with the exception of Esselte. Enterprises included in the table are those with a significant media interest (e.g. Esselte with 16 per cent), but their ranking is based on the turnover of the whole enterprise. In line with this, the rank of News Corporation is based on total turnover, but figures for its European subsidiaries have been given separately. The turnover of public broadcasting institutions has been calculated as the sum of advertising revenue, fees and other income. Turnover figures for 1989 were in many cases only available in the middle of 1990 and thus have had to be omitted.

Sources: Company reports, press announcements, archives of the Media and Politics Study Group, Hamburg.

Thus in the process of internationalization a market structure is being set up which is dominated by multi-media and multi-national enterprises such as Rupert Murdoch's News Corporation Limited, Silvio Berlusconi's Fininvest Group, Bertelsmann or the Compagnie Luxembourgeoise de Télédiffusion (CLT).

Radio and television programmes such as television serials or sporting events have been traded in an international and largely free market for a long time. New developments are occurring not so much at the production level, but rather in the distribution of programmes to the audiences. 'For an integrated communication market comprising all stages from production, through transmission to resale', deregulation of national radio and television markets is an essential precondition (Hoffmann-Riem, 1985, p. 184). The EC television directive of 3 October 1989, for example, has this precise aim.

Seen in this way, the process of internationalization affects all economic, legal and organizational interests which contribute to the establishment of a comprehensive radio and television market. The process thus includes more than merely the distribution of transfrontier programmes in the form of 'natural spillover', as has been known for a long time. The consequences of the emerging internationalization of European broadcasting for programme quality are foreseeable: the programme range will be less varied and standardized. Programmes with a national, regional or local basis meet with hardly any international interest. They will only be viable in future if geographically limited partial markets are established, or maintained, alongside the international market. What is more, so far the commercial television stations of western Europe have shown only a small proportion of home-produced programmes. Instead, they broadcast mostly low-priced imports from the USA (cf. Sepstrup, 1989, p. 35), which as a rule have already covered their costs on the large single American market and can be sold abroad very cheaply.

Television

In western Europe in 1980 there were 21 public and three private television stations with a total of 37 channels. By 1987, 78 channels could be received in the 18 countries of the EC and EFTA. In the middle of 1989 the number was 91 (see details in Kessler and Schrape, 1990). Whereas at the beginning of the 1980s national operating areas and public broadcasting monopolies dominated the European television landscape, by 1989 there were already more private (47) than public (44) channels. In addition to the 68 channels with a full range of programming, which, as in the past, constituted the majority of stations, twelve specialized channels and eleven Pay-TV channels have been set up. Yet more television channels are being planned, of which twelve will be broadcast via the satellites Astra, TDF 1, TV-Sat 2 and BSB.

Table 5   Television channels in western Europe according to languages of transmission and type of programme

	Full-range channels	Specialized channels	Pay-TV	Total
Dutch	3		2	5
English	8	11[1]	3	21 + 1
Flemish	3			3
French	10	1[1]	3	13 + 1
German	15	2[1]	1	17 + 1
Greek	2			2
Italian	8			8
Portuguese	2			2
Scandinavian	14		2	16
Spanish	3			3

Note:

1   One programme with presentation in English, French, German.

Source: prognos, from Kessler and Schrape, 1990, p. 27.

As Table 5 shows, 22 channels are broadcast in English, 18 in German and 14 in French. The remaining programmes are distributed among various languages.

Programme-hours are increasing at an even greater rate than TV stations. Growing competition, particularly among commercial television providers, and lengthening broadcast hours are a direct result of the greater number of providers. From 1987 to 1989 the output of broadcasting hours increased by some 26 per cent, from 308,948 to 388,800 hours. These figures say little, of course, about the degree of 'Europeanization'. The majority of both new and old programmes are broadcast nationally, as in the past, just as competition for audiences and advertising revenue is still mainly conducted in national markets. International cross-frontier broadcasting via cable and satellite is only slowly gaining ground. Hitherto it has mainly been commercial providers in France and Germany who have used satellite technology to transmit their programmes across frontiers. They are not, however, aiming at a pan-European public, but at television viewers in other countries who share their languages. This strategy is thoroughly sensible: linguistic and cultural barriers to the reception of programmes and advertising messages are avoided in advance. German, as the most widespread language, is spoken by 88 million people in western Europe, and French by at least 66 million. Italian is spoken by 62 million people, English by 59 million and Spanish by 39 million. Unlike their German and French counterparts, Italian and Spanish stations have no need to broadcast their programmes across frontiers; almost the entire Italian and Spanish-speaking public can be reached inside the respective national borders.

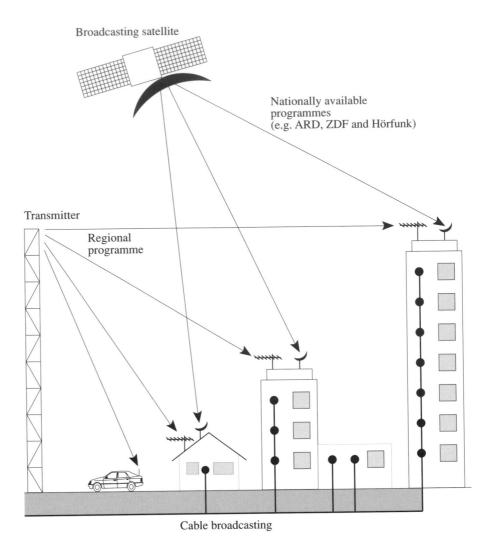

Broadcasting satellite

Nationally available
programmes
(e.g. ARD, ZDF and Hörfunk)

Transmitter

Regional
programme

Cable broadcasting

How a satellite works (credit: Arnold, W. (ed.) (1984) Die elektronischen Medien, Heidelberg, p. 167).

Television providers in the smaller language areas in Europe are at a disadvantage. In these countries a relatively large number of homes are connected to a cable network, so that national programmes have to compete with those of outside providers. (In general, the degree of cabling in Europe is low in comparison to the USA: only twelve per cent of all European households are cabled. In only four European countries does cable TV have an influence worth mentioning: Belgium, the Netherlands, Switzerland and the German Federal Republic.) Furthermore, these providers can not make use of the language-area strategy, since hardly any viewers outside their own country understand their language.

As far as television providers, and transfrontier channels in particular, are concerned, further rises in the level of provision will depend on the spread of cable and satellite television. Additional terrestrial television broadcasting frequencies are available in only a few countries such as the United Kingdom, Switzerland and Austria. By contrast, more than 80 satellite transponders are now available in western Europe for transmitting television programmes. The number of individual receivers for satellite programmes is also growing, even though this market is still in its infancy. At present, cable remains the main distribution route for these programmes.

The meteoric increase in the production and distribution of television programmes has met with great public interest in Europe. Watching television is numbered among the most important spare-time occupations in western Europe. Virtually every household has a television set; the average European spends more time in front of the television than in eating, washing or in making social contact.

Table 6   The development of cabling in EC countries

| | Households cabled by 1989 | | Change since |
	Millions	**%**	**1986/7 (millions)**
Belgium	3.35	97.1	+ 0.05
Denmark	0.58	26.4	+ 0.29
France	0.40	2.0	+ 0.15
German Federal Republic	5.43	21.7	+ 2.51
Greece	–	–	–
Ireland	0.32	32.0	+ 0.04
Italy	–	–	–
Luxembourg	0.05	35.7	–
Netherlands	4.30	78.2	+ 0.70
Portugal	–	–	–
Spain	–	–	–
United Kingdom	0.28	1.3	+ 0.08

Sources: prognos, from Kessler and Schrape, 1990, p. 31; author's calculations.

In 1989, according to GfK television research, the average daily viewing time for citizens of the German Federal Republic over 14 years old was 153 minutes, while in cabled households the time amounted to 165 minutes. The immense television consumption in Europe has some quite unwanted consequences, as Peter Muzik stresses:

> The British too, with 218 minutes on average the keenest viewers in Europe, ahead of the Spaniards and the French, have had to admit that their hobby is a wonderful contraceptive: in answer to a questionnaire 42 per cent of women confessed that they preferred a television set in the bedroom to all other pleasures.
>
> *(Muzik, 1989, p. 79)*

Radio

Since the runaway commercial success of television, radio has been considered a subsidiary medium in Europe, and is chiefly used at times when television is inaccessible. Yet radio possesses specific qualities which are not found in other media, or are present only in embryonic form. Among these are its great mobility and topicality, and its high degree of intimacy, as when radio is used as a mood lightener or as a substitute for interpersonal contact (cf. Rogge, 1988). In these ways radio has a specific social relevance which is reflected in the way it is used. Despite the huge consumption of television, in most European countries radio remains the medium used for the most hours per day.

Unlike television, radio makes few technical, organizational or professional demands on the production, distribution and reception of programmes. At the same time, as an electronic medium, radio offers listeners a high degree of accessibility, with opportunities for participation. This is true both of production studios and programmes. Typically, radio stations are locally based (if only for technical reasons), providing programmes to individual towns or communities located around an antenna. The German Federal Republic, with its regional radio networks, is an exception compared with other European countries.

Table 7   Public and private/commercial radio provision in western Europe

	Public	**Private/commercial**
Belgium	several (RTBF, BRT) few local stations	strong competition since 1981
Denmark	DR, regional programmes	no commercial competition
Finland	strong public radio, 9 local stations	commercial competition
France	public, few local stations	strong commercial competition
Ireland	RTE, few local stations	strong commercial competition
Italy	RAI, few local stations	strong commercial competition (c. 4000)
Netherlands	strong public radio, no local stations	many pirate stations (400–10000)
Norway	NRK, regional branches	no commercial competition
Spain	RNE, few local stations	strong commercial competition
Sweden	SR, extensive network of local stations	no commercial competition
Switzerland	SRG, with extension to local areas	commercial competition since 1983
United Kingdom	strong public radio (BBC) active locally	commercial competition (Independent Radio)

Source: Kleinsteuber, 1991, p. 277.

Table 7 gives an overview of the current state of public and private radio in Europe. In the last two decades the latter has developed extremely rapidly. In Italy, for example, where the first radio station outside the public network was founded in 1967, there are now 4000 commercial stations. In Denmark and Norway, on the other hand, no commercial stations exist, though there are a few hundred private non-commercial stations in northern Europe which, although financed partly by advertising, do not attempt to make profits. (On non-commercial local radio see details in Kleinsteuber, 1991 and the section below on mass media and regions.)

Since commercial radio stations pursue identical economic interests, their programming is remarkably homogeneous, regardless of national frontiers. In spite of the most varied legal requirements, content is dominated throughout Europe by music and entertainment programmes, mainly in magazine form, and with a great deal of pop music. Private commercial stations reach substantial audiences and must be considered a permanent feature of the European media scene.

Whereas television is clearly affected by the different media policies adopted by European institutions, radio attracts almost no political attention. On the contrary, it has been expressly excluded from the two most important documents on European broadcasting. Neither in the Council of Europe's 'European Agreement on Transnational Television' nor in the television guidelines of the EC are there any requirements concerning radio. There are, moreover, no plans for future regulations.

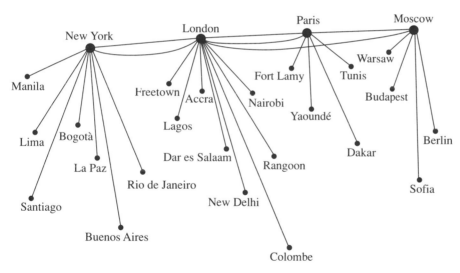

International structure of news agencies (credit: Singer, M. R. (1972) Weak States in a World of Power. The Dynamics of International Relationships, New York/London, p. 190).

News agencies

In view of the fact that 'Europeanization' has not gone very far either in the print media or in electronic media, it is appropriate to consider the role of the news agencies in Europe. For there is no doubt that the news agencies, as the procurers of news, play a central part in the international news network. Without them, a 'European public' would be unthinkable. Apart from reports by the correspondents of individual newspapers or stations, what happens in the world reaches most recipients only via the agencies.

Traditionally, the news agencies have exercised a gatekeeper function in the communications network (that is, they make decisions about which events are newsworthy and should be reported and which are not). From the news reports they receive, they put together a news service for various client groups, giving each group a survey of the national and international events of the day (cf. Höhne, 1984, p. 130). The ability to report on events throughout the world requires considerable technical and staff resources. The necessary means are obviously not available in all countries in equal measure.

There are currently 180 news agencies in over 120 countries in the world. Four large ones, however, known as the 'Big Four', dominate the news market. These are the Associated Press (AP) and United Press International (UPI) from the United States, and two European agencies, Reuters of the United Kingdom and the French Agence France Presse (AFP). Besides the Soviet agency TASS, the German press agency Deutsche Presseagentur (dpa), which is likewise represented by correspondents in almost all parts of the world, is of considerable importance. The organizational form of these agencies differs. The British agency Reuters has been a public limited liability company since 1984; the French AFP is an independent institution operating on economic principles. The German dpa is, by contrast, financed by newspaper publishers and broadcasting bodies.

In addition to these. there are, of course, many other national agencies. Not only is the supply of media in Europe exceptionally good, the provision of news agencies is as well. This is not surprising: all important innovations in the media field and its technology have taken place in Europe, as did the establishment and organization of the news agencies needed for a world-wide flow of information. At present, 24 European countries have their own news agencies, the only exceptions being the tiny states. Twelve of these 24 agencies have an influence on the international market beyond the borders of their own countries. Apart from Reuters, AFP and dpa, there are, for example, the Italian and Spanish agencies ANSA and EFE.

The European news market is especially hard fought-for. Six further agencies from America and Asia are also seeking to supply it. To improve their competitiveness, some agencies not only issue their news in several languages, but offer specially selected reporting to various regions. The most polyglot is the American agency AP: their services appear in English, French, German, Dutch and Italian.

The dense media provision in Europe is interesting to the agencies in two respects: not only is there a strong demand for news, with good possibilities of profit, but the European market also provides the economic potential the agencies need for their capital-intensive operations in other markets. The large European agencies are thus confronted in their home markets by two main problems: how to secure the best position for themselves, and, once established, how to defend that position against national and international competition.

*These contrasting pictures of Reuters demonstrate changes in technology over
the last fifty years (credit: Reuters Holdings plc).*

The achievements agencies are capable of producing in order to compete in the
news market can be well illustrated by British agency Reuters, which, since its
foundation in the middle of the last century, has gained competitive advantage
through a 'high-tech' and diversification strategy within the information sector (cf.
Weischenberg, 1985). Whether it was the use of radio for news transmission
(1923), satellite transmission (1962) or computer-controlled telecommunications
(1964), Reuters has been in at the start, either as initiator or participant. The

company began by supplying stock market quotations and economic news, then was able to establish itself and expand further as a news agency. In the process it was transformed into an information business which also offers new services with commercial applications. In its range of products Reuters follows the principles of the 'high-tech' sector: the more efficient manufacture and functional improvement of products, the squeezing of conventional products out of the market, the introduction of new ones.

The economic news system especially follows these principles. Reuters' customers can call up information or receive it conventionally by teleprinter services as they need it; via the Monitor System they have direct access to the national and international finance markets. Reuters still distributes its media service mainly by telex to several thousand daily papers and radio stations in 150 countries. In the middle 1970s the agency, with a local television company in New York, tested an entry into the new media with their 'Row Grabber', a cheap and rapid television text system. All in all, thanks to its technological infrastructure and diversification, Reuters has become one of the largest communications concerns in the world. Its emphasis has shifted from general media services to the distribution or provision of call-up facilities for business information; the 'classical' media services now account for only six per cent of Reuters turnover.

Summary of Reuters product range

Reuter Media Services
Foreign Language Services
Reuter Newsbank

Economic news
   Finance and Commodities
   Reuter Money Report (RMR)
   Reuter International Security Report (RISR)
   Reuter International Commodity Report (RICR)
   News Retrieval (Reuter Minotor)

Quotation products

Contributed data products
   Reuter Monitor Money Rates
   Reuter Monitor Bonds
   Reuter Monitor Equities
   Reuter Monitor Commodities
   Reuter Monitor Shipping
   Reuter Monitor Oil

Dealing products

Interface products

Special traffic
   North America
   News View
   Row Grabber

Source: Weischenberg, 1985, p. 497.

From the economic standpoint, the European news market differs only in non-essential ways from the other media markets in Europe. Like them, it is capital intensive, demanding great staffing and technical resources, and is dominated by a few companies. Language barriers are overcome by multi-lingual products. Yet the organization of European agencies retains national characteristics; there is at least one agency per country. These national characteristics are not, however, reflected in the flow of news; both in Europe and globally, the large news agencies dominate.

Every smaller national agency is dependent on the large agencies' news material, which they then pass on. On this point the 'Big Four' are frequently accused, especially by developing nations, of seeing the world from a western perspective. This refers not only to the fact that news events in North America or western Europe are given undue prominence compared with those in the developing world, but also to the fact that news content is often full of stereotypes and prejudices against non-western cultures and interests. Agencies are thus accused of creating a distorted view of the world which is reproduced beyond its countries of origin. Due to their financial and technical superiority agencies are said to define media images which have little or nothing to do with the problems of developing countries.

Compared with the stark political, economic, social and cultural contrasts between highly developed western industrial countries on the one hand and developing countries on the other, the countries of Europe are relatively homogeneous. Yet even here, media attention is inequitably distributed. The United Kingdom, France and the German Federal Republic clearly dominate mainstream European news, while the politically and economically less influential countries, such as Denmark, Portugal or Ireland, are more marginal. It is no coincidence that the three most significant western European news agencies are British, French and German.

Mass media as a means of European integration

Pan-European or national newspapers?

European newspapers typically retain, as they have traditionally done, close identification with their countries of origin. How could it be otherwise? As the oldest mass medium, the newspaper is deeply rooted in national traditions and reflects in many ways not only national cultures and information habits, but also the very varied regional and local information requirements. To a greater extent than in television, language barriers function as boundaries for specific circulation areas – a newspaper 'dubbed' like a film, and using foreign material on a large scale, could simply not exist. Today – despite the mergers and disappearances of recent decades – the European newspaper scene is still one of great variety. This generalization, however, must be qualified somewhat as we look more closely at the newspaper sectors of a few sample countries.

In 1990 the German Federal Republic (not counting the new federal states) was at the forefront of European newspaper production, with 356 dailies, of which 343 were local and regional subscription papers – an indication of the great importance readers still attach to newspaper reports of local news and information, in spite of numerous new local radio stations. Only a few German newspapers attain any national significance: for example, the *Frankfurter Allgemeine*, the *Süddeutsche Zeitung*, the *Frankfurter Rundschau, Die Welt* and *Die Tageszeitung* – and three of these have extensive regional information.

With a total circulation of about 26 million copies, an average of 400 newspapers is available to every 1000 German citizens. Notwithstanding the increase in so-called 'one paper areas' (areas in which there were previously two or more competitive newspapers), since the 1970s and the emergence of dense regional circulation areas (for example, the Axel Springer publishing house in the north, the Süddeutsche Verlag in southern Germany or the WAZ group in the Ruhr area), the situation has been one which even the critics of the German journalists' association describe as 'variety despite concentration'. (For an overview, see Meyn, 1990.)

That does not mean, however, that the Germans are the 'European champions' in newspaper reading. This honour belongs quite clearly to the British. Of the 25 European newspapers with the largest circulations, 15 are British (and all of these are national papers, since regional papers in Britain have very little significance – unlike those in a similarly centralized France). The European leader, with a print-run of 5.2 million copies, is the British Sunday newspaper, the *News of the World*, followed by the German *Bild-Zeitung*, for which German unification has meant an increased circulation totalling about 4.9 million. In third place is the popular British tabloid, the *Sun* (4.4 million). It is notable that in the United Kingdom seven different Sunday papers rank in the top 25 European titles; in Germany only *Bild am Sonntag* attains a comparable circulation. Weekly newspapers thus dominate the reading habits of the British far more than those of other Europeans.

The outstanding newspaper laggards are the Italians, whose leisure time is directed far more at the television than is other Europeans'. Thus only three Italian titles are found among the leading European ones: the weekend editions of *La Repubblica* and *Corriere della Sera*, and the *Gazzetta dello Sport* which heads the list of favourite papers. Every Monday the latter gives full coverage of the previous weekend's football events, a type of newspaper which can hardly be compared with the more serious weekly papers in other countries. It appears that on the whole Italians use their media more for entertainment than for information. They also seem to object much less to advertising than do their European neighbours: for example, *La Repubblica* heads the list of European newspapers with the most advertising revenue (followed by the Finnish newspaper *Helsingin Sanomat, Bild-Zeitung* and the other Italian paper, *Corriere della Sera*).

Table 8a   Top 25 titles by circulation, 1989

Title	Publishing interval	Country	1989 total circulation[1] ('000s)
1 News of the World	Sundays	UK	5240
2 The Sun	Mon–Sat	UK	4419
3 Bild-Zeitung	Mon–Sat	Germany	4095[2]
4 Daily Mirror	Mon–Sat	UK	3146
5 Sunday Mirror	Sundays	UK	2969
6 The People	Sundays	UK	2651
7 Bild am Sonntag	Sundays	Germany	2228
8 The Mail on Sunday	Sundays	UK	1927
9 Sunday Express	Sundays	UK	1899
10 Daily Mail	Mon–Sat	UK	1737
11 Daily Express	Mon–Sat	UK	1582
12 Rudé Právo	Mon–Sat	Czechoslovakia	1300[3]
13 Sunday Post	Sundays	UK	1291
14 The Sunday Times	Sundays	UK	1283
15 Neue Kronenzeitung	Sundays	Austria	1270
16 W.A.Z.	Mon–Sat	Germany	1242
17 The Daily Telegraph	Mon–Sat	UK	1108
18 Neue Kronenzeitung	Mon–Sat	Austria	1030
19 Daily Star	Mon–Sat	UK	902
20 Sunday Mail	Sundays	UK	882
21 La Gazette dello Sport	Mondays	Italy	848
22 La Repubblica	Fridays	Italy	830
23 Daily Record	Mon–Sat	UK	773
24 Corriere della Sera	Saturdays	Italy	754
25 Ouest-France	Mon–Sat	France	767

Notes:

1   Paid-for

2   West German editions only

3   Unaudited

Source: National circulation audit services/Carat International.

Table 8b   Top 25 titles by advertising revenue, 1989

Title	Publishing interval	Country	US$ million
1 La Repubblica	Tue–Sun	Italy	301
2 Helsingin Sanomat	Mon–Sun	Finland	294
3 Bild	Mon–Sun	Germany	211
4 Corriere della Sera	Mon–Sun	Italy	208
5 Daily Express	Mon–Sat	UK	185
6 Daily Mail	Mon–Sat	UK	182
7 Le Figaro	Mon–Sat	France	175
8 The Daily Telegraph	Mon–Sat	UK	167
9 Daily Mirror	Mon–Sat	UK	157
10 Financial Times	Mon–Sat	UK	150
11 The Sun	Mon–Sat	UK	135
12 W.A.Z.	Mon–Sat	Germany	118
13 La Stampa	Mon–Sun	Italy	113
14 Dagens Nyheter	Mon–Sat	Sweden	110
15 Le Monde	Mon–Sat	France	106
16 El Pais	Mon–Sat	Spain	100
17 Süddeutsche Zeitung	Mon–Sat	Germany	97
18 The Sunday Times	Sundays	UK	90
19 Il Sole 24 Ore	Mon–Sun	Italy	87
20 Frankfurter Allgemeine Zeitung	Mon–Sat	Germany	84
21 Il Messagero	Mon–Sun	Italy	79
22 Neue Kronenzeitung	Mon–Sun	Austria	78
23 Svenska Dagbladet	Mon–Sun	Sweden	75
24 Sunday Express	Sundays	UK	77
25 De Telegraaf	Mon–Sat	Netherlands	76

Source: National advertising monitoring services/Carat International. Based on rate card costs; excludes classified advertising. Methodology of surveys and actual discount levels vary.

The French newspaper scene is completely different. Not by chance, only one French title is found among the top European newspaper circulation figures: the regional group *Ouest-France* (in 25th place). On the whole, the French newspaper sector is clearly dominated by such regional groups; this is the result of a breakneck concentration process since the 1950s and the decline of once–renowned national papers such as *Le Monde, Le Figaro* and *France-Soir*, which to the provincial reader seemed to be more Parisian than truly national. The days when French people were enthusiastic newspaper readers (at the start of the century they were still in second place worldwide), are in any case long gone: today according to circulation figures, they rank only sixteenth (cf. Liehr, 1990).

It is not only language barriers that impede the pan-European circulation of European newspapers and even news content, and will do so well into the future – the completely different consumer habits outlined above are also a barrier.

Collaboration between the *Frankfurter Rundschau*, the French *Libération*, the Spanish *El País* and the British *Guardian* in the exchange of correspondents' reports, or the ambitious project of a European cultural magazine with identical content in national languages (*Lettre Internationale*) are at present rather the exception than the rule. It is true that print media are distributed beyond national frontiers, but foreign newspapers, which are on sale particularly in railway stations, airports and holiday areas, are usually not directed at local citizens but rather at holiday-makers or business travellers who do not want to forego their usual reading matter.

A search for print media with a Europe-wide distribution reveals almost exclusively European editions of American publications: the *International Herald Tribune*, published in Paris (by the *New York Times* and the *Washington Post* jointly), of which the 'Atlantic edition' has been aimed primarily at Americans in Europe since the 1920s, the European editions of the *Wall Street Journal, US Today*, and the magazines *Time* and *Newsweek*. The British *Financial Times*, which, as the leading European business newspaper, is distributed throughout Europe, also belongs in this category.

The European – *currently (1992) enjoying a circulation of 350,000 (credit: The European).*

To date (1992), the most ambitious (and the only) project for a European newspaper was initiated in Britain by the late Robert Maxwell. *The European* is distributed weekly in 15 western and eastern European countries and has attained a circulation of 350,000, comparable to that of the *Süddeutsche Zeitung*. With its blend of correspondents' reports from various European countries, cultural and leisure features (which include Europe-wide coverage of events and TV programmes), and many large, full-colour pictures, the newspaper still contains little that would not be done as well or better by a serious national weekly or daily, or any number of specialized magazines. Only its effort to report and comment more comprehensively on the politics of the European Community raises it above the national newspapers with which it competes. Whether that will be enough to turn *The European* into a genuine and indispensable source of information must be doubted. The paper is meeting problems of acceptance in almost all European countries and, given the demise of Robert Maxwell (and of much of his business empire) in 1991, its future remains uncertain.

More typical of current transnational trends is the co-operative adoption of magazine formats by major European publishers. This does not mean that content is exchanged, but that concepts proven successful in one country are adapted for similar market niches in others. Thus the German publisher Gruner + Jahr decided to discontinue its own women's magazine, *Viva*, and replace it with a German version of

Four versions of Marie Claire *for April 1992 – and four very different images produced for the French, Greek, German and UK markets (credit: Marie Claire copyright).*

the French *Marie Claire*. In Italy, Mondadori are producing an Italian version. Following the same concept, major French publisher Hachette is distributing its women's magazine, *Elle*, almost world-wide (for instance, in Japan, China and Brazil, among other countries), and the German publisher Burda distributes its fashion magazine, *Burda Moden*, in eighteen countries, including an edition for the former Soviet Union.

This list could be continued, though it includes only target magazines (mostly for women) with a large proportion of pictures and advertising which do not conflict with any extreme national differences. In photo-journalism, which meets no language barriers, exchanges, international collaboration and the placing of national titles in other countries are very common. Examples include the long-standing co-operation between the German magazine, *Stern*, and the American *Life* magazine (which fell victim in its home country to the flood of television and now appears only occasionally); the numerous editions of the German *Geo-Magazin* (among others in France, Spain and the United Kingdom); or the Swiss publisher Ringier-Verlag, whose travel magazine, *Globo*, consists principally of translated text from the American *National Geographic Magazine*. This type of collaboration, then, is a world-wide trend which is not limited to Europe.

The question as to what Europeans are learning about each other from this type of international media co-operation is quickly answered: little or nothing. The ideal objective in the global magazine market is to eliminate any 'disturbing' national peculiarities editorially in the course of transferring the format, so that in most cases the readers are not even aware that they are handling a product of foreign origin. The motives for such collaborations are purely economic: economies of scale and the transfer of proven concepts minimize the risks to publishers in a magazine market which is largely saturated in the major European countries, and help them open up markets outside Europe.

Television programmes in the European single market – soap operas without frontiers?

One of the greatest fears accompanying the setting up of a unified, economically oriented European single market in the electronic media is that of being swamped by cheap American serials, against which national productions, or even European co-productions, will be unable to defend themselves. This fear has two essential components: one is cultural, based on the belief that excessive consumption of non-European programmes will work against the development of a common 'European cultural identity' (or, to put it more realistically, that it will undermine long-established national cultural identities). The second component is related to industrial and employment security, European film and television production industries hardly being able to withstand unprotected competition from the United States. In order to understand and correctly evaluate these threats, we must first examine more closely why the USA has such a dominant global role in both production and the international trade in television programmes (and in cinema films).

First of all, the United States, with about 250 million inhabitants, is the largest, most unified single-language television market in the world. This means that programmes (mostly serials) produced and broadcast there are as a rule already amortized in the home market by the first broadcast over nationwide commercial networks and mass repeats ('reruns') from local stations, that is, they have recovered their production costs. About a quarter of all advertising fees in the world are paid in the USA and it is the strength of the American advertising industry which finances the commercial television system, that makes it possible to produce television serials that are unimaginable in Europe. Hollywood studios spend enormous sums to implement their projects. As a rule it can be assumed that only one out of 100 ideas for television productions is developed to maturity and actually broadcast. That an idea should fail to be to the public's liking (a few spectacular exceptions notwithstanding) is thus relatively improbable.

In a thoroughly commercialized television system, the drive for high viewing numbers (which determine the price a network can charge its clients for advertising spots) requires the general direction of the programme to be towards the lowest common denominator – to 'mass taste'. From the start of cinema and

This listing for a cinema in Stuttgart, in Germany, demonstrates the dominance of the US in European cinema as well as in TV.

television, the United States, as a multi-cultural country of immigrants, has gained great experience in producing programmes for people with widely varying social, ethnic and cultural backgrounds; this capacity has never been developed to such a degree in the national television markets of Europe.

This has led to what the Canadian communications experts Colin Hoskins and Rolf Mirus have called a unique 'cultural discount' for American productions – a low 'cultural entry threshold' into markets outside the USA (Hoskins and Mirus, 1988, pp. 499–515). The attentive viewer of US television serials notices that the sets seem to be interchangeable and that only very slight regional references are shown (for example, by the end of the series, the 'ranch' theme had almost completely disappeared from the serial 'Dallas'). Hollywood's decades-long experience in the international distribution of its productions represents the other major factor in the success of American productions.

The most convincing argument for purchasing American programmes is their uncontested low price. Since the production costs have normally been recovered in the home market, the production companies can afford to match their prices to the purchasing power and the demand of individual target markets. For example, a thirty-minute American serial episode costs about $40,000 in Italy; in Bermuda it would cost only $40. Even if American production companies have to calculate more finely nowadays, and are increasingly dependent on foreign markets due to greater competition and shrinking ratings at home (as a result of the viewing public being divided among more and more cable channels), an American serial can still be bought for only 10 to 15 per cent of the cost of a European production.

The stars of Eldorado*, a first attempt at a pan-European soap opera, are shown relaxing on the set in Spain. So far (1992) it has not attracted as much support as some US and Australian imports (credit: Rex Features).*

It has frequently been asked why traditional European film-making countries like France, Italy and the United Kingdom, do not export to the United States to the same extent. The regular viewing of foreign television programmes, however, which is quite common in much of Europe, would be unimaginable in the United States, where (in terms of mass viewing audiences) exposure to and understanding of other cultures is undeveloped. An average American viewer can not be expected to accept a dubbed or even subtitled programme. In short, the 'cultural threshold' for European productions is so high that entry seems impossible. To date, no European television serial has succeeded in gaining access to one of the three dominant commercial networks. (The only American showcase for European television programmes is the subscription-financed Public Broadcasting Service, which, however, attracts only three per cent of the public.)

Interestingly enough, the resistance to European programmes also affects British productions, which one would think most likely to succeed in the United States. For years the British producer Granada TV, for example, has tried in vain to sell its successful serial *Coronation Street* in the USA. Even its offer of a free test of a whole sequence met with no success. The risk of failure was simply too great for the American networks; they believed (perhaps correctly) that the actors' unfamiliar Lancashire accent would cause American viewers to switch channels – a vision of horror for every commercial television provider, not only in the USA. (The fact that the British public, by contrast, did not seem to be worried by the Texan idiom of the 'Dallas' actors serves as a further indication of the high degree of cultural isolation in the world of American television.)

It is characteristic of American programme-makers that they prefer to study the European market closely with a possible view to recruiting successful directors or buying ideas and remaking them in the USA. The latest tendency, given the emergence of the European single market, is to look for strong European partners and to produce directly in Europe for the foreign market.

As regards the fear that Europe could be overrun by a wave of American productions if no protective measures are taken, mere economic factors suggest that this is highly probable. If the situation is looked at more closely, however, it becomes clear that certain other factors must also be taken into account. In the first place there is, as there always has been, a pronounced liking for home-produced programmes in all European countries. No American serial attained the ratings of *Black Forest Clinic* in Germany, *Coronation Street* in the United Kingdom, or *Alone against the Mafia* in Italy. In the public systems there are only a few American serials which have managed to reach the prime-time slot between 7.30 and 10.30 p.m. This is, of course, no indication of quality, but a plain cultural fact. The argument over whether the expensive European co-production *Euro-Cops* is 'better' than *Columbo* or *Kojak*, or a cheap Italian film from the 1970s better than a Hitchcock or Lubitsch film from the 1940s will be left, with some relief, to the critics. Debates about cultural superiority, however defined, seem inappropriate to the present discussion.

The second factor in a consideration of the mooted American threat to European programming is the irrefutable connection between the commercialization and the

'Americanization' of media systems. We must consider not just 'European television' as an undifferentiated whole, but also its growing commercial elements and their possible and probable effects on the public providers. The following table shows that the proportion of bought-in productions is generally far greater with commercial European providers than with public or state-owned ones, the proportion of their own productions being correspondingly smaller (comparable data for each station are hard to obtain and do not show the latest position, but they do indicate clear tendencies).

Table 9   Programming in selected TV channels, 1987; proportion of programme-hours in percentages

Public	O	C	P	R	*Private*	O	C	P	R	*Programme hours*
German Federal Republic										
ARD	51.4	13.5	13.5	21.6						3700
ZDF	49.4	11.4	19.0	20.2						3950
					Sat1	29.2	9.3	43.0	18.5	6500
					RTL+	15.2	4.5	54.5	25.8	6600
France										
A2	37.7	28.8	17.7	15.8						5500
FR3	50.0	4.5	25.5	20.0						5500
					TF1	25.7	18.6	30.0	25.7	7000
					La Cinq	17.9	19.6	32.1	30.4	5600
					Canal+	11.7	0.0	18.2	70.1	7700
Italy										
RAI	56.8	2.7	13.8	26.7						14,400
					Italia-1	23.5	1.5	48.5	26.5	6800
					Canale-5	27.3	1.5	45.5	25.7	6600
Spain										
RTVE	62.1	0.8	29.1	8.0						8580
United Kingdom										
BBC	61.2	0.9	6.9	31.0						11,600
					ITV	56.9	1.4	25.0	16.7	7200
					BSkyB	5.7	21.6	48.8	23.9	8800
Average percentages	52.7	8.9	18.9	20.5		23.7	8.7	38.4	29.3	

O = Own productions   C = Contract or co-productions   P = Purchases   R = Repeats
Source: Sonnenberg, 1990, p. 106.

It is clear that in-house productions make up the majority of programmes for the public providers listed here, although with considerable variations (between 62.1 per cent for Spanish radio and television and only 37.7 per cent for the French Antenne 2). The trend to contract and co-productions is most noticeable in Germany and France and usually works in favour of the home (or European) private film industry. Commercial television stations, on the other hand, show little inclination to steer capital into steep production costs; bought-in programmes are generally in the majority. The only exceptions to this are the British ITV (Independent Television) companies, which, under a public supervisory body unique in Europe (the Independent Broadcasting Authority), have to meet a relatively high standard of programmes. Yet even with ITV, the proportion of in-house productions is lower than it is for the BBC.

The theory that high public acceptance and low market prices ensure that mainly American productions are bought by the commercial providers is substantiated in table 10 (even though, dating from 1985–6, it depicts a relatively early stage in the commercialization process.

Table 10   Percentages of American programmes on EC television channels

	Station	Public		Commercial	
		1985	1986	1985	1986
Belgium	RTBF	7	7		
	VRT	5	10		
Denmark	DR	4	9		
France	A2	3	5		
	FR 3	9	11		
	TF 1			10	15
	Canal Plus			–	37
German FR	ARD	4	15		
	ZDF	16	7		
	3sat	–	10		
	1 plus	–	8		
	RTL+			7	15
	Sat 1			25	38
Greece	no data				
Ireland	no data, but above average high imports				
Italy	RAI 1	12	16		
	RAI 2	24	19		
	RAI 3	7	7		
	Rete-4			33	66
	Canal-5			67	59
	Italia-1			–	68
Luxembourg	RTL			24	31
Netherlands	NL 1	15	23		
	NL 2	14	8		
Portugal	no data				
Spain	TV 1	12	12		
	TV 2	9	19		

**Table 10   Percentages of American programmes on EC television channels –
continued**

	Station	Public		Commercial	
		1985	*1986*	*1985*	*1986*
United Kingdom	BBC 1	12	12		
	BBC 2	5	12		
	ITV			9	6
	Channel 4			32	29
	Sky			31	26
	Super Channel			–	15
Average percentages		7.3	11.7	26.4	33.8

Source: Sonnenberg, 1990, p. 109.

If the 1986 data are compared, the proportion of American productions in the
commercial providers' programming is consistently higher than in the public sector (though here again ITV, whose proportion of American programmes is even
dropping, is an exception). On average the public providers devoted only 11.7 per
cent of their total programming to American productions, while the proportion
among commercial stations was 33.8 per cent. National differences are considerable: the European leaders in 'Americanization' are quite clearly the media mogul
Silvio Berlusconi's private Italian channels Italia-1 (68 per cent), Rete-4 (66 per
cent) and Canale 5 (59 per cent).

The Danish communications researcher Preben Sepstrup has come to the conclusion that Americanization and commercialization are in direct relation to each
other: the higher the degree of commercialization in a media system, the higher, as
a rule, the total proportion of American productions, and the greater their likelihood to occupy prime time slots (Sepstrup, 1989, p. 46).

If one takes this finding as empirically proven, current EC policy on transnational
media must be viewed extremely critically. The recently issued EC television
guidelines (which must be embodied in national legislation within the foreseeable
future) state: 'The [EC] agreement provides for the free exchange of all services
duly supplied against payment, and this shall occur regardless of their cultural or
other content' (EC, 1989, L 298/23). The 'free exchange' of television programmes is thus explicitly included among the free exchange of services.

However, placing television programmes on the same footing as other services, ig-
noring their special cultural nature, can cut the ground from beneath any media
policy based on cultural considerations. In the end, this could even threaten public
TV systems, which are invariably based on culturally determined national legal
systems. This 'economistic' attitude in EC policy thus favours those providers
who, as we have seen, are contributing nothing worth mentioning towards the
European orientation of television programming but rather the opposite. Sepstrup
argues correctly that the price viewers would have to pay for the political realiza-
tion of a European single market would be the disappearance of public television
and an overall increase in the American content of European television.

It would appear that many EC politicians have now become aware of this argument. A rethinking of the primarily economic view of television is not taking place, however, because only on the economic level does the EC have legitimate power to impose regulations on television. Neither the EEC agreements – nor the Single European Act provides a mandate for EC institutions to assume a cultural role. Any cultural classification of television would thus be tantamount to abandoning European rules.

Instead of this, an effort is being made to subsidize the European film industry through the comprehensive assistance programme 'Media 92', in order to enable it to compete with Hollywood. About 200 million Ecus will be spent in the next few years on subsidizing scripts, sales and so on. Whether these subsidized productions will eventually reach television, and thus form a counterbalance to the dreaded Americanization, must for the moment be doubted. So far, EC politicians with special interest in the media have not been able to reach agreement on compulsory quota regulations, which have repeatedly been requested by the French and which would be the only way of assuring access to broadcast time for European productions. Definition of this matter in the television guidelines has so far been non-committal and vague, as no member state is prepared to hand over such far-reaching powers to the EC.

Mass media and regions: the example of non-commercial local radio

In 1984 European television was still in its infancy, compared with the current explosive increase in channels and commercialization. Many media politicians hoped that once limitations on channel numbers were removed, television would be able to grow into an important local or regional communication medium. Thus the green paper 'Television without Frontiers', in which the EC Commission introduced its media policy, stated 'The medium of television in particular will help to develop and sustain the consciousness of a common European culture and history and their many-faceted richness' (Kommission der Europäischen Gemeinschaften, 1984, p. 28).

Today, much of this prediction must be qualified. It has become clear that as a rule the new commercial television stations have only a very slight interest in replacing cheap American serials with 'consciousness promoting' European productions. In addition, the expectations of regional or local television have not been fulfilled: compared with national providers, regional stations, in so far as any exist at all, are playing a small and diminishing role. The reasons are easy to see. First, television requires expensive and complicated technology; this alone makes it hardly suitable for short-range communication. Secondly, commercial providers are dependent on high ratings for adequate advertising revenue. They thus aim from the start at a national or even transnational market, and serve regional needs at most with 'window programmes' when the licensing authorities force them to. Television, especially in its commercial version, seems in the current state of development to be quite unsuitable for special regional needs.

In most countries the chief local and regional medium is still the daily paper. In recent years, however, some very interesting developments have been taking place in the 'forgotten medium' – radio – which seem likely to establish a third type of mass medium: largely non-commercial local radio stations operating alongside the familiar public and commercial organizations (for a survey see Kleinsteuber, 1991).

If one looks at European developments since the 1970s, radio has unquestionably undergone a meteoric rise. Italy, for example, has experienced since 1976 a wave of new stations outside the public sector, so that there are currently about 4000 radio stations. With the exception of Scandinavia, similar developments have taken place in all European countries, a trend which, in television-fixated media politics, has attracted surprisingly little attention. By far the majority of these stations are, however, purely commercial, whether legally founded, as in the German Federal Republic, or operating illegally as 'pirate' stations, as in the Netherlands, or without any legal supervision, as in Italy.

Despite its diverse origins, however, this form of commercial radio makes very little use of its special opportunities for local communication. Characteristically, such stations quickly link up into so-called networks (this started first in Italy) in order to enlarge their distribution area and thus their advertising revenue; they also tend to focus their output on easily consumable music programmes.

This means that in the niches left open by both commercial radio and public providers with national distribution, a third type of radio, aiming neither at profits nor at geographical expansion, has been able to establish itself. This comprises stations set up on local initiative, by groups or even by individuals who want to broadcast alone or in co-operation.

In the UK the best-known examples of non-commercial local radio are the network of BBC local radio stations.

This type of radio started in the United States, where as early as 1949 Station KPFA, the first example of so-called 'community radio', was founded in the university town of Berkeley, California. Today some 140 such stations exist across the country. Similar developments can be seen in Canada and Australia, where such stations are often located outside the urban centres and cater for the particular cultural needs of ethnic minorities. Another feature of the community-radio model from the English-speaking world is that it is usually financed by listeners' contributions and broadcasts only a very limited amount of local advertising. Some types of similar local radio stations have grown up in Europe, mostly independently and in ignorance of the North American and Australian models.

If one contrasts the situations in the different countries, one finds several basic types of local radio which have grown out of the specific requirements and conditions of their regions. First there is the southern European type of 'free radio' as it arose in Italy in the 1970s; politically militant stations which were nevertheless soon suppressed by commercial competition. These created the impetus for experimentation – mostly illegal – in many countries. This type of station is still found in Italy (now under the label 'democratic radio' or 'information radio'), in Spain (as '*emisoras municipales*' or community radio stations), in France (as 'collective radio'), in Belgium (as 'free radio'), and to an extent in Ireland (as 'community radio').

In many cases these radio stations began illegally and were subsequently legalized. Their forms of organization vary from the firmly established 'listeners' radio' on the North American model, like Radio Popolare in Milan, to the pure enthusiasts' radio which gives free access to everybody, like Radio Air Libre in Brussels. The content is clearly aimed at the communication needs of sub-cultures and ethnic minorities.

In northern Europe (Sweden, Denmark and Norway) there is a different type of local radio, the so-called *naerradioer* or neighbourhood radio stations. Unlike those of southern Europe, these local stations are set up 'from above' in best Scandinavian welfare-state tradition as instances of 'popularized radio culture', and, not least, to forestall the kind of uncontrolled and illegal development found in Italy and France. The central feature of this type of radio is that local groups come together as management associations and then receive transmitting licences. Since the beginning of the 1980s neighbourhood radio has experienced turbulent beginnings in all three countries. At present almost 900 such local stations are active or licensed: about 300 in Denmark, 400 in Norway and 160 in Sweden. In Norway and Denmark at least it has been noticeable recently that stations have been financing themselves almost solely from advertising, without, however, being allowed to make profits.

In many other European countries there are either hybrids of these two basic types of non-commercial local radio, or the process of establishing it is still in its earliest stages. Most remarkable are the numerous Dutch local radio stations; originally these were allowed to transmit only through cable networks, but since 1988 it has been possible to receive them via aerial. The example of the Netherlands makes it clear that the argument (frequently advanced in the German Federal Republic) that the scarcity of radio frequencies justifies limiting the types of broadcasting allowed is invalid if stations really concentrate on the immediate local neighbourhood, to which there are no technical obstacles. Further hybrid types exist in Switzerland (Radio LoRa), in the German Federal Republic (the previously piratical and now legalized Radio Dreyeckland in Freiburg), in Finland and, since 1989, in the United Kingdom with advertisement-financed community stations.

As well as the trend to commercialization, European local radio in the last fifteen years has shown a recognizable tendency to return to the neighbourhood and its sometimes highly specific communication needs. The programmes are as multifarious as the regions and the human beings who live in them (detailed case studies appear in Kleinsteuber, 1991). Their umbrella organization, the *Fédération Européenne des Radio Libres*, was urging as early as 1988 that the local radio movement deserved appropriate political (and financial) support from the European Community, such as the independent European film industry enjoys under the 'Media 92' support programme. However, a European cultural radio policy has not so far been forthcoming.

The Europe of the future – opportunities and dangers for the mass media in Europe

European 'cultural identity'

Around the start of the 1970s the concept of 'cultural identity' appeared in the developing world. For them, modernization and development increasingly meant subordinating their own traditions and values to western patterns. This process was also seen as 'cultural imperialism', and the growing dissatisfaction with it is reflected in various declarations by UNESCO, which organized world conferences on international cultural policy in Venice in 1970 and in Mexico City in 1982. The final declaration of the Mexico conference proclaimed each culture (understood as a 'unique and irreplaceable totality of values') to be the most effective way in which a people could demonstrate its presence in the world, and rejected any form of cultural domination as the denial or impairment of a people's identity (Deutsche UNESCO Commission, 1982). In the media world, this led to an extensive UNESCO inquiry into the international exchange of news and information, the result of which was a demand for a 'free and balanced flow of information' which might act similarly to the industrial nations' principle of the free flow of information (Deutsche UNESCO Commission, 1981).

This short review of the beginnings of the debate is enough to make clear that a simple transposition of the problem to Europe is not possible. Europe is not part of the developing world – the growing penetration by American television programmes is not the same as the extensive, or possibly total, loss of a people's own cultural means of self-expression. For a citizen of Senegal or Kenya, say, for whom western cultural domination is synonymous with strong European influences, any discussion about Europe's cultural autonomy would hardly be comprehensible. Thus we are dealing with a concept that is subject to numerous variables.

The four most important of these are:

- Cultural identity can refer to widely differing geographical areas, cultures and historical backgrounds, and is borne and claimed by equally dissimilar social groups, from ethnic groups, through nations, to entire regions of the world. The basis for the development of cultural identity is thus first a certain number of common cultural features which (at least temporarily) push divisive forces into the background.

- Secondly, cultural identity seems to be highly dependent on a real (or perhaps only an imagined) cultural threat from outside. Like every form of common consciousness it draws a frontier between itself and other, foreign, cultural values.

- Finally, if cultural identity is to develop, there must be a minimum of social and political capacity for its expression and self-assertion. If this is lacking, the final consequence is usually the complete destruction or transformation of the affected culture.

- In positive terms, cultural identity may be defined as an attitude derived from a common language, history, tradition and (often religious) set of values which is understood by a sufficiently large group (as a rule a nation, people or language group) to be part of its collective feelings of belonging together. This definition necessarily involves inherent negative components: identity with one group also means non-identity with others. In view of the social and economic realities which increasingly transcend groups and nations, these negative, divisive factors undergo constant erosion. From this process arise the beginnings of a higher collective identity (even if nationality has very recently shown itself to be extremely effective as a force for creating identity in multi-ethnic nations and regions, as in eastern Europe and the former Soviet Union).

Current debate about a 'European cultural identity' has received fresh impulse from the advent of the single market and refers to the sort of identity which transcends nations and regions. The debate arose in the middle of the 1980s from widespread dissatisfaction, particularly among conservative intellectuals, with the faltering EC integration process. The criticism was that the idea of 'Europe as a community of values' had become lost amid incomprehensible arguments about agricultural subsidies and the steel industry, butter mountains, brewers' purity ordinances and drug-licensing. This debate should be seen primarily as 'conferring identity' in order to give new impulse to the (western) European unification process. Its common starting point is an extremely broad definition of unique European values as a basis for collective cultural identity.

This view finds academic expression particularly in the work of the social philosopher Hermann Lübbe. For him, European culture lies in a 'richness of content' which has shown itself 'in all parts of the world to be universalizable' and which has found expression in the development of norms (such as, for example, the subordination of politics to legal constraint). The fact that 'definitive works from our culture' are found right round the world is an 'expression of their power to define'. The core of European culture is the formation of a 'universal intellectual and technical civilization' which does not cut across any specific national or regional 'cultures of origin'. These latter should however, as 'original European units' be guarded and made 'visible' by means of (traditional humanistic) education (Lübbe, 1989).

The well-known German researcher on Europe Werner Weidenfeld, whose work is focused more on the linking of identity with the factual unification process in the EC, argues in a similar vein, as, for example, when he points out the 'normative power of supranational institutions' (Weidenfeld, 1984) or enquires directly about the 'identity potential' of joint European policy (Bertelsmann Stiftung, 1988).

This version in particular of the debate on identity has nourished among critics the suspicion that the 'resounding speeches about a common European culture are nothing but an ideology designed to awaken enthusiasm for the forthcoming 1992 EC single market, which above all will benefit the large economic enterprises of the twelve countries' (Pöttker, 1989, pp. 17–18). It is difficult to postulate from this any particular need for the protection of European civilizing values. If these values are indeed 'universal', as is often asserted in the course of this debate, then they are valid for all those nations, societies and cultures which have been or are being determined, or even only decisively influenced, by Europe. This would include the whole of North America, industrial countries outside Europe, such as Australia, and also the so-called 'élites' of the developing world, all of which are characterized by universal European culture – a cultural concept which could then no longer be classed as 'western'. Furthermore, who could seriously threaten these globally dominant cultural values, and thus justify any debate about the defence of European cultural identity? A 'cultural centre' outside Europe, in relation to which Europe might find itself dependent, defies the liveliest imagination. On this topic the French intellectual Luc Bondy declared as long ago as the mid-1980s that the question of a European identity was neither central nor capable of being answered unambiguously.

What about the actual linguistic, historical, social and cultural conditions within Europe itself, which after all must form the basis for the development of a cultural identity? Europe is (in 1992) 32 nation-states with 67 languages, not counting dialects. At the national level alone this multiplicity is frequently repeated in marked regional identities, which are in more or less stark conflict with the prevailing national identity and which meet any proposed supranational identity sceptically, if not with rejection.

Even the bitterly contested slogan 'Europe of the regions' can hardly any longer encompass the multiplicity of cultural realities on this continent. It must be taken into account that even the Europe of the twelve EC countries, as a 'gathering of the remnants of empires' (Bondy, 1984, p. 29) manifests the most varied cultural ties and overlaps with other countries and regions.

Thus France is a cultural centre for the francophone communities of Belgium, Switzerland, Canada, West Africa and the Pacific area, just as the United Kingdom represents the linguistic and cultural centre of the Commonwealth. The Scandinavian countries practise highly institutionalized co-operation in cultural policy, while the German Federal Republic can be counted as the centre of the German-speaking area.

An inquiry instituted in 1977 by the EC Commission (most of those questioned were Belgian) led to the conclusion that such linguistic or historical connections within a 'sphere of influence' were far more influential than geographical propinquity (for example, Belgium–Germany) or membership of the European Community (Wiesand, 1987, p. 89). Furthermore, countries outside Europe also affect Europe as a cultural area – this can be clearly seen from the current multi-ethnic composition of the population in large cities. To give a particularly extreme example, for an average school in the middle of London, around 170 different languages will be spoken in the pupils' homes (Hearst, 1987, p. 4). This alone is almost enough to rule out any talk of cultural identity, whether British or European.

Despite this, the concept of cultural identity is increasingly employed in discussing the media, initiated by the spread of transfrontier satellite programmes and the foreseeable scarcity of programmes to fill a growing number of channels. Difficulties experienced hitherto with the pan-European distribution of transnational programmes could be a first indication that the many linguistic barriers and 'cultural identities' within Europe have far stronger effects than do the features thought to be common to all.

On closer inspection, however, it becomes clear that the highly varied cultural and political media problems within the EC alone can hardly be explained by the concept of identity. A look at the experience of several west European countries is interesting here:

- In Scandinavia, discussion about identity resulted in an attempt to set up a jointly-run satellite network (NORDSAT). This incipient transnational collaboration, to date the most extensive (which has now foundered due to the high cost), aimed quite clearly at the Scandinavian cultural area, and thus showed itself to be contrary to ideas of pan-European cultural identity. Furthermore, traditional centre–periphery tensions in some Scandinavian countries (for example, Norway) have moved the problem of maintaining regional identities closer to centre stage (Bakke, 1986, pp. 135, 138).

- Beneath the discussions about identity in France and the United Kingdom, lurks the attempt to keep their own strongly developed media industries internationally competitive, in order to be able ultimately to serve world markets through the consolidation of their positions in their own supra-European cultural areas.

- In the German Federal Republic, discussion about cultural identity was for a long time overlaid – and rightly so – by negative historical experiences of nationalism. If the concept of cultural identity is raised, it is usually in the context of media politics over the demarcation of areas of competence between the Federal Government and the EC on the one hand, and individual Federal states on the other, and these conflicts are hardly comparable with those between the countries and regions within Europe.

- Finally, Luxembourg knows no kind of identity debate. As a classic 'spillover' country and as the home of an internationally operating media concern (CLT), Luxembourg's media policy has from the start been transnational and pan-European (Bakke, 1986, p. 138).

The structural differences within Europe are reflected in national media policies and determine what is understood by cultural identity or media culture in different countries, regions and sub-regions. A level of external, media-based cultural threat great enough to push these differences into the background is hardly imaginable.

These few indications suffice to show that a sensible approach to the problems of a culture oriented development of European media will hardly be possible by appealing to the concept of 'cultural identity'. It appears that this form of the current debate has to be understood as a mirror image of an EC policy which at the core is centralist. Against this centralization there stands the enormous diversity of the European media scene, on the protection and development of which many writers are increasingly focusing their attention.

If we now substitute the term 'cultural diversity' for the concept of 'cultural identity', both positive and negative factors can be much better identified. The German media lawyer Wolfgang Hoffmann-Riem rightly points out the misuse of the concept of identity, particularly when a truly free flow of information and opinion across frontiers is defined politically as 'dangerous' (for example, over decades of the east–west confrontation). Such a definition of identity with reference to the media is incompatible with 'general western European cultural and political values' (Hoffmann-Riem, 1985, p. 182).

Instead of this he advocates that a maximum of diversity should be the criterion which determines whether or not media 'deserve protection' as elements of a national culture. Such media diversity has at least four aspects:

- *objective* diversity (a variety of specialisms and topics);

- *content* diversity (catering for all types of information and opinion relevant to the society; equality of opportunity);

- *person-related* diversity (access to the communication system for all groups within the population); and finally

- *geographical* diversity (local, regional, national and supranational content represented in the total offering).

He concludes that those media developments must be perceived as negative that wish to impose norms on cultures, to limit opportunities for expression, to hinder the integration of society and opportunities for collaboration, or to restrict individual choice of media content. Media systems which are, by contrast, based on 'diversity' have to take into account the cultural values accepted or struggling for acceptance in their society. In the course of this it will become clear whether the particular society possesses enough collective traditions, values and assumptions to be able to create an identity for itself. Changing the theme from cultural identity to diversity of communications makes it possible to accommodate social and political change. Creativity and innovation should not stop at national frontiers. Neither should they be impeded by the submergence of any society's potential for diversity (Hoffmann-Riem, 1985, p. 183).

The above discussion will, it is hoped, have made clear that the criterion of diversity, which aims at the most comprehensive, untrammelled and democratic development of highly varied cultures, suits not only the European situation, but also the situation of nations and multi-cultural regions, much better than the idea of cultural identity does. With this in mind, discussion about the future and the necessity of public broadcasting as a cultural factor in Europe can be carried on much more fruitfully.

Television for Europe?

In a Europe which is beginning to grow together economically and politically ever more closely, the question arises as to what contribution the media, and particularly television, can make to European cultural integration. Opinions on this subject are divided. A number of people foresee a European identity created by cross-frontier, pan-European television programmes; others see only commercial programmes of further diminishing quality which will destroy Europe's cultural diversity and lead to the loss of cultural identity. Satellite television does indeed open up new perspectives: people of different languages could, by receiving programmes in their own tongues, come nearer to each other and develop a better understanding of each other. But it is equally possible that the smaller nations could sacrifice even more of their own culture, as they would hardly be able to defend it against the three large language areas of English, French and German.

There is agreement on one thing, however: a European television initiative is essential to European integration. How and in what form it will be possible to bring this about remains unclear.

Following the discussions about 'Television without frontiers', stimulated by the EC Commission's green paper of the same name, various transnational initiatives were launched relatively early. However, these were predominantly based on national media systems. That some initiatives towards a 'European television' are to be found among them is due to Europe's public providers, who did not wish to leave the field to the commercial providers without a battle. 'European television' should above all be characterized by specifically European programme content. The central problem remains, however, how to overcome language barriers. At present three different concepts are being tried or discussed: multi-language programmes, lingua franca programmes and language-area programmes (cf. Faul, 1987, p. 78ff.).

Multi-language programmes

As early as the beginning of the 1980s the European Broadcasting Union (EBU) had given birth to a multi-language programme: the five-week 'Eurikon' project in which the IBA (Britain), RAI (Italy), ORF (Austria), NOS (Netherlands) and ARD (German Federal Republic) took part. In the course of this experiment the same programme was broadcast simultaneously in various languages. The results of this trial were thoroughly satisfactory, and the experience gained was passed on in 1985–6 to the so-called Europa-TV, the community programme of ARD, NOS, RAI, RTP (Portugal), and RTE (Ireland). This had to be ended after 14 months because of inadequate financial support by both its operators and the EC Commission.

172

In addition to financial problems, overcoming language barriers proved to be extraordinarily laborious: productions by the various public providers were broadcast in the original language, and in the other participating countries either dubbed or sub-titled. This had to be done for each first broadcast. The aim was that in this way the programme content should foster a common consciousness among the viewers, despite their different languages. Europa-TV received very positive critical response for its specifically European conception, even if, despite a potential audience of 3.5 million households, it was able to achieve no measurable viewing rating.

A third multi-language programme project of the EBU is *Eurosport*, a European sports programme which was broadcast first via the ASTRA satellite and now via the ECS-1 satellite. As well as 17 EBU members from 15 countries, one commercial provider, Sky TV (now BSkyB), a subsidiary of the Murdoch group, also participated in the consortium. The multi-language Eurosport programme was composed of sports material from the EBU members; the transmitter was operated and advertising revenue gathered by Sky TV. On 6 May 1991 *Eurosport* had to stop transmission, however. At the request of the competing channel, Screensport, the Commission decided that co-operation between two potential competitors such as Murdoch and the EBU consortium was anti-competitive and put other sports television providers at a disadvantage. Only after the sale of the Murdoch share to the French private television TF1 was *Eurosport* again able to broadcast on 22 May 1991.

A further multi-language programme, the European television cultural channel (ARTE), is now active after a long gestation period, which, although originally a Franco-German initiative, explicitly intends to draw in other European partners. In April 1991 the French television station La Sept and a specially founded subsidiary of the public broadcasting institutions in Germany set up the cultural channel in the legal form of a 'European economic syndicate'. The initial total budget of about 120 million ECU is intended to help develop alternative programmes representing European culture in its entirety and thus make a contribution to the integration of Europe – there is no certainty of success.

With all multi-language programmes, the problem of whether to dub or use subtitles arises. Both procedures have advantages and disadvantages. Subtitles retain the audio-visual integrity of the programme and are low in cost; their disadvantage is the reading they demand of viewers, which affects the comprehensibility and the acceptability of broadcasts. Compared to this, dubbing is relatively expensive and falsifies the audio-visual context of the production; it does, however, permit undisturbed reception of the broadcast. Both processes share the unavoidable disadvantage of distorting the original programme content.

As far as the translation of television programmes is concerned, Europe is polarized. The larger countries such as France, Italy, Germany and Spain dub their programmes; the smaller and multilingual countries – Belgium, the Netherlands, Switzerland and Scandinavia – use subtitles. Subtitles tend to be used in the United Kingdom too. Interestingly enough, people throughout Europe are satisfied with the prevailing systems.

Lingua franca programmes

That the British virtually never need to translate is due to the role of English as a modern lingua franca[1], a generally understood means of communication. Although German constitutes the largest language population in Europe, English has grown into a pan-European and world-wide language of conversation, particularly in the television world. A consequence of this is that in 1992 most European lingua franca stations are based in Britain: BSkyB, Super Channel, Children's and Arts Channel, Lifestyle TV, and MTV-Europe among others. Of these, however, only BSkyB and Super Channel could possibly be termed 'European' stations in the narrow sense, the other English-language broadcasts having a more specialized character which stands in the way of a European orientation of the programmes.

In 1982 the commercial Sky TV was the first European satellite station. In 1989 it changed its name to Sky One (because there have been more Sky programmes in the mean time) and belongs to British Sky Broadcasting (BSkyB), 48 per cent of which is owned by Murdoch's News International. BSkyB was set up in 1990 out of a merger of Murdoch's Sky Television with British Satellite Broadcasting. It is still the most significant satellite broadcaster in Europe. In addition it has a range of co-operation agreements for linking up with programmes with regional trans-mitters in lightly cabled countries such as Italy, Spain, Monaco and France, and also in Canada and Hong Kong. The channel offers an extremely high proportion of entertainment material – over 70 per cent. The proportion of topical news is less than one per cent. In the field of films and serials the station has, at 70 per cent, the highest proportion of American imports in the whole EC. So there are no initiatives from Sky One for a 'European television', although the station claims to produce about 40 per cent of its programmes itself (Videoclips) and to pay for half of its total programming in EC countries.

Super Channel is another commercial entertainment station with a range hardly comparable with that of Sky Channel. It was originally British but is now partly owned by the Italian company Videomusic, and the British Virgin Group. The originally almost solely British slant of the programmes was replaced in 1987 by a European perspective; instead of 80 per cent British productions, the same pro-portion was devoted to continental European productions. Specifically European programmes were broadcast, such as weather, news, business reports and a maga-zine covering various aspects of the EC. Just one year later, in 1988, diminishing advertising revenue made budget cuts necessary, and this area of programming was sacrificed. Since then the Super Channel's programming has come to re-semble BSkyB's, though the proportion of films and serials is still perhaps some-what smaller.

Neither station can be unequivocally classed as lingua franca, since they also show non-British films in the original version; nor are they unequivocally European in their orientation. The language level of their programmes is none too high. Besides entertainment programmes, music and sport are their most important com-

---

[1]   Lingua franca ('the language of the Franks') was a mixed tongue traceable back to the early Middle Ages which was preferred in the Mediterranean region for trade between Christians and Arabs and was in use until the nineteenth century.

ponents. It is with such culturally unspecific programmes that the operators hope to achieve the widest possible distribution regardless of geographical and cultural identities, and with it, commercial success.

Language area channels

The term 'language area channels', refers to stations targeted at specific European language areas, in particular the large ones such as the German or the French. (Channels in English are considered to be lingua franca channels in this classification. Nevertheless some efforts are being made to set up an anglophone cultural language channel, even if those have not been particularly successful. Super Channel was originally conceived as one such). For the most part the public television providers in large countries co-operate with those of smaller countries sharing their language.

The francophone channels TV5 and TV Sport, the German-language station Eins Plus ('1+') and 3sat, and the Scandinavian TV3 are language area channels in this sense. At the most, TV5, Eins Plus and 3sat can be considered 'European' channels. TV Sport is the French counterpart of the English Screensport, a specialized channel without any specific European content. The successful commercial TV3, on the other hand, is expressly directed at the Scandinavian area only.

The participants in TV5 are television companies, including commercial ones, from France, Belgium, Switzerland and Canada. The programming avoids American films completely and instead transmits programmes exclusively from the parent organizations, RTBF, TF1, A2, FR3, SSR, and CTQC. In 1988 TV5 had the largest distribution in Europe after Sky Channel and Super Channel. Its long-term target is clearly to grow into a world-wide French-language television service. In future the programming will be more closely integrated and the number of in-house productions is expected to rise.

The first language-area station was 3sat, in which ZDF, ORF, and SRG take part. The Swiss Schweizer Rundfunk and the Austrian broadcasting organization together hold only 30 per cent of the shares, so that ZDF (the Second German Television Channel) carries the main financial and programming responsibility. Since the end of 1984, 3sat has been transmitted via telecommunications satellite and fed into the cable networks of the three participating countries. As far as content is concerned, in-house productions are emphasized and their scope extends to eastern Europe. Programming consists mainly of the participating public stations' repeats, the selection of which is claimed to be based on the more demanding cultural standards.

Eins Plus on the other hand is the German station ARD's satellite channel; their sole partner, SRG, is responsible for only 18 television evenings per year. Eins Plus has so far been distributed only via the cable networks in the Federal Republic of Germany. While broadcasts like *Europe Our Neighbour*, *This Week in the European Parliament*, or *Travel Routes to Art* illustrate the channel's claim to be specifically 'European' or 'cultural', in fact peak-time viewing consists of repeated German, and often American films. All in all, hardly any impulses towards a 'European' television are emitted by Eins Plus.

All three of these language area channels may be classed as full-range stations which set their own cultural standards and aim to carry the culture of their own language area beyond their own frontiers. In every case, however, low budgets make it impossible to support a 'European' range of programmes. The language area channels can stay afloat only with help from the parent companies. They represent not so much an initiative towards European television as the desire of the public providers in Europe to take part in the development of satellites.

It has thus become clear that anyone who wishes to use television to further the cause of European integration faces a whole series of problems, of which language barriers are the foremost. The existing lingua franca stations are too much oriented towards the standards and objectives of American commercial television to serve any aims worth mentioning with regard to cultural policy. Language area stations on the other hand, though they might seem an option worth considering in respect of cultural aims, are dependent for their implementation on the politically regulated fee income of public providers and their willingness to support such projects. At the same time, the linguistic targeting of these programmes limits their distribution potential.

For theoretical and practical reasons, multi-language programmes thus offer the only possibility of success in producing European television which, while respecting the cultural and linguistic diversity of existing cultural areas, can make a reasonable contribution to European integration. It is to be hoped that following political union a multi-lingual European transmitter can be set up. The technical process for simultaneous transmission of multi-lingual programmes already exists in the D2 Mac-Satellite transmission system. Whether this technology can be used depends, as so often in Europe, on solving the question of standards.

Advertising in Europe – the pan-European consumer?

The European mass media – press, radio and television – not only inform, entertain and advise the public; they are also, in various ways, carriers of advertising. This means that they are dependent to a considerable degree on advertising revenue to finance their editorial activities.

The scale of the western European advertising market is indeed impressive. In the 12 countries of the European Community and the non-EC countries of Austria, Finland, Norway, Sweden and Switzerland as a whole (eastern Europe does not usually appear in current advertising statistics), there are 354 million people who together generate a gross national product of DM9.2 billion – the richest region in the world. In 1990, western European firms spent about DM95 thousand million on selling their products to consumers. Annual rates of increase in advertising budgets have as a rule been between 11 per cent and 14 per cent since the mid-1980s, a clear indication that the advertising market is not at present exhausted. Although one of the most important reasons for this advertising boom is doubtless the founding of new commercial television stations in many European countries, television is by no means the primary advertising medium, as one might suppose from the omnipresence of television advertising spots. With billings of

DM37.7 thousand million, European newspapers still attract the lion's share of advertising expenditure; television occupies second place with DM22.1 thousand million, followed by general magazines (DM12.6 thousand million) and business magazines (DM7.3 thousand million). Outdoor advertising on walls, billboards or continental advertising pillars retains its traditional importance – at DM5.6 thousand million it still occupies fifth position, well ahead of radio (DM4.3 thousand million) and cinema publicity (DM650 million) (Stern Advertising Department, 1991, pp. 2–3).

Obviously the large industrial countries – with Germany, the United Kingdom, France and Italy in the lead – spend many times more on advertising than the small European countries and the relatively poor countries in southern and south-western Europe. In united Germany alone firms invest DM39 thousand million in advertising. By the year 2000 as much as 60 thousand million is forecast – Germany would then account for about 40 per cent of all EC advertising expenditure.

It is clear that one cannot speak of a standard European advertising market, even in economic terms; the differences between countries and regions are too great, and national regulations and other constraints on advertising are too varied. The dream of pan-European consumers who may be reached by a unified strategy in all western European countries is, as it always has been, hardly achievable. A few examples will illustrate this point.

Newspapers in the United Kingdom, Germany, the Netherlands, Luxembourg, Norway and Sweden obtain between 62 per cent and 66 per cent of their revenue from advertising; Finland is in the lead with 77 per cent. Greek newspapers bring up the rear with only 25 per cent – an advertising revenue which has already been reached in the former eastern block country Czechoslovakia. In addition, newspaper penetration and reading habits are so varied (as we have seen earlier in this essay) that, in the advertisers' view, any unified Europe-wide strategy is hardly possible.

The situation with magazines is similar. Despite the large number of different titles, there is hardly one type of magazine which is available in every country. Even the widespread type of 'topical illustrated', according to the most recent Europe-wide analysis (Stern Advertising Department, 1991), exists in only 12 countries, as does the business magazine category; only 10 countries have 'reveal-all' scandal-sheet newspapers or magazines of the type known in Germany as 'yellow press'. In this sector, too, there are considerable differences in public habits, and therefore in potential customers: in the United Kingdom and Italy, magazines are by no means as popular as in Germany and France, the leading 'magazine countries' in Europe. In Finland an advertiser can reach about 60 per cent of the population through a single issue of *Pirrka*, the largest magazine in the country. In Portugal, on the other hand, even in six months the total of 38 magazines are read by only 35 per cent of the adult population.

In every country, television transmission time is limited; demand is still always greater than supply. Norway and Sweden still allow no television advertising; in Belgium only the French-speaking commercial regional stations accept so-called institutional advertising (business is done principally in this area by the

What goes down well in one country in Europe and accords with local legislation may well be totally inappropriate and even illegal elsewhere (credit: Marshall Aver).

Luxembourgeoise RTL), and in Denmark there is advertising so far on only one of the two national stations. Differences between public television broadcasting in the individual countries are also notable: whereas the British BBC remains completely free of advertising (and is therefore of no interest to the advertising business), in Germany, ARD and ZDF are financed by advertising to the extent of 20 per cent and 40 per cent respectively (though only before the important 'prime time' between 6.00 and 8.00 p.m.). Similar figures obtain for other public television providers in Europe.

State-owned RTVE in Spain, however, with 97 per cent advertising finance, is the great exception. Commercial television stations accept advertising round the clock (within certain maximum limits), but in many countries, for technical reasons, it reaches only about half the public.

There are also numerous and sometimes very different limits on advertising certain products, especially cigarettes and alcohol (which, despite reasonable arguments for a ban, are unanimously regretted by the advertising industry). Cigarette advertising is allowed on Spanish television and in Portugal only in the introductory phase of commercial television. The United Kingdom makes an exception only for pipe tobacco and cigars. Manufacturers would be able to run a European advertising campaign for spirits in only half the countries, and in Portugal only after 10.00 p.m. Comparable impositions also exist for radio advertising. In this field, far-reaching harmonization can be expected in future, when the EC's television guidelines are adopted into national law. No lifting of bans on tobacco and alcohol advertising is planned, however.

Pan-European satellite programmes, mostly in English, are still suffering from viewer ratings too low to be really interesting for a European advertising strategy. Knowledge of the English language in European countries is much lower than one might think, and many Europeans clearly overestimate their actual knowledge. The proportion of those who claim to understand English well varies between 9 per cent (in Spain and Italy) and 51 per cent (in the Netherlands). A simple language test carried out annually by media planners shows, however, that only one per cent (in Italy) to 28 per cent (in the Netherlands really understand an English-language advertising message (Stern Advertising Department, 1991, p. 3).

In western Europe there are about 1.2 million billposting sites – no small number. Here too the advertising industry laments big national differences: in Greece there are hoardings in only three towns, and they are so concentrated that up to 64 posters may be placed above or beside each other, so that the individual product is overwhelmed. The size of individual posters also varies considerably.

European cinema advertising mostly features expensive, film-like sequences aimed predominantly at a youthful public. The restrictions here lie in the limited target audience and the relatively high production costs.

After enumerating these and other differences, F. Jürgen Stockmann, media planner for the agency Lintas, draws a trenchant conclusion:

> The standard European market does not exist. The national and cultural differences are too great, the mentalities too varied, the language barriers too high, ways of using the media too widely divergent. In the United Kingdom/Ireland or Benelux/France, in Scandinavia or in the German-speaking area there is already wide-ranging media overlap. But no transformation that will alter the structure is in sight.
>
> *(Stockmann, 1989, p. 239)*

This does not mean, however, that advertisers will not make intensive efforts to identify and contact supranational target groups. In a large-scale study called 'Eurostyles', 15 European market research institutes investigated the motivation and behaviour of 24,000 western Europeans, and concluded that a gradual convergence of habits of consumption and life-styles in all countries has produced similar 'life-style types', though in different proportions in different countries (see Höfer, 1991). Thus in all countries there exists – to name but one example – the so-called 'Euro-dandy', the young, urban, pleasure-seeking middle-class European, whose habits and preferences show the same basic structure, whether British, German or Spanish. The advertisers are thus able to calculate their chances in individual national markets and tailor the quality of the product, the packaging, the advertising media and the message to suit this 'Euro-dandy'.

On the other hand, national stereotypes are also intentionally used in the creation of product images, and these stereotypes obstinately assert themselves, despite growing similarities in life-style. For example, espresso coffee packaging is very often designed in the Italian national colours, regardless of whether the contents come from Italy. The Spanish car manufacturer Seat has aggressively advertised its German technology and reliability ever since it was taken over by Volkswagen (although many models still originate from Seat's co-operation with Fiat). And perfume manufacturers who fail to print the magic trio 'Paris – Milan – New York' as a place of origin are criminally reducing their chances in the market.

Differences in national mentality also have a decisive effect on what most Europeans consider 'good advertising'. These differences, which are distinct from the nationally overlapping types of life-style, are of prime importance for mass products without specific target groups. Höfer gives the following examples:

> In advertising the Italians like things loud, in market-trader style, shot through with elements of Commedia dell'Arte. The British on the other hand prefer their national humour, while finding advertisements for hygiene products embarrassing. The French like the text to be a three-part argument ('first of all..., and then..., finally...'). They value picture sequences, pseudo-editorial reporting. They enjoy quotations from serious cultural sources, hate grammatical errors and tolerate anglicisms only with very innovative dynamic products.
>
> *(Höfer, 1991, p. 33)*

National preferences, which could be amplified indefinitely (Spaniards dislike vulgarity, Germans feel cheated by advertising), have led to one and the same mass product being marketed under a different name or in different packaging in every country in Europe. When the brand name is the same, the product behind it is often modified from country to country. Only very few international brands – say Coca Cola or Nike sports goods – can be marketed throughout Europe and the world with a single image or advertising theme, because the product has already been introduced and 'all' that is needed is to present its name and image over and over again.

The simultaneous existence of divisive and common elements, national differences in mentality and trans-frontier life-styles, will determine the nature of European advertising for years to come. 'Euromarketing', as Stockmann says, still means, as it has done in the past, 'Plan Euro-strategically – but transpose nationally' (Stockmann, 1989, p. 242).

Commercial or public broadcasting?

The outstanding characteristic of present-day broadcasting in Europe is undoubtedly the dramatic alteration in the structure of ownership of the electronic mass media. In nearly all countries, private commercial radio and television providers have appeared alongside the state-owned or publicly controlled systems. But the apparently simple process of granting broadcasting licences marks deep-rooted changes in the most varied areas, which the British communications researcher Denis McQuail has briefly sketched as: '... turning aside from the previous form of public broadcasting, entry of financial considerations into electronic media via advertising or direct payments from viewers, the introduction of new media or media services as economic products ...' (McQuail, 1986, p. 633).

Privatization was worked out very differently in different European countries: for example, in France the previously state-owned station TF1 was sold; in the German Federal Republic publishers were given preferential treatment when broadcasting licences were granted; in the United Kingdom there was extensive public control over the commercial sector; in Italy there was a largely *laissez-faire* privatization with a heavy intrusion of capital from outside the sector. Nevertheless, the national impulses for this development are largely identical:

> Reasons of industrial policy, to further the development of new information and communications technology; a disinclination to venture public funds in high-risk enterprises; consumers' wishes for greater choice, a wider offering; the search for lucrative investment opportunities for free capital; new technologies looking for applications, and finally the phenomenon of commerce, which shows us proven examples of how capital and technology can collaborate.
>
> *(McQuail, 1986, p. 633)*

How this process has led to the building-up and strengthening of internationally operating media concerns has already been fully described earlier in this essay.

This commercialization of part of electronic mass communication has led to a new organizational structure which has become known as a 'dual broadcasting system'. At first sight this concept suggests a somewhat static state, rather like a 'peaceful co-existence of systems', but this image is hard to reconcile with the dynamic process of commercialization. Already, dual broadcasting systems that have existed over long periods of time outside Europe – particularly in Canada and Australia – have shown that the public sector has been driven step by step to the edge, and with ratings of about 20 per cent is currently playing a kind of gap-filling role, by providing information and high-quality entertainment for those viewers whose taste is not catered for by commercial broadcasting, dominated as it is by light entertainment (see Kleinsteuber, Wiesner and Wilke 1991).

If the core problem of this development is to be understood, it must first of all be made clear that public and commercial broadcasting providers differ fundamentally in their understanding of 'public'. A British study describes it thus:

> Public broadcasting is the attempt, in the era of electronic communication, to give a concrete form to the idea of the public as a component part of the democratic community ... In this connection public broadcasting, as an embodiment of the public domain, moves most starkly into conflict with every form of broadcasting organized according to a market economy, as the two systems differ from each other fundamentally in the way they see their public and what ideas about the social relationship between broadcasting and public and between individual members of the public inspire their activity. The market approaches human beings as individual consumers ... Public broadcasting on the other hand is under an obligation to approach its listeners and viewers as rational citizens and to place at their disposal that information on which alone public discussion can be based.
>
> *(Broadcasting Research Unit, 1985, quoted by Schiller, 1986, p. 663)*

This makes it clear that the maintenance of cultural diversity in the media is inseparable from the protection and development of the public sector.

On the programme level, this (admittedly ideal) differentiation means many-sided public broadcasting which aims to balance (not to be understood in a party political sense) its total offering between entertainment, information and advice, and thus fulfil its cultural policy of social integration. As a result, mixed programming has dominated both public radio and public television for many years. Mixed programming recognizes 'the public's overlapping preferences and interests', and starts from the recognition that

> in the course of an evening, listeners and viewers are constantly forming new minorities and majorities, and that interest in any particular topic can be nourished and increased, so that a minority can be turned into a majority. In other words, overlapping identities form the basis of traditional programming policy.
>
> *(Hearst, 1987, pp. 4, 6)*

As it has turned out, 'Europe's public broadcasting has consistently striven to offer its customers a cultural diversity of which millions of people previously were completely unaware' (ibid.).

In order to meet its programming responsibilities, public broadcasting has grown, wherever it exists, into one of the most essential tools for the 'production of culture' (for example, in the Federal Republic of Germany today, hardly one cinema film is produced without ARD or ZDF participating as a co-producer).

However, this traditional interpretation of the term 'public' no longer appears fully to meet the needs of many people. With the expansion of programme supply, and especially the appearance of new commercial providers, the integrative aims of public broadcasting are filtered out by the sheer quantity of programmes by commercial suppliers. Hitherto there have been only a few studies of changes in usage. The research accompanying the introduction of commercial television in the Federal Republic of Germany (the cable pilot project in Dortmund, North Rhine Westphalia), hitherto the most comprehensive, does, however, show a clear slackening of the educative power of public providers overall, and an equally clear trend towards entertainment programmes (Landesregierung Nordrhein-Westfalen [Land Government of North Rhine Westphalia], 1989, pp. 262, 263).

The cultural effects of this will essentially depend on how the two elements in the dual broadcasting system interrelate in future. It is possible to imagine stronger competition between the two systems for large majority ratings, which would 'result in giving the customer what he wants, even if it does him harm' (McQuail, 1986, p. 635). This tendency can be observed today in many European countries. It is equally conceivable, however, that what is offered may become more clearly differentiated, with the advertisement-financed commercial providers concentrating on popular entertainment programmes, while the public providers concentrate on the less popular informative programmes. This would be very much what the commercial providers want, and in the dual systems in Canada and Australia it has to a large extent already come about.

A veritable vicious circle now confronts the public providers. How can licence fees – the essential source of income for public systems – any longer be justified, if in the course of competition public programming becomes ever more similar to that of the private stations? Or, in the alternative case, how can public financing of high-quality information and entertainment continue to be justified if, while admittedly meeting the cultural aims of broadcasting, it no longer reaches the majority of tax-payers? Thus both possible developments may lead to a gradual marginalizing of public broadcasting, until, in its present form, it finally disappears. That such a scenario is not simply plucked from thin air is shown not only by the already mentioned events in Canada and Australia (where for a long time there has been no fee financing), but also by the still debated plans of the British government to convert the public BBC into a type of Pay-TV, where those who tune in are the only ones who pay. That would be the beginning of the end for public broadcasting as a cultural force in its present form.

It is still scarcely possible to assess the effects this would have on the overall understanding of culture and the general acceptance of social subsidy for the 'production of culture'. The French media researchers Lange and Renaud, for example, in their study of the future of the European audio-visual industry, consider it urgently necessary to call for a European cultural media policy guaranteeing that the production of (audio-visual) material shall not be wholly subjected to market forces (Lange and Renaud, 1989, pp. 136–7).

The development of the media in Europe, and with it media policy both in individual countries and at the EC level, is at a crossroads. Either the continent takes thought for its deep-rooted cultural traditions, among which has always belonged public support for broadcasting and culture, or it gives way to short-term economic temptations and jeopardizes a store of diversity unparalleled in the world.

Conclusions

Official publications often express the opinion that the media will be the central force in the formation of something like a European identity. For example, under the heading 'On the way to media development on a European scale' the EC states: 'Audio-visual media have a cultural dimension which the Community would like to promote in the same way as the technical and economic aspects of this sector' (EG, 1988, p. 53). At first sight it does indeed seem plausible that a continental media market, a 'television without frontiers' as the EC was calling for as early as 1984, might bring about European ways of thinking better than almost any other force could. What could possibly bring Europeans closer together, intensify contacts between them, and strengthen mutual understanding, if not newspapers and television which go into almost every household in the Community?

It should have become clear in the course of this study that such a view is too simple, that the roads already taken can lead to utterly different and unwanted destinations. Many contradictions which make up Europe's uniqueness were established in its past history, and serve to underline how difficult it will be to draw up a sensible media policy for Europe. As already outlined, Europe was the birthplace of modern media technology and the closely associated idea of press freedom. Fundamental experiences from Europe spread across the world; without Europe, today's global media scenario would be unimaginable.

Europe's role in world history emerged from its achievements, which constitute both its strength and its weakness. Its strength lay not least in successfully developing through exchange (that is, through intercultural communication, and in spite of its babel of languages and multiplicity of cultures and regions) a certain uniformity which allowed the much debated European culture to come into being. But the weakness of the European character is equally noticeable: history has seen not only the constructive and fruitful cultivation of European intellectual life but also the most terrible wars based on prejudices and stereotypes. Even today these divergent forces continue to have their effects, as in the nationality conflicts in the multi-national country of Yugoslavia, or the unresolved minority conflicts from Ireland to Corsica.

It should certainly also be seen as a sign of strength that Europe has engendered a variety of innovative media, from the first newspapers in the world, to the prototype of public service broadcasting on the BBC model. Needless to say, today we find highly developed and powerful media systems in all European countries. This makes the almost complete lack of pan-European media all the more remarkable. It is ironic that the few pan-European media there are – newspapers like the *International Herald Tribune* or television stations like Sky Channel – are either under American management or show an especially large proportion of American programmes.

'Eurocrats' within the EC have sketched the outlines of a future European media scene. Print media have shown themselves to be unsuitable, all their European markets being practically saturated. In addition, print media are as a rule monolingual and their relatively high transport costs work against multi-national distribution. Furthermore, the tabloid press in Europe is particularly well-developed; its market share is greater than elsewhere, say in the United States or Japan. These publications, with their tendency to exaggerate the sensational and focus on sex and crime, repeatedly pass on or recreate prejudices against neighbours. When something outrageous occurs they are always quick to recast it in simple stereotypes and to ignore any more detailed explanation. Little momentum towards European understanding is to be expected here. More likely, new 'football wars' will be whipped up and tomorrow's scapegoats created, all for motives of profit. In such publications it is nearly always 'the others' who are blamed for defects in one's own country. Greater mutual understanding requires more sophisticated language than that of the tabloid press.

Thus it falls to television and its Europe-wide providers to reduce the deficiencies in understanding and breathe new life into the idea of Europe. Above all, television is a medium which works with the power of the picture, so it manages relatively easily to make itself understood across national and cultural frontiers. In addition, it has the advantages of the latest technological developments such as satellites and multi-channel sound. A single stationary television satellite can already bring up to 16 programmes per antenna into every house in Europe; and it is possible to equip these with more than one sound channel and offer soundtracks in several languages for a single programme. But in line with European conditions, television providers hitherto have almost always been commercially oriented: first because the competing public providers are usually limited by national laws and distribution areas, and secondly because the EC obviously favours commercial providers.

Yet surprisingly enough, many of these pan-European enterprises have failed even in commercial terms. The multi-ethnic and multi-cultural continent proved itself too unwieldy: the programmes (mostly English-language) were accepted by only small numbers of viewers; the language barrier was too high. Furthermore, viewers' expectations and habits across the continent were too widely divergent. What might have been well-received in Norway was not necessarily successful in the Netherlands or Spain. Finally, advertisers held back because too much of their message was lost. In other words, a European television without frontiers, though technically possible and politically desired, is clearly much more difficult to achieve than is sometimes supposed.

Even when providers are active across Europe, however, as are a few general programme categories like sports, music or news, which can be economically self-supporting, that does not mean that they are able to advance European identity. One reason for this is that the take-up is surprisingly slight, since viewers identify primarily with their own various language groups (for example, the francophone area of France and parts of Belgium, Switzerland and Luxembourg). A further reason, moreover, is that the programmes themselves have hardly any European orientation. A high proportion of material comes from the United States, the absolute leader in the production of entertainment material – so much so that it slips easily into commercial programming. The news channel CNN International, which is available in Europe, even transmits directly from the USA and offers no sort of European view of world events. Thus a paradox is thrown up: European commercial television providers, with their transfrontier marketing strategy, are bringing about the Americanization of their own programme content. This is all the more significant in that the public providers, with their strongly national character, are increasingly being pushed into a defensive position.

It is possible that politically engineered efforts to shore up European identity by means of European television will turn out to be unworkable. After all, coexistence without any common pan-European medium is part of the European tradition. That has not prevented the establishment of the EC, which has led to a level of mutual understanding never previously reached – all despite the hegemony of national media. The question remains whether the European ideal is not better served by careful continuation of European traditions. Among these are a high degree of local and regional media, national rather than European media, public service providers in broadcasting, and sensitivity to niche markets and cultural peculiarities.

Hitherto the large commercial providers have been responsible for increasing the proportion of American productions on television. They have neither contributed much to the advancement of European culture, nor promoted pan-European understanding or the breaking down of national prejudices or stereotypes. It remains hard to see how they could profit from a European media policy.

That is, of course, not to say that there is no need for a European media policy.

The major commercial interests know very well how to look after themselves. What is needed is the strengthening of the cultural elements in Europe, an active policy to protect European creators of culture, against, among other things, the migration of their jobs to Hollywood. The EC's recent audio-visual initiatives are certainly a good beginning. Yet the question remains as to whether they will be enough to stem the tide. It would be an irony of history if, on the continent where the development of the modern mass media began, the media were 'colonized' and the continent handed over to the commercial calculations of outsiders. Commercial interests alone, it seems, will manage neither to preserve the existing European cultural scene nor to create a positive European identity.

References

BAKKE, M. (1986) 'Culture at stake' in MCQUAIL, D. and SUINE, K. (eds) *New Media Politics – Comparative Perspectives in Western Europe*, London, Sage.

BERTELSMANN STIFTUNG (ed.) (1988) *Europäische Defizite, europäische Perspektiven – eine Bestandsaufnahme für morgen*, Gütersloh, Bertelsmann.

BONDY, F. (1984) 'Europa ohne Grenzen' *Aus Politik und Zeitgeschichte*, B 23–24, 21–30.

CARAT INTERNATIONAL (1990) *European Newspaper Minibook*, London, Carat International.

DEUTSCHE UNESCO KOMMISSION (ed.) (1981) *Viele Stimmen–eine Welt: Bericht der Internationalen Kommission zum Studium der Kommunikationsprobleme unter dem Vorsitz von Sean McBride an die Unesco*, Konstanz; Universitätsverlag.

DEUTSCHE UNESCO KOMMISSION (ed.) (1982) *Weltkonferenz über Kulturpolitik*, Mexico City/München.

FAUL, E. (1987) 'Ordnungsprobleme des Fernsehens in nationaler und europäischer Perspektive', *Publizistik*, **32**(1), pp. 69–92.

FÉDÉRATION INTERNATIONALE DES EDITEURS DES JOURNAUX (FIEJ) (1991) *World Press Trends*, Paris, FIEJ.

HEARST, S. (1987) 'Ein Bildschirm für alle? Weltweites Fernsehen und kulturelle Identität', *epd Kirche und Rundfunk* (49), Juni, pp. 3–6.

HÖFER, P. (1991) *'Stil ohne Grenzen'*, *Zeitmagazin*, **26**, 21 June, p. 32.

HOFFMANN-RIEM, W. (1985) 'Kulturelle Identität und Vielfalt im Fernsehen ohne Grenzen: Zur Diskussion um die Sicherung der Vielfalt im internationalisierten Rundfunk', *Media Perspektiven* (3), pp. 181–90.

HÖHNE, H. (2nd edn 1984) *Report über Nachrichtenagenturen: Neue Medien geben neue Impulse*, Baden-Baden, Nomos Verlagsgesellschaft.

HOSKINS, C. and MIRUS, R. (1988) 'Reasons for the US dominance of the international trade of television programmes', *Media, Culture and Society*, **10**, pp. 499–515.

HUNZIKER, P. (1988) *Medien, Kommunikation und Gesellschaft: Einführung in die Soziologie der Massenkommunikation*, Darmstadt, Wissenschaftliche Buchgesellschaft.

KESSLER, M. and SCHRAPE, K. (1990) 'Fernsehmarkt Westeuropa', *Media Perspektiven* (1), pp. 25–32.

KLEINSTEUBER, H. J. (ed.) (1991) *Radio–das unterschätzte Medium: Erfahrungen mit nicht-kommerziellen Lokalstationen in 15 Staaten*, Berlin, Vistas.

KLEINSTEUBER H. J., WIESNER V. and WILKE P. (1991) 'Public broadcasting im internationalen Vergleich: Analyse des gegenwärtigen Standes und Szenarien einer zukünftigen Entwicklung', *Rundfunk und Fernsehen*, **39**(1), pp. 33–54.

KOMMISSION DER EUROPÄISCHEN GEMEINSCHAFTEN (1984) *Fernsehen ohne Grenzen. Grünbuch über die Errichtung des Gemeinsamen Marktes für den Rundfunk, insbesondere über Satellit und Kabel. Mitteilung der Kommission an den Rat*, KOM (84) 300 endg.

LANDESREGIERUNG NORDRHEIN-WESTFALEN (ed.) (1989) *Viel-Kanal-Fernsehen. Begleitforschung der Landesregierung Nordrhein-Westfalen zum Kabelpilotprojekt Dortmund*, Bd. 15.

LANGE, A. and RENAUD, J. L. (1989) *The Future of the European Audiovisual Industry*, Manchester, Media Monograph No. 10, The European Institute for the Media, University of Manchester.

LIEHR, G. 'Die französische Presselandschaft', DEUTSCH-FRANZÖSISCHES INSTITUT in Verbindung mit ALBERTIN, L., CHRISTADLER, M., KIERSCH, G., KOLBOOM, I., KIMMEL, A. and PICHT, R. (eds) (1990) *Frankreich-Jahrbuch 1990*: *Politik, Wirtschaft, Gesellschaft, Geschichte, Kultur*, Opladen, Leske & Budrich, pp. 173–206.

LIPPMANN, W. (1922) *Public Opinion*, New York, Macmillan.

LÜBBE, H. (1989) 'Modernität als kulturelle Herausforderung' in BONUS, H. *et al.* (eds) *Herausforderungen für die Politik*, München, Schriftenreihe des Bundeskanzleramtes, Bd. 6.

LUYKEN, G.-M. (1989) ' "Europa 1992": Auch ein Binnenmarkt für die Medien?', *Rundfunk und Fernsehen*, **37**(2–3), pp. 167–79.

MCQUAIL, D. (1986): 'Kommerz und Kommunikationstheorie', *Media Perspektiven* (10), pp. 633–43.

MORIN, E. (1988) *Europa denken*, Frankfurt, Campus.

MUZIK, P. (1989) *Die Medienmultis*, Wien/Stuttgart/Bern, Verlag Orac.

PÖTTKER, H. (1989) 'Europäische Kommunikations-Kultur–Einführung, *Medium*, **19**, Januar-März, pp. 17–18.

ROGGE, J.-U. (1988) 'Radio-Geschichten: Beobachtungen zur emotionalen und sozialen Bedeutung des Hörfunks im Alltag von Vielhörern, *Media Perspektiven* (3), pp. 129–51.

SAXER, U. (1990) 'Sprachenbabel in Europas Medien', *Media Perspektiven*, pp. 651–60.

SCHILLER, H. (1986) 'Die Kommerzialisierung der Kultur in den Vereinigten Staaten', *Media Perspektiven* (10), pp. 659–72.

SEPSTRUP, P. (1989) 'Implications of current developments in west European broadcasting', *Media, Culture and Society*, **11**(1), pp. 29–54.

SINUS (1988) *Sowjetische und amerikanische Politik im Urteil der Deutschen in der Bundesrepublik*, München, Gesellschaft für Sozialforschung und Marktforschung mbH.

SONNENBERG, U. (1990) 'Programmangebote und Programmproduktion in den Ländern der Europäischen Gemeinschaft', KLEINSTEUBER, H. J., WIESNER, V. and WILKE, P. (eds) *EG-Medienpolitik: Fernsehen in Europa zwischen Kultur und Kommerz*, Berlin, Vistas.

STERN ADVERTISING DEPARTMENT (1991) *The Media Scene in Europe*, Hamburg, Initiative Media.

STOCKMANN. F.-J. (1989) 'Werbemarkt Europa: Zahlen-Fakten-Folgerungen', HUFEN, F. and HALL, P. C. (eds) *Fernseh-Kritik. Das Medien-Monopoly Europa*, Mainzer Tage der Fernsehkritik, Band XXI, Mainz, v. Hase & Köhler Verlag, pp. 233–42.

WEDELL, G. and LUYKEN, G. M. (1986) *Media in Competition: the future of print and non-print media in 22 countries*, Hamburg, Intermedia Centrum/Manchester, European Institute for the Media.

WEIDENFELD, W. (1984) 'Was ist die Idee Europas', *Aus Politik und Zeitgeschichte*, B 23–4, pp. 3–11.

WEISCHENBERG, S. (1985) 'Marktplatz der Elektronen: Reuters auf dem Weg zurück in die Zukunft. Eine Fallstudie zum Profil künftiger "Massenkommunikation"', *Publizistik* (4), pp. 485–508.

Essay 4
Everyday culture

Prepared for the Course Team by Wolfgang Kaschuba, Professor of European Ethnology, Humboldt University. Translated by Monica Shelley, Ulrike Hill and Ian Holt

> The lives of strangers are the best mirrors in which to recognize ourselves.
>
> *Goethe to Charlotte von Stein*

Horizons of everyday life: national, regional, ethnic and social aspects of identity

'Typical' is a word that crops up in all European languages. Without thinking, people use expressions like 'that's just typical', 'typical of Robert', 'typical of a man' or 'typical of a woman', in the street or in the pub, among friends or during marital disputes. We use this word to describe particular, frequently-recurring ways of behaving which we may find either endearing or irritating, but which appear to us to be characteristic of a situation, person or gender. We use the word to describe cultural practices and, at the same time, to classify or identify them according to type. This is a way of carrying out everyday cultural analysis, in which we use our own experiences and perceptions as the standard by which we then judge the characteristics and peculiarities of others. This is not a completely arbitrary or subjective process since, in most cases, it involves an unconscious reference to certain rules of everyday life which we take for granted and to which we expect our own behaviour and that of others to conform. So 'typical' used in that sense means that we have recognized, or believe we have recognized, a specific social, personal or gender-related variant within the framework of general rules.

These two elements – our attitude towards everyday life itself and the manner in which we observe and classify it – represent basic guidelines, as it were, by which we define 'culture'. This is not culture in the traditional sense, transmitted through the work of artists such as Homer, Shakespeare, Mozart or Picasso, but rather in the broad, anthropological sense: the social organization of everyday life with its various systems of significant rules and values and the way in which the individual comes to terms with them.

The word 'typical' seems to be on our lips particularly often when we cast a classifying eye at the behaviour of people of other countries and nationalities. 'Typically English!', 'Typically German!', 'Typically French!' may often be heard when we come across something – either at home or abroad – which is literally 'foreign' to us. This can be triggered off by someone's looks or their dress, their body language or their social behaviour. The deciding factor is that we detect in their way of being different a behavioural repertoire which sets *them* apart from *us,* from our own lifestyle, which we think of in essentially national terms.

These national stereotypes may well seem anachronistic to us in the light of modern media and lifestyles and with the prospect of European rapprochement and unification. In western Europe, at least, the trend seems to be for national particularities to become less distinct, to recede into the background of our consciousness. Intercultural contacts through travel and migration of labour are becoming more and more frequent; the media constantly improve their coverage of foreign news and we see the same brand names on hoardings and in supermarkets whichever country we are in. All this decreases our sense of being abroad when we cross European borders today.

On the other hand, there is still an ever-present – perhaps even increasing – need to confirm 'national identity', which cannot be ignored. Advertisements for domestic car models, the reporting of international football matches, the staging of national holidays – all these provide us with countless and thoroughly welcome opportunities to celebrate our national feelings. It would be too simplistic to explain all this away as a product of media hype. In many respects such occasions seem to arise out of a deep-rooted need for a particular kind of communal identity that is felt by all of us. The coming together of Europe is therefore perceived by some people not only as an opportunity and a benefit, but also as a destabilizing factor, a threat that we might lose our own particular identity within the broader landscape of a uniform European culture.

Such questions of identity crop up again and again in the field of everyday culture. This may be on a small scale, in social relationships, or in the confrontation between men and women, or on a large scale at the level of international relations. These systems of identity-formation and identification have thus become major concerns of the social and cultural sciences today.

Concepts and categories

The systematic, scientific preoccupation with everyday life is still a relatively young subject of academic study. Sociology used to be concerned mainly with large social systems and social structures; the historical sciences concentrated largely on the development of the history of ideas and institutions, while ethnography and folklore research were more interested in the prominent and supposedly archetypal elements of a culture than in its unspectacular, normal processes. It was not really until the 1970s and 1980s that everyday life was accepted – in Germany, at least – as being worthy of serious scientific study.

In the wake of this new orientation – above all in the realms of sociology, historical research and the cultural sciences – concepts for the documentation and analysis of everyday culture were developed using various approaches. On the one hand, research tracked the historical development of both material and intellectual ways of life. Questions were posed about the process of modernization in society during the last two centuries and about its costs – a fresh look was taken at the

Raymond Williams 1921–1988, English cultural historian and sociologist (credit: Times Newspapers Ltd.).

way in which 'history' operated. A second approach demonstrated an interest in the differences that find expression in the lifestyles of various social groups, that is to say, in the class-specific elements of everyday culture. A third approach revealed a new multiplicity of cultural models and practices in the sphere of everyday experience and activity; this approach has brought about a diametric change to the ideas we used to have about the homogeneity and linearity of historical living and learning processes. For instance, we used to have a simplistic conception of linear development from the extended to the nuclear family, from the 'superstitious' way of thinking of the pre-Enlightenment era to our modern 'rationality'. Fourth – and most important – the everyday world cast more light on the subjective aspects of historical and present day society, on a history of experience and awareness that has been revealed only through research and which centres on specific subjects and actors. Most of all, research into the everyday has provided real insights into the culture and lives of peasant and working-class families.

A precondition for these new ideas was consensus on the broad definition of culture which, in the words of the English cultural historian and sociologist Raymond Williams, relates to 'the whole way of life' (1963, 1971). Culture has now come to mean all the material and spiritual activities of human beings – the outer, societal frame of reference as well as the inner self-image of the subjects at a particular time and within a particular environment. Concern now is with the 'other side' of society, where culture may be defined as operating at the level of reality, with experience, of everyday behaviour, and with the reflection of these in the thinking of those concerned.

So the question of how we actually acquire culture, how social behaviour turns into accepted cultural practice, something that we 'own', is no longer answered in the conventional way, by reference to 'primary socialization', or to old-fashioned schooling of the child in social matters. The new approach is to regard 'enculturation' as a form of secondary socialization extending through childhood and beyond in what is, in fact, a lifelong process of induction into social roles and identities. Important structures for this process of cultural initiation are, for instance, adolescent peer groups, colleagues in the workplace or the domestic relationships that develop between neighbours. These operate both as central configurations and carriers of our everyday culture.

There are two major approaches to research into everyday life – one is to look at *ways of living*, the other at the *living environment*. The first has an emphasis on patterns of work, earning a living, family life, nutrition and leisure. Here the researcher is looking for the rules and principles which underlie the organization of life, making it appear not just accidental, but rather predetermined by membership of a certain social group in a particular country at a certain time. The second looks at those structures of everyday experience which are to be found in the cultures of all groups and sub-groups; it investigates those rules and systems for making sense and meaning which mediate in the interaction between the individual and society and which are, in turn, differentiated by the distinction between class and group membership. This living environment must be understood as a network of social connections and movement, of communicative and interactive configuration.

There are three concepts from the domain of cognition and knowledge which are often used in discussion of the social and cultural sciences to explain differences between larger societal units or, as the case may be, their cultural practices. These are: mentality, ethnicity and regional consciousness.

Mentality means the sum of historical, geographical and societal influences that add up to a shared world of thought and feeling. Examples of mental attributes that are allotted to people from different geographical areas are a greater or lesser degree of industriousness, devoutness, openness and gregariousness. Such attributes are often extended to include ethnic characteristics, or supposed 'tribal characteristics' that define the essential nature of the people. Physical and biological attributes are usually added to psychological attributes – appearance, colour of skin and hair, speech and gesture, for example – which when put together are alleged to constitute a common *ethnic identity*. It is not disputed that there is such a thing as ethnic difference. But the fact that past and present debate on the subject has been marked by the misuse of these ethno-cultural concepts so as to discredit, or discriminate against other races, does not make it easy to use these terms in a neutral way. The history of ethnology, in particular, which emerged in the nine-teenth century as the study of supposedly 'uncivilized' colonial peoples who had yet to attain the standards of European culture, serves to demonstrate the ideologi-cal ballast that weighed this concept down.

Much more recent, and more realistic, is the concept of *regional consciousness*, which has come into use in recent years with the emergence of new regional political movements all over Europe. It is based on a subjective relationship that people have with their environment and towards their experience. And this means an orientation which also draws on science and literature, geographical areas and political boundaries. In many ways it also seems to incorporate intangible cultural elements such as language and dialect, features of landscape and historical bor-ders, eating habits and traditional festivities.

Culture as historical concept

Any view of culture assumes, of course, that it has evolved historically and that it is subject to constant change and transformation. It is experience, which has emerged bit by bit and become ordered, where rules and patterns are not simply repeated mechanistically but are examined and modified again and again in the course of everyday life. This approach accepts that our present-day culture con-tinues to build on countless historical layers and amalgams created in previous so-cieties and epochs.

One of the best-known supporters of this type of cultural-historical perspective was the cultural historian and sociologist Norbert Elias, who described this multi-layered process of cultural change as a 'process of civilization', a continuous pro-cess of generating social norms and values that bind individuals in ever increasing measure to social conventions and oblige them to be observed. Industriousness and diligence, punctuality and discipline, education and cleanliness, self control and control of the instincts – these were values which were sanctioned gradually by religion and the idea of civilization and given the status of ethical imperatives.

Some critics label this perspective 'culturalism', accusing it of over-emphasizing the 'soft' content, which is open to interpretation, at the expense of 'hard' facts and structures. They fear that historical reality will be broken up and diluted into an incomprehensible mass of impressions, feelings and moods. These critics for-get, however, that our picture of historical reality is always a cultural construct in itself, both because it has been constructed from those historical sources that hap-pen to be available, and because we have interpreted this evidence in some way. As yet we know not too much, but too little about the historical world which ex-isted beyond the mists rising from those sources.

Culture as a concept of social identity

There is another view of culture which is not opposed to the one just described, but has a rather different emphasis. In this version culture is perceived as a foil to reality, which throws social differences and hierarchies into sharp relief. This view is based on the precept that different forms of living and working have produced cultural practices over long historical periods which are not only different from each other, but are perceived as differentiating factors: these factors are actively used as such by different sub-groups. Culture is thus used as a means of social self-portrayal and as a marker of social position.

By now we are aware of the amibiguous nature of culture and know how difficult it is to divide it up along abstract, very clearly defined lines. The so-called Anglo-Marxist concept of culture, as formulated by Edward P. Thompson and Raymond Williams in the 1960s and 1970s in particular, has played an essential part in this academic learning process. Both these authorities see the connection between culture and social structure as one where those concerned determine their own social status through their everyday behaviour. They interpret and define their social reality by conforming to certain cultural traditions and patterns and rejecting others. Class and social strata affiliations will, of course, predetermine and limit this choice.

All analyses of forms of living and styles of culture in western European societies confirm that there are still significant differences in the material as well as the intangible ways in which life is organized, which can be traced back to systematic privileges relating to income, housing, education and opportunities (or lack of them) for consumption. Behavioural studies show that these groups are fully aware of their social and cultural differences.

Culture as a national stereotype

Finally, as I have already mentioned, culture is most commonly connected with nationality. 'National culture' and 'nation of culture' are two identifiable concepts from the era of nationalism since the late eighteenth century. This epoch has seen repeated calls for a coherent national culture to be cultivated and protected in order to safeguard the spiritual existence of the nation.

But perceiving culture in this way, i.e. as unique to nations, within the framework of political and spatial separation, meant that the supposedly different nature of a 'foreign society' was used as a cause, or pretext, for isolationist policies. Since the end of the eighteenth century, that link, which is supposed to bind a culture to a nation, has been known as the 'people'. This 'people' is welded together by a common language, religion and history, and needs to separate itself from everything foreign so as to preserve its own character. But it has been suspected for some time that in most European countries this much vaunted historical unity of national community was nothing more than a deliberately fostered myth. There are few countries where language, religion and history combine to present us with a truly homogeneous and uniform view of the past.

The cultural sciences

Culture and everyday issues have received increasing attention from a range of disciplines in recent years. From different starting points, these have developed shared ideas and solutions to the problem of 'cultural understanding'.

Ethnology, whose true task is to compare different societies and cultures, has developed in recent years from the investigation of less developed societies to include the study of developed industrial cultures. The methodological approaches used have become important to all research into culture because they make a considerable contribution to the understanding of cultural systems in neighbouring disciplines. Using an ethnological approach, culture is seen as a range of symbolic and ritualistic possibilities of communication between individuals and groups which is expressed through language, gestures, signs and values. The aim of the scientist is to communicate to his own group or society how a different ethnic group lives within its own culture and how its different horizons of thought and values are constructed, in order to facilitate a cultural dialogue.

In contrast, *ethnography* is concerned with internal cultural phenomena, particularly those of the indigenous society. It also investigates the norms and rules, the symbols and gestures of cultural communication, its aim being the decoding of what Bausinger calls the 'cultural grammar of everyday life'. Its preferred approach is to use hermeneutical and microanalytical procedures; that is, to interpret and elucidate individual phenomena, whose meaning is investigated within the framework of small societal and cultural contexts. An essential prerequisite for this ethnographic analysis is that investigations into the interaction of the many factors and details be carried out only within a limited section of society, within a village, for example, a group or even an individual life history. The main area of interest is always how everyday life is experienced and how that experience is assimilated by the individual.

There are many links to the *sociology of culture* and to the *anthropology of culture*. The former is concerned in particular with the investigation of the social organization of living space and life styles; it also assumes that a sense of belonging to a particular social group is expressed in concrete cultural values and patterns of practical life, or, as the case may be, that it is just those patterns and values that constitute the existence, 'the reality of life' of these groups. The way in which objects and gestures of everyday culture take on the characteristics of symbolic signals is perceived to be of special importance.

While the sociology of culture deals primarily with the change and development of social constellations and cultural forms, the principal concern of the anthropology of culture is long-term phenomena, the structures and forms of our culture in the sense of basic genetic patterns. These patterns and symbolic structures are to be found partly within the realm of history, partly at the level of comparative cultural analysis, where structural similarities and functional modes in different cultures and societies are being investigated.

Besides related theoretical perspectives and methodological approaches, what links all these cultural sciences to a certain extent is a particular view of the everyday within society and what constitutes the normal life of the people. This is certainly a step forward, when you consider how long cultural research was dominated by investigation into issues that were thought to have something special, something of a culturally higher value about them.

Everyday culture and environment: what is ours and what is foreign to us

So far the discussion has touched on distances, on ideas of what constitutes 'being foreign' and misunderstandings between whole societies. National differences – or perceived differences – are not all that matter. There are other conflicts within our society: the differences between what we perceive as ours and what is foreign to us generate lines of division which run right through social situations and cultural configurations, making themselves felt as a structural problem throughout everyday life. There is no such thing as *the* family life or *the* food culture. The same issue can take on different, even opposing, meanings in the perception of those concerned, depending on whether you're talking about the working or the middle classes, about women or men, about people in urban or rural, in Christian or in Moslem communities. I want to introduce three basic variants to this problem of perspective as we make this journey into the everyday world: the principles involved in the experience of social inequality, in the experience of uneven historical-cultural development and in the experience of gender-related ambiguity.

Inequalities

We are at a strange in-between stage just now in the discussion of structures, hierarchies and social disparity in contemporary society. Must we – or should we even – still talk of a 'class society' in the traditional sense? Or has post-war affluence and post modernism provided us with a new social order, where social disadvantages do still exist, but must be ascribed to different aspects such as race, gender, ethnic origin or age?

In the 1960s and 1970s the situation still seemed reasonably clear. Politically-engaged social research in western European countries involved investigation into working conditions and income, into housing and consumerism, opportunities in education and life aspirations. It was concluded that there were still systematic characteristics in the unequal way in which advantages were distributed. It was also easy to recognize social class profiles within societies. These were characterized by inequality of opportunity and by the way in which these inequalities were passed on to the next generation of children. Despite educational reforms and the improvement in material circumstances in general, upward mobility remained severely limited. 'Fate by class' was just as apparent in the biographies of British workers, male and female, or French children of the middle class, though on a considerably less dramatic scale than between the wars.

In the 1980s, this perspective became more and more questionable. The argument was that the idea of 'class' was no longer relevant in everyday life, that the social awareness of living in a 'class society' no longer existed.

> Differences of social class are losing their relevance to the real life
> world, and with that the idea of social mobility, in the sense that it is
> possible for the individual to become aware of transition from one
> extended group to another.

(Beck, 1986, p. 158)

We cannot argue with the fact that in the societies of the post-war years there was a general improvement in incomes and housing conditions, in opportunities for consumption and leisure with, at least on the surface, less evidence of the traditional form of 'proletarian poverty' except, of course, for the large groups of long-term unemployed, where this is still very much in evidence. More noticeable today are the social disadvantages that result from gender. This is because the new generation of women will no longer be quiet and accept traditional ideas about role identity. And as far as ethnically related disadvantages are concerned, the situation of large groups of foreign families and foreign workers in all western European countries demonstrates the emergence of a new group of the 'socially underprivileged'. In terms of employment opportunities and choice of career, in terms of quality of housing and quality of life, these groups form a new 'lowest' lower class whose all-round disadvantage can hardly be doubted.

So has the old scheme of social stratification disappeared, where the way of life and lifestyle of workers' families was regarded as being quite separate from those of the bourgeois middle class? Apparently not:

> ... workers have remained workers, despite considerable convergence of income and status ... Workers are still differentiated from salaried employees and civil servants not only by training, by the degree of stability of their career development and income differentials, but more particularly by the physical nature of their work, the above average level of stress that results and recently, a higher risk of unemployment as well.
>
> *(Mooser, 1984, p. 225)*

This indicates that there is hard, as well as circumstantial, evidence pointing to the existence of 'objective' class differences which affect social position. More important, the existence of social inequalities is clearly apparent: it is expressed through societal perceptions. A Gallup poll in Britain in 1980 showed that 28 per cent of those questioned had a very precise awareness of their relative social class positions; a further 41 per cent had a pretty good idea of where they stood (Winck, 1986, p. 49f.). Even if the concept 'working class' as a self-description is no longer much in vogue outside England – though 'middle class' certainly is – peoples' descriptions of their own situation still locate them within a class society.

Pierre Bourdieu, the French cultural sociologist, was primarily responsible for investigating the practice of 'distinction' – of being culturally different and aware of this difference – as a system of social self-orientation in modern societies. He sees this as the systemization of different individual experiences and of symbolic forms of expression which work themselves out in lifestyle and everyday culture in patterns resembling those of class. His concept assumes a system of what he terms incorporated (consciously or unconsciously held) forms of awareness and value structures, whose application enables individuals to experience a sense of belonging to a certain cultural practice and thus to a certain social formation. Social and cultural identity is thereby defined in practical everyday activity by deviating from that of other classes and transposing social differences into consciously held social distinctions. Bourdieu calls this systematization of behaviour and orientation the 'cultural habitus' and is able to provide striking evidence of how fine distinctions in style and taste provide precise information about the group or strata the individual belongs to in the form of coded symbols. This is most noticeable in the way a person dresses: this conveys certain immediately recognizable 'tribal characteristics' (Bourdieu, 1979).

This business of styles is more than just a game of fashions and minor differences. The behaviour of other individuals and of other groups seems strange and disconcerting to us so that we cannot understand it. Every member of society knows which restaurants, which theatres, which shops are not for them, but only for others. They know that their own rules of behaviour and speech wouldn't be right there, quite apart from not being able to afford it. It is the foreign element within our own society which frequently surrounds itself with real fences and barriers.

Uneven development

The concept of uneven, or out-of-step, development is rather a metaphor for what we might term anachronism in an extreme case and perhaps cultural backwardness or just provincialism in a milder form. Our understanding of economic and technological, social and cultural processes usually includes an assumption of a certain societal standard which we should or must not fall too far behind.

Uneven, or out-of-step development can occur in many different ways, as in this example (credit: Magnum).

The concept of uneven development is normally used to describe behaviour which has already been abandoned by the majority of society and is perceived as outdated. The images here are to do with contrasts that are typical or, sometimes, raised to the level of a stereotype as in modernity and tradition, rationality and irrationality.

One of the classic and most widely cited juxtapositions is the comparison of 'modern' town and 'traditional' country. Over the last two centuries in particular, this image has had a strong influence on the perception of societal developments and processes. And where working conditions and educational opportunities are concerned, or technology and communication, it is the country or village, which has been cast in the role of the backward and outdated. In many respects the facts are, of course, undeniable: as far as what is modern is concerned, the country was always backward. Even today you can sometimes detect a kind of collective inferiority complex in country people when they are obliged to compare their infrastructure and culture with that of large towns.

On the other hand, there has long been another aspect of this town–country comparison where the advantage really goes the other way. This is the image of the 'sick town' and the 'healthy country'. The nineteenth century's critique of civilization characterized the town as a negative centre of industrialization, traffic, noise, dirt and stress. Alexander Mitscherlich's image of the 'inhospitality of the towns' in the 1960s should be seen in the perspective of that critique. In contrast, the farming community and the countryside were still thought of as 'natural', a piece of 'unspoilt nature' where people lead a more authentic, culturally healthier life. From Romanticism to Art Nouveau, German literature and painting have diligently cultivated this topos of the 'intact countryworld'; much of this nostalgia for the countryside is still with us to this day.

There is a third facet to this image: the country as rubbish tip for the urban world, absorbing its traffic and waste and supplying it in return with energy from agricultural monocultures and nuclear power stations. This contrasts with the postmodern myth of the town, ascribing a new attractiveness to urban life.

So uneven or out-of-step development is used not only to describe *conditions* which can be identified as historical paradoxes in terms of their juxtaposition in time, but also *perspectives* of perception and evaluation which can transform themselves over and over again, along with the images which reflect them. More important, however, than this way of looking at things from the outside, is the question of how uneven development is perceived from the inside, what lies at the bottom of it and what rules of logic it obeys.

The country (inappropriate though this collective singular noun is!) used to be more custom- and tradition-oriented than the town, probably because its material resources and opportunities were so restricted that it could not afford the more risky experiments. So the latest innovations did not always reach the villages straightaway; this meant that villagers often had to seek them out in the industry, shops, cinemas, bookshops of the town. This can often be a disadvantage but it can be a chance for a breathing space, an opportunity for reflecting on fashion and modernity. When there is a time lapse, things may be sorted out in a calmer manner, with more thoughtfulness and care; irrational detours and cul-de-sacs are avoided.

Another way of illustrating the principle of uneven development, which is almost as popular, is the comparison between the everyday world and the world of religion. Historically, the division in western Europe between the two is relatively

recent: until the secularization of the nineteenth century, when the values and norms of societal life came to be perceived as worldly, religion and everyday life were in a symbiotic relationship. The basic rules and rituals of everyday life were derived from religious patterns and central ethical and moral principles were judged from a religious viewpoint: in western Europe to be human meant to be a 'Christian human being'. Some of those people who were not leading a Christian life, or going to church on a Sunday risked being excommunicated, not only from the church, but from the social community as well.

Today, of course, this religion-based identity is no longer a societal principle, i.e. a principle for those educated in a mainstream Christian tradition in western Europe today. It can be quite a shock suddenly to stumble upon life norms of a strong religious character within one's neighbourhood, perhaps amongst Jewish, Turkish or Pakistani families. What counts today for the 'enlightened' western European is a 'rational' attitude to life. Religious denominations and religious practices are a private matter within that context. This has become a kind of basic tenet of western civilization, the legally formalized version of freedom in the way you conduct your life.

Since the war, daily, even weekly, churchgoing and other forms of piety have diminished dramatically in all western European countries. And yet, at the same time, against all the predictions, there has been a counter reaction which has manifested itself most noticeably in demonstrative forms of religious practice. The phenomenon of the Catholic pilgrimage, for instance, brings millions of people out onto the streets every year and not just in Latin countries. These processions and pilgrimages are joined not only by the older generations, but also by a great many adolescents and young adults. When asked why they are taking part, many of them play down religious reasons, pointing more to family or local traditions and more especially to the shared experience and the community feeling which is generated on these occasions. Most of them take part in such events not as individuals, but as members of their peer group or with friends. For them the pilgrimage is not something that is separate from everyday life, but serves as a continuation of it in a form that is organized and experienced in a different way (Scharfe, Schmolze and Schubert, 1985). Religious rituals represent an affirmation, an experience of the senses in modern disparate societies. Is this to do with the old habit of looking backwards to the past, or does it represent a new freedom in the choice of cultural forms of life and experience?

We cannot fudge the issue by explaining these phenomena away, by giving them simplistic labels such as 'belief', 'superstition' and 'reason'. Such black and white cut outs may enable us to keep our cultural map in order, but they leave out the motivations and perceptions of the people concerned. Such behaviour is certainly uneven, out of step, not only because it is no longer shared by the majority, but also because it clearly makes it impossible always to find rational solutions to problems. That is one side of the argument. The other side requires cultural understanding from the onlookers; it demands that they think themselves into the *Weltanschauung* (philosophy of life) of those whom they regard as backward. This change of perspective is rarely undertaken – perhaps with good reason – for in many cases it would undoubtedly become irritatingly clear that such traditional ways of behaviour are based on feelings which are familiar to everyone. These are feelings such as insecurity and loneliness within the mass society, feelings of help-lessness, which are simply searching for active forms of expression. The difference between the old and new magic is not so very great: trust in the beneficial effect of medical cures, human biorhythms or soothing music is generally based more on faith than on knowledge. In the final analysis it is 'subjective reality' which alone decides what is useful and helpful.

This concept of uneven development is, of course, a product of the modern world. This is a world of very fast and differing rhythms of development, where traditional attitudes can mean not only shortsightedness and prejudice, but also cultural protection. Looking back in this way helps people in an increasingly complex world and environment to sort things out, to distinguish, as it were, what matters to them and what they consider relevant to their repertoire of social and cultural behaviour, from what does not belong nowadays. It is a variant of that selective perception which protects people from being swamped by information and problems. And what of those stamped as backward or old-fashioned? They may well regard materialistically-oriented modernity as a sign of craziness. Uneven development can be observed and judged from two different points of view.

Ambiguities

It has long been held that culture, and everyday culture in particular, is marked by gender-specific forms and accents. Yet awareness of the deep-seated differences between men and women in their experience and interpretation of everyday life has developed only gradually since the 1960s, through the international women's movement and women's studies. To claim that men have drawn much in the way of practical conclusions from that insight would be an exaggeration.

It was not until the 1980s that research in history and the cultural sciences took up in any systematic way the question of female and male-related experience within society, and especially that of the gender-bound outlook of research itself. It was female historians, in particular, who opened up the history of the way in which male and female 'gender characters' had evolved, the history of the process of determining those cultural forms and norms which were presented as 'natural', and as biologically and anthropologically based characteristics of men and women (Hausen, 1977). The way in which women are assigned to a domestic and mothering role, while men are required to prove themselves in their career and in the eyes of the world, has a long history that goes back to premodern times. Gender characteristics were given their final form, however, at the birth of bourgeois society in the eighteenth and nineteenth centuries. It was then that the ideological images of female and male were translated into social roles, reinforced by political and legal systems, by religion and by education in the home and at school.

Our everyday life, the life of a society still structured on patriarchal lines, shows how very much alive these traditions and pre-ordained roles still are. This can be illustrated in small gestures:

> A man whose wife is shown on the wedding photograph with her arm
> around his shoulders is considered a henpecked husband. If a man holds

his wife's hand when going for a walk, it will be with the back of his hand to the front i.e. leading in 90 per cent of all cases.

(Mäder, 1990, p. 151)

It also shows in more important matters:

> Domestic work and the upbringing of children are still almost exclusively the domain of women, whilst men are prepared from childhood for the task of proving themselves in a career and in public life. It is precisely this 'appropriate' family orientation which ensures that women's ability to earn a living fails in most cases to fulfil the classic dimensions of a career role. This, in turn, reinforces yet again the structurally unequal position of the sexes, both in working life outside the home and in politics, culture and public life.

(Frevert, 1986, p. 313)

This relatively new view of gender requires a fundamental change in our everyday awareness, not only for research, but even more for us as a society. Many familiar, apparently self-evident truths and ways of seeing ourselves – from the male perspective in particular – are increasingly being questioned. Awareness and experience with regard to gender are genuinely ambiguous – they do indeed have two different meanings in almost all everyday situations. While only limited practical conclusions have so far been reached, we still have a long way to go before we can claim that equality between the sexes has been achieved. However, there has been some softening of those deeply-entrenched definitions of 'male' and 'female' that have been in force for almost two hundred years. The cultural anthropologist, Martine Segalen, sums up the situation in French society:

> Following the victories women have won in the political and educational spheres, society is now slowly maturing. Women are better educated than their mothers were and are trying to define their new social roles … As early as the immediate post-war years, the powerful pressure of the idea of equal rights for all citizens brought about considerable changes in legislation. Even though practice sometimes lagged behind, a number of laws were passed establishing the equality of the sexes in education, the handling of property, wages and social rights.

(Segalen, 1990, p. 365ff.)

In the autumn of 1990 the journal *Nouvelle Observateur* conducted a survey among its female readers on changes in female feelings and life perspectives under the headline 'After twenty years of struggle – are women happy?' The results sounded as though there had been a considerable growth in self-confidence. More than 80 per cent of the French women questioned could no longer imagine a satisfactory life without a career and insisted on this basic right as a matter of course; 82 per cent were able to conceive of a happy life without a partner; 76 per cent regarded motherhood as the most important moment in a woman's life, whilst 53 per cent thought that life without children is also acceptable, marriage was less important, with only 37 per cent seeing it as a central event in their lives (*Berliner Tagesspiegel,* 13 January 1991).

The situation in Germany, England or in Scandinavia demonstrates very similar trends. In response to a survey of adolescents' views on work, pay and housework carried out in 1983, 88 per cent of girls thought that employment was equally important for both sexes, 80 per cent wanted equal pay for both sexes and 90 per cent were of the opinion that working couples should share housework (Ward, 1987, p. 212). A Finnish survey in 1985 stated 'that the integration of Finnish women into work showed the highest percentage of all western industrial societies' (more than 65 per cent of women are in gainful employment) and that the role of the mother in particular was free of many traditional norms and fetters (Sallinen-Gimpl, 1988, p. 134ff.).

Measured against the opportunities of their grandmothers and mothers, the younger generation of women are much better able to determine the ways in which they will run their lives. But comparison with the past and with the fate of women in previous generations is, of course, only one perspective. The other perspective takes as its point of reference the actual situation in society and the desires and needs which can be formulated from that situation; measured against this yardstick of true equal rights and equality of opportunity between the sexes, the balance sheet looks a lot less rosy.

As far as the employment market and wages, opportunities in education and promotion are concerned, equal conditions are as yet nowhere to be found. There is a clear north-south divide across Europe: the situation looks distinctly better in the Scandinavian countries than down in the Mediterranean regions.

A particularly important example of the far-reaching effect of the way that gender-specific symbolic forms and rules govern everyday behaviour is spatial behaviour. This has been demonstrated very clearly in recent years, most particularly by French researchers. An investigation into the daily life of French cafés and bistros, for instance, confirmed how much of the public space that appears to be accessible to everyone is actually reserved as a male domain. The regulars are mainly young single men, white and blue collar workers and craftsmen, who determine the dominant culture and style of communication in the café with their talk about work or football, gambling on the horses or playing boules. Modes of greeting, offers of drinks, the way they sit or stand, their manner of speech and body language clearly dominate the scene, demonstrating the male 'egalitarianism of the bistro' (Bozon, 1982, p. 142). In this male domain women are accepted as guests only on sufferance. They adapt, evade, behave defensively and almost apologize for their presence – or mostly stay away from this particular space.

Examples like this, which can be found just as easily in other countries, explain why women's research as well as women's movements underline over and over again how decisive gender-specific differences in spatial behaviour are for social participation. Both the way in which people behave and the images that spell out the conventions of space occupation express what and how much space a person can claim, which role opportunities are open and which are closed. If you add the men-only territories of the pub and the sportsground to the danger areas of the streets and parks at night, where women may not go because they feel uncomfortable or are not safe, it then becomes clear what this spatial restriction means for women: the loss of a social world.

Everyday norms and values

The social conventions and norms which regulate our everyday behaviour, which protect us to some extent from what you might call behavioural anarchy, do not manifest themselves to us as abstract principles and values, but as very concrete connections and configurations in our social lives. These rules, conveyed through social structures, enable us to distinguish right from wrong, sensible from senseless. And there are always two arguments to hand to serve as yardsticks of what is right and sensible: first, the reference to tradition, that is to say the historical origin and endurance of certain values; second, the emphasis on social conformity and normal behaviour.

Naturally, there are many ways in which access to these values can be gained, from school and work, from media consumption and literature. From this broad spectrum of possibilities I shall choose three quite different, but particularly important learning environments. These range from the micro world of the family to society as a whole. First, the family as a training ground for feelings and roles, then the home environment as an aesthetic practice ground and finally the relationship between citizen and authority as a model for political order.

Sense of family

The idea of the family unit and family values is part of our basic historical-anthropological equipment. Long before bourgeois society had confirmed the family as the basic unit of social order, family ties and obligations were regarded as central in all societies and cultures. Although times, cultures and continents might differ in their understanding of 'family', in recent years western European models have carrried out tasks which are essentially common or, at least, similar. The family is a community that shares work and property, and it is the place for biological reproduction, and passing on social customs.

To this day the farming family shows how much everyday life is determined by the relationships between couples and between generations, by work and gender roles, by the systems of family relationships and inheritance. It demonstrates the importance of this model of the 'family as production unit' and as a means of securing the family's survival through the generations. The ties to house and farm span whole generations and the way in which individual lives have to submit to the overall interests of the family have made their mark on the biography of the individual. Those ties determine work and leisure behaviour, choice of partner and sexuality – in short, the whole of life. In the case of the aristocracy the goals of preserving feudal property and asserting the family's status imposed obligations on each new generation. While many of these traditional attitudes still linger on, they have been forced to adapt to the conditions of life in an industrial society and in cultural modernity.

The working-class family accepted – or, rather, was forced to accept – a strict division between working and domestic life, since the whole rhythm of everyday life was determined by the dictates of industrial work. These affected consumption and housing, living conditions and opportunities for leisure. Lack of money, living space and time for relationships, meant that family life was often forced to expand to include the neighbourhood and the street. The bourgeois family, on the other hand, retreated behind a protective fence of private domestic life, where the main focus of attention was the cultural training and education of the children. At the same time, households were gradually becoming smaller with fewer children, so that by the beginning of this century, the standard four person nuclear family had been achieved – at any rate in western Europe (Segalen, 1990; Frevert, 1986).

Today's European prototype of family life is what has been labelled as the 'bourgeois' family model. This is the nuclear family, which prefers to withdraw into the privacy of the home and concentrate on educating and caring for its children. Older, traditional forms of the family may still be found, particularly in the rural regions of Europe where agriculture and the ownership of farm land still play an

Gustav Doré (1832–1883), the Alsatian artist, visited London and recorded what he saw in 1869. This is Dudley Street in Seven Dials – a vivid example of working-class life led largely in public (Grant & Co., London, 1872).

important part. In Sicily, for instance, the basic model of the patriarchical-Catholic family is still widely accepted. The concept subsumes a strict hierarchy of values and roles: the man takes the role of provider for the family and thus is its representative in the eyes of the world; he owes it to his wife and to his 'masculine honour' to ensure a secure income. This means that only his work is productive, because it produces income. Women's work, on the other hand, whether it be working on the family's land, taking in work at home or housework, is not considered 'work', but rather as quasi private family duty. This division of roles is kept up as a fiction for the benefit of the outside world, even when men are unemployed, because male dominance and female subordination are part of 'family honour', which forces women to accept the discipline. This ideological and cultural construction is so conclusive and inescapable, that the woman would be almost compromising her own dignity if she did not perform this role. This is particularly true in southern European communities, such as Sicily, where cultural traditions and norms make it difficult to adopt a new set of beliefs and practices.

> Many Sicilians are prevented from acting in accordance with their own belief in a more contemporary form of living for fear of the possible lack of understanding and the anger of those around them. There are still important 'attributes of a respectable family' handed down over the generations which lead to uneven development between idea and reality.
> *(Devaux and Halva, 1986, p. 263)*

What still exists completely openly in Sicilian society is covert and less obvious elsewhere. To put this in a positive way, the family is still the most important agent for socialization and enculturization; family ties and a sense of family still provide central systems of human orientation. Expressed more negatively, the one-sided and rigid determination of roles is still evident in many ways, even in modern family forms; the achievements of the family in terms of education and security are borne mainly by the women.

Since the 1970s the importance of the family as the primary agent of socialization has been acknowledged once again. Even in socialist societies, where the attempts of state institutions to provide care and education in early childhood remained more of a programme than an accomplished fact, what was frowned on for a long time has become the official line in recent years. The pedagogical party line in the former Soviet Union, for instance, required that most children of crêche age should be cared for by their families once more (Projektgruppe Curriculum Familie, 1978, p. 43). During the 1960s and 1970s numerous attempts were made in western societies to replace the close ties of the care provided by the nuclear family with more open forms, such as 'anti-authoritarian education', *Kinderläden* (crêches, or, more literally, child shops), freely organized child care groups or the shared care for children that occurs in communes. Many aspects of these experiments have come to nothing. Others, however, have fertilized new ideas which have become part of today's relationships and family life: common law marriages, housing communes and women who consciously choose to be single parents.

This is the second feature of today's family life: that it exists in new, modified forms or even outside the traditional family configurations. This is true for almost half the population in some European countries. Some statistics may cast light on this new 'demographic revolution'. In France, for instance, the average number of children per woman fell from 2.6 to 1.9 between 1930 and 1960 and in the Federal Republic of Germany from 2.3 to 1.4. Approximately a third of the adult population in western European countries is permanently single yet, at the same time, the number of divorces has trebled since 1960. For the year 1984, the percentage of births out of wedlock was 18 per cent in France, 17 per cent in Great Britain, and 40 per cent or more in Sweden and Denmark. Single person households amounted to 22 per cent of the whole in the Netherlands and Great Britain, to 24 per cent in France and to as much as 30 per cent in the Federal Republic of Germany and Sweden in 1981; in Paris today, half of all households are one-person-households. In Sweden only a quarter of all households fit the original European 'standard model' of the married couple with one child (Roussel, 1988).

Some alarmists fear the worst when they consider this family scenario, which is both real and statistically accurate. For them it heralds the dread vision of the decline of the family. A more considered judgement is that:

> The end of the twentieth century is characterized in western countries
> by the co-existence of several forms of marriage. Alongside the classical
> marriage, a more flexible and fragile form of union is allowed; single
> parents, especially single women, now have civic and social rights. This
> familial pluralism is part of the changes taking place in a society which
> is undergoing a transition from an industrial to a post-industrial era
> within an international context which is substantially different from that
> which existed for the countries which were industrialized in the fifties.
>   *(Segalen, 1990, p. 373ff.)*

So there is no need to lament the demise of the family: on the contrary, we should learn to value the growing plurality of different forms of families and relationships. A fairly extreme example of the 'old' and 'new' models of family life for a woman makes it clear what has actually changed. In the 'old' model, a woman was 18 years old when she got married; at that time she had a life expectancy of another 35 years. She bore six live children, and after the birth of the last child, she had a life expectancy of a further 23 years, having spent 13.5 years of her life in pregnancies and breast feeding. Today, the average Frenchwoman marries at the age of 23; at this point she has a life expectancy of another 54 years. She gives birth to two live children and, after the birth of the second child, she can expect another 47 years of life. She has spent a total of only 1.9 years in pregnancies and breast feeding (Segalen, 1990, p. 365). This represents a dramatic change in the family cycle, that is, the sum of chronological and biographical episodes in the family.

We also know that reliable long-term forecasts, particularly in the area of demography or the development of populations and families, are especially difficult if not impossible. Demographic processes do not follow a straight line, but rather one which seems to swing backwards and forwards, where each new generation orientates itself anew, often assuming an opposite stance to that of its parents as far as its generative patterns are concerned. So it is not only economic conditions and individual ideas about the future that matter, but also the way in which societies perceive their past and future.

The birth of children out of wedlock has taken on a different significance from the way things were. An illegitimate birth today is a far less traumatic event, especially for women, than it used to be.

> The modern 'free partnership' is just as different from the traditional couple in its attitude towards fertility. Even if the birth of a child is not totally excluded *a priori*, the idea of a child is in no way used to legitimize the couple or to provide a reason or guarantee for the couple's relationship.
>
> *(Béjin, 1988, p. 185)*

Even while the old rigid forms are being discarded, new individually tailored forms of existence, complete with new, public legitimization and protection, confirm that the 'sense of family' is not to be allowed to fade away. To put it more simply, thinking in terms of family relationships and family ties still has a strong influence on behaviour, especially in situations of need and crisis.

It is even more difficult to produce quantified estimates and statistical forecasts when we come to the question of family forms and their great variety. It is becoming increasingly clear that modern and traditional patterns are combining in ever new ways. This means that we should take great care about applying labels such as 'modern' and 'traditional' or 'progressive' and 'outdated'. Two different examples taken from Europe may illustrate this.

In the farming families of an Irish village, all major purchases and acquisitions are discussed and decided upon together by the couples, though

> … this cannot prevent occasional differences between partners. Nora bought a washing machine three years ago. It is electric, but not automatic, so that she has to switch to the different washing cycles and fill the machine with water and drain it by hand. Meanwhile, she discovers that she could have had an automatic machine for relatively little more money. But she does not dare to talk to Johnnie about a new washing machine because this would mean admitting they had made a bad purchase; alternatively he would say that they could not buy a new washing machine every three years.

> Shared decision-making on issues like education for the children, where to go on holiday etc. are other examples of thinking as partners; while this is not new in farming families, it should be remembered that there are many more opportunities for decision-making and choice than there were a few decades ago.
>
> *(Hallerstein-Teufel, 1984, p. 140ff.)*

In most village families the partners each decide for themselves on how the money they earn should be spent: the woman decides on the income from the sale of the eggs, the man on the proceeds of the sale of the animals. The man usually has the last word. Nowadays, however, especially amongst the younger families, more and more couples leave decisions about money to the one who's best at it.

> This West German family has more 'alternative' tendencies:

> It's my husband who generally takes our son to the crèche in the mornings, I take over when my appointments are later. He needs

fetching in the afternoon and I try to work that in with my appointments; but, of course that is not always possible. My husband and I sit down with our diaries and discuss appointments, for instance, who takes on evening sessions and who is at home for how long. In the week we generally arrange it so that just one of us is there all the time.

(Innovatio 3, 1991)

But to mix traditional relationships and family patterns with progressive ideas is a difficult balancing act for everyone. Constraint or support, safety or adventure, closeness or freedom are needs which coexist often enough in relationships and which have to be accommodated, contradictory though they are.

Many of our idiomatic expressions reflect and encapsulate this uncertainty. The idea of a 'companion for life' became a well-established concept in middle-class terms; the notion of 'companion for a portion of life' is now circulating in the singles culture. Does this refer to a consciously short-term perspective of the relationship? Or is it just a way of disguising a real need for security with irony?

Home environment

Anyone looking at the European magazine market can see how important housing and furnishing is for us in our everyday culture from the sheer quantity of periodicals on the subject. Our homes and our immediate environment serve as the basis of a local identity, which we all build up and cultivate, so as to preserve a space for rest and reflection in our increasingly mobile lives. At the same time housing needs are becoming diametrically opposed. On the one hand, we need a comfortable dwelling which promises privacy and intimacy; on the other we want to present the desired public image of our lifestyle. The ideal would seem to be a well-balanced relationship between both – hard to achieve.

> Instead of preserving a permeability between private and public and the simple transition from being alone to being in company, it happens not infrequently that the private sphere is barricaded off so as to shut out what is seen as the powerful public eye.
>
> *(Flade and Roth, 1987, p. 21)*

The domestic environment has become more isolated and anonymous, lacking in communication. This is shown by surveys which include both detached houses and high-rise flats. Yet when asked, occupants express an amazing degree of satisfaction with their housing situation. Studies, whether undertaken in England, France or Germany, frequently record a surprisingly high proportion of positive answers. Does this mean that people are satisfied with their housing conditions?

Probably not. Psychologists treat this reaction rather as evidence of 'resigned adaptation' to living conditions which have to be accepted and tolerated, since they are so important.

> Man adjusts his expectations to reality, thus reducing the gap between his original hopes and the way things actually turn out. The social psychological theory of cognitive dissonance points the same way. To admit that you live in an exceptionally bad area, that the

accommodation is too cramped, the layout of rooms particularly inconvenient and the building structurally unsound and dilapidated is inconsistent with a positive self-image and a need for recognition; moving house would be tantamount to admitting failure. So the results of opinion polls of housing conditions do not reflect degrees of satisfaction so much as expose mechanisms of self-defence.

(Flade and Roth, 1987, p. 73)

Such questions and problems are, of course, relatively recent in the history of housing. In previous centuries a choice of living environment, comfort and space for individual development and withdrawal into privacy were out of the question unless one owned a castle or a town residence. A large living space and privacy were a privilege of the rich. People of the lower and middle classes – that is, 90 per cent of the population – were lodged, rather than housed as we would expect today. Well into the nineteenth century farmhouses contained just one, all-purpose room. It was only gradually that separate areas for cooking, living and sleeping developed within it, perhaps with the addition of a small separate room. Separate living rooms, furnished for effect, were the prerogative of a small group of wealthy farmers. Naturally, living conditions were extremely crowded. From what it is possible to reconstruct, it appears that there were often five to ten people of both sexes, old and young, living and sleeping together in one room. Intimacy and privacy were unobtainable and, apart from a table and a few benches or chairs, there was hardly any furniture. Beds, chests and cupboards were as rare as proper tableware.

Working-class housing in the nineteenth century was not much different as far as overcrowding was concerned. At the beginning of our century normal housing, both in rural settlements and urban blocks of rented accommodation, was made up of a kitchen and one room, with perhaps one small room more, a total of barely 30 square metres living area for a family of between five and eight people. There was no inside water supply and the water closet was in the backyard. Life went on as before in the kitchen-cum-living room; there was no separation of sexes or generations and no private space whatsoever. Furnishings were sparse, and apart from being somewhere to eat and sleep it was hardly a place you could spend time in. Because people lived in a mainly urban environment, a strangely 'half-open' structure of working-class housing developed. This was a form of housing where hallways, courtyards and the street became, in effect, a part of the living space. Most communicative activities, household chores and children's play had to be shifted outside the home.

Because it was so difficult to improve housing conditions and the growth of industrialization required frequent moves, working families tended to purchase certain household items which had a 'modern' prestige value, such as cast iron stoves, mirrors or crockery. These represented a small piece of quality which the family could take with them when they moved and turn into cash in the pawnbrokers in times of crisis (Niethammer and Brüggemeier, 1976).

After the First World War, house builders mostly concentrated on creating more living space for this mass housing sector. While the the dwellings got slightly larger, they were crammed close together and on top of each other so as to make most economic use of the area available for development. The outside environment was not considered important, since 'life goes on inside'. This was also true of the ghettos created by the concrete blocks and satellite towns of the 1960s and 1970s, with the slums, depression and vandalism which are consequently to be found in these 'walled-up worlds' (Schild and Sywottek, 1988).

These historical contrasts, and the fact that similar housing conditions can be found in some urban housing areas and rural regions even today, serve as a crucial reminder of how recently our modern functional and aesthetic ideas of housing have evolved. As far as the vast majority of the population is concerned, modern housing has only recently undergone the transformation from unattainable luxury to being part of the normal expectations of everyday life. In Germany, for instance, the living area per person in 1960 was still 20 square metres, but by 1980 it had risen to 30 square metres; an inside bathroom and toilet are now standard. The idea that each child should have its own room, that adults should have their own living or workroom, is now either a matter of course or, at the very least, an achievable aim for middle-class families. Most of all, the domestic environment is now recognized as an accepted medium for the display of one's life style and social prestige. Whatever style we choose, we make a conscious statement to those around us about how we live, or the impression we want to give of how we live, by the way we furnish our houses.

Despite all the different styles of the last three decades, certain basic aesthetic patterns have survived. These are clearly associated with differences in social position and social taste. Italian designer furniture or Swiss leather settees remain exclusive by virtue, of course, of their price. But there is also a certain aesthetic sense that tells us that furniture like that does not fit the self-image of certain social groups and classes. Families of workers or the farming community would not feel comfortable with such furniture, because it is not appropriate to their circumstances. The young, dynamic professional couples of today who want to live in airy and sparsely but expensively furnished rooms regard the built-in cupboards which dominated almost every living room in Germany in the sixties with horror. Yet the cupboard monster, or a variant of it at least, has survived in the flats of young German workers; while they no longer want the closed, heavy constructions which represented solidity and bourgeois comfort for their parents, they still remain true to that style of furnishing by grouping cupboard and open shelving elements together so that the function remains similar.

Public housing in Germany has also adapted to the development of new forms of family life and life styles. Housing communes are no longer just for students but are, at least in urban areas, relatively common. Conversely, the civic housing construction industry tends more and more to build small flats for single person households. Blocks of flats are laid out nowadays more like houses, where architecture and environment are no longer separate but are open to one another. Where new building is taking place in both rural and urban areas, attempts are being made at 'ecological' housing by combining communicative housing with environment-friendly building. This does, however, look like a middle-class trend, a chance to show the world how modern – even post-modern – you are. Your house becomes clothing – a new outfit, a personal statement.

Much is reflected in housing: the history of settlements and architecture, techno-logical and aesthetic developments, material living conditions and styles of furnishing, social needs and the norms of civilization. The home environment has always been subject to the regulations and norms that apply to everyday culture. What is beautiful and what is ugly, what is neat and what is untidy, what is proper and what is exotic, are concepts which to this day are determined not only by subjective taste and what is available, but also to a large degree by social conventions.

The standards of social behaviour of a given society are reflected in its domestic life, in the external appearance and inner order of its housing. Clues, such as the carefully-tended front garden, the immaculate living room, the ostentatious chandelier, or, at the other extreme, the lovingly staged chaos of young people's housing communes, reflect not only subjective preferences and needs but also, to a high degree, the desire to be socially seen-as-such and recognized.

In Germany, for example, it is not enough for the flat or house to be clean. The pavement in front has to be swept diligently at least every Saturday afternoon, as you can observe every week in the south. A French or Italian visitor is left shaking his head in wonder at a phenomenon that he cannot comprehend. The well-known concept of 'German cleanliness' might have led them to expect something of the kind. What might not necessarily be common knowledge is that it can all be explained in simple historical terms. The authorities of the eighteenth and nineteenth centuries issued regulations to make the citizens responsible for their share of public cleanliness. This was supposed to teach order and cleanliness – important basic social values which were to be instilled into them, so that they became 'second nature'. On the other hand, a middle-class German might not quite understand why the French bourgeois family protects its home so carefully against outside influences and visitors, why they prefer to meet in a bistro rather than at home for a cup of coffee. And for a French working-class family the rules of the game might be quite different again.

It is difficult to disentangle the individual strands of historical and social housing culture in order to orientate oneself, they are so interwoven with national patterns. This may be why, in our attempts at explanation, we take refuge so easily in clichés such as '*deutsches Heim*' (German home) or 'Englishman's castle'. On the one hand these convey stereotyped images of domestic life as a bourgeois idyll, created mainly in the ninetenth century as part of the development of a bourgeois aesthetic. On the other hand, they contain some informative pointers to characteristic elements of style which are widespread throughout the country and are not present in the same form in neighbouring countries.

These differences are epitomized in national bedding cultures. This is not a story about sex, it is about the nightly restless tossing and turning in strange bed and pillow combinations that takes place in any European hotel. The French *grand lit* with its round bolster and tucked-in blankets seems like a nightmare to many German double bed-sharing couples, making them think longingly of the idyll that awaits them in their beds at home. Their monstrous wooden beds, on the other hand, with their heavy feather covers and high pillows, generally come as a shock to Italian visitors who are used to lighter beds and bedding. European standard beds and standard bedding are now evolving in modern hotels which will be a compromise between national styles.

There are, of course, other examples of national characteristics in housing and the domestic environment. *Gemütlichkeit*, the very German concept of feeling comfortable and 'at home', may take very different forms. This is what two German exchange students reported about their stay in England:

> We were simply not used to an island climate. Why, we asked
> ourselves, didn't our host families have heating like we take for granted
> at home? Later on we noticed over and over again how modestly people
> live over here. It struck us as funny that they had an artificial fireplace
> in the middle of the room, of all places; this was the same in every
> house, as we found out from other students. It was a plastic fireplace
> with pieces of artificial wood and a gas flame … Was this imitation of a
> fireplace supposed to evoke the atmosphere of the English country
> house, even in flats? Once the TV was switched on, then the flame in
> the fireplace would be turned on as well, and strangely enough this
> generated an infectious *Gemütlichkeit*; if room temperatures were low,
> the hospitality was all the warmer.

The *englischer Kamin* (English fireplace) which can be fuelled not only by gas, but also by electricity, can also be found in many flats which are equipped with modern central heating. This symbol of British life has exercised the eyes and imaginations of tourists for generations. They ask, too, whether it represents nostalgia for the aristocratic country manor style of living or if it is just an example of bourgeois *Gemütlichkeit*. And since I know of no British fireplace statistics it may be that this *englischer Kamin* is really no more than a film and tourism stereotype.

The traditional British fireplace can be found in many homes in the United Kingdom. It is still an important focus, even with younger generations …

... a student household chose to make the fireplace the centrepiece of the living room – even though it is a stage prop made of plaster with no chimney in sight! (credit: Marshall Aver).

The Dutch window is a special architectural feature, often emphasized by being placed on a bay, expensively framed, furnished with an ornamental grille, picked out in colour and, while it is normally curtainless, laid out and decorated in a very personal style. It could take up a whole chapter in the history of European architecture on its own.

The Dutch tradition of emphasizing and ornamenting façades with windows goes back to the fifteenth century. The philosophy behind it transmits the message of sociability, of looking out onto wide, distant expanses, of being 'open to the outside and to the inside', which also tells us that behind these windows 'there is nothing to hide' (Beutel, 1976, p. 87). Foreign tourists are both astonished and fascinated by this revelation of domestic inner life through large, uncovered windows. They do not expect to be able to see straight into living rooms and kitchens, into the heart of everyday situations and family life. Here it seems to be positively encouraged. They seem to say: 'We have nothing to hide'. But if you put this to the test, you will sometimes be disappointed to discover that behind the Dutch window there is often a cleverly positioned room layout or dividing wall which sets limits on the inquisitive gaze, after all. Perhaps this window, which is claimed to be as much a part of Dutch life as the piazza in Italy or the pub in England, is now only a gesture in response to a cliché which has burgeoned over the years; it represents a dialogue between local people and strangers which has become so popular that no one wants to curtail it, even though it has become meaningless.

Our ideas of national domestic lifestyles are shaped not only by correct and incorrect images of home life but also, to a considerable degree, by characteristic architectural set pieces. For instance, Mediterranean architecture and landscape are associated – correctly, no doubt – with images of pulsating and communicative life on the streets, the *piazza* or the *corso* of an evening. And the areas surrounding the parks in London or the garden city layouts of Berlin seem to influence the social micro-climate and the people through the architectural characteristics of buildings and landscape – sometimes warming, sometimes cooling it. In recent years, attempts have been made in many European countries to reproduce characteristic architectural and communication features of urban and rural life in new building projects. This was because the monoculture of concrete, purely functional housing developments of the post-war years had turned out to be isolating, impersonal and lifeless in terms of communality. These attempts to counteract the desolation of modern city life with buildings and landscaped areas which are more strongly oriented towards community living are presently in the experimental stage. Their initiation has been disadvantaged by the expectation of a success which is probably not achievable by architectural means, but only through complex social policies. Then, as now, it was noticeable that it was not the national styles of architecture which were capable of supporting life in the literal sense, but rather those of regional and traditional origin. These are styles of houses and settlements which might, for instance, bear the stamp of specific geological and climatic conditions, as in the Mediterranean area; they might have evolved in response to economic requirements as in the case of urban working-class districts, or been built in accord with regional traditions where indigenous building methods and raw materials were linked with functional and symbolic forms as, for example, in Scandinavian wooden buildings.

But with the industrialization of house building and furniture production, regional and national characteristics were gradually eroded over the decades. Living space within and between houses also fell victim to industrialization and mass production. Were we to be transported to an average city flat, be it in Madrid, London, or Berlin, we would probably all have difficulty in identifying where we were if we just had to rely on furniture and style. Details would provide the best clues – the nostalgic prop of a paella pan on the wall of a Spanish kitchen, a false fireplace with simulated flames in a London flat or a roaring stag above the settee of a living room in Berlin.

Who knows what else 'post modernism' might have in store for us? Maybe architecture will reach further back into history, reviving the styles of the Tudor, Empire and Gothic periods. And might there be a trans-European interchange – Tudor style in Moscow and Rococo style in London?

Citizens and authority

When people consider the relationship of the citizen to the state, to government administration and order, to political opinion-forming and decision-making processes, they often refer to the existence of national mentalities which have evolved over time. These permeate the whole of political culture and its institutionalized forms as well as everyday practice – the dealings that every citizen has with officials, administrative bureaucracies, laws and regulations.

Everyday life, in particular, seems to bring national characteristics into focus. Just think of those standard situations like dealing with no-parking signs, traffic in towns, encounters with the police and dealings with authority. We know from our own experiences of travel and holidays that, while other countries may have the same rules of behaviour and traffic signs, they are interpreted with considerable 'national' differences. In Italy, British drivers get irritated because they believe that they are supposed to drive on the right; in practice, however, Italian drivers demonstrate that almost anything is allowed. At the other extreme, anyone exceeding the speed limit in Switzerland will get a nasty surprise from a police force which exacts a cash fine with totally un-Romanesque pitilessness. And in Paris if anyone is dutiful enough to stop at a pedestrian crossing when the light is red, it is probably a German tourist. There is certainly truth in the claim that these small examples of everyday behaviour do not arise by chance, but can be traced back to traditional attitudes to rules and authority that have been handed down through history.

Indeed, this assumption is itself a part of history. Two hundred years ago the German philosopher, Immanuel Kant, wrote of the typical German attitude to authority:

> Amongst all civilized peoples it is the German who submits most
> readily and durably to the government under which he is living and is
> furthest from experiencing any desire for reform or opposition to the
> established order. His character is a mixture of reason and apathy.
>
> *(Kant, 1975, p. 667)*

And in his *Essay on the History of Civil Society*, Kant's contemporary, the Scot Adam Ferguson, passed a very different judgement on the British tradition:

> The history of England, and of every free country, abounds with the
> example of statutes enacted while the people or their representatives
> assembled, but never executed when the crown or the executive was left
> to itself.
>
> *(Ferguson, 1966, pp. 166–7)*

He sees this as a tradition where the people kept a sharp eye on those who led them, never simply submitting to being ruled.

Irrespective of how right Kant or Ferguson were, the Germans still have a reputation for obedience to authority, just as the British feed off the myth of their long history of democracy and civil courage. In France ambivalent thoughts about the legacy of the French Revolution in which scepticism was balanced with pride predated the bicentenary of 1989. In any case, our everyday experiences appear to bear out what has been learnt from history, so far as others are concerned, at any rate. This is how a Greek student reported her experience in Germany:

> The Germans accept many directives from the government or from the
> authorities. I find that everything here is governed by some institution
> or other. The state represents some sort of higher authority which
> provides for and takes care of its citizens. And people rely on this.
>
> *(Fremde Deutsche, 1986, p. 109)*

Compare the completely opposite reactions of a young German woman on a Greek ferry:

> My head is really buzzing with the noise! People shouting: 'Come here!', 'Look out!', crying children, scolding mothers, fathers trying to grab a seat ... I see that the Greeks are no good at organizing anything. They are quite calm and collected beforehand but once the journey starts they are all the more excitable. I am sorry for the man below decks who directs the cars into the hold of the ship. He must be so hoarse afterwards that he can't speak!
>
> *(Rheinischer Merkur, 8 March 1986)*

Obviously German tradition is not entirely made up of the Prussian's blind obedience to authority, that Wilhelminian bourgeois spirit described by Heinrich Mann in his novel *Der Untertan* (The Underling) in such graphic and horrifying detail. To a large extent that arose from a style of writing in Germany that aimed to mythologize 'national history', where subordination and loyalty towards the ruling power were upgraded into central historical principles. Recent German research in social history has revealed that this principle of obedience imposed from above was quite often counterbalanced by a principle of disobedience or insubordination from below whereby agricultural workers, craftsmen, and industrial workers defended their way of life and interests.

Still, it's true to say that in comparison with France and Britain, Germany's rulers and representatives of authority (none of whom lost their heads on the guillotine) cast considerably longer shadows, many of which reach as far as the present. In Germany, abstract ideas of loyalty and respect have had a much greater effect on perceptions of the functions of government and institutions than on the other side of the Rhine or the Channel. 'The state' as embodied in its officials and offices comes across as a neutral and objective, non-human institution. Remote from the lower levels of society, its exalted status also enshrines and protects the individual civil servant, even down to his obstinacy and pedantry. The new social movements and citizens' initiatives of the last two decades show that things do not have to stay this way for ever. They have struck new, critical and irreverent notes in German political culture and the courage to stand up for one's individual beliefs is no longer foreign to this country.

Of course, more research needs to be done on the 'other side': public administration and its practices. Unfortunately, there are as yet no studies of 'national' police mentalities which would help us to reassess our images of the casual *carabinieri* in Italy, the politely helpful bobby in London, the lenient *flic* in Paris and the pedantic and petty-minded German policeman. I suspect we may come across changes here as well.

The relationship between state and authority in Mediterranean countries, where the theory and ideology of the 'welfare state' is far less deep-rooted than in western and northern European countries, appears to be a phenomenon in its own right. Observers and critics speak of a special 'state of mind', of a very particular relationship between the autonomy of the private individual and the authority of the state. The example of Sicily is of particular interest here:

217

> In the society of Southern Italy the cornerstones of the private sphere –
> family, kinship and godparenthood – are considered to be the only
> institutions that can guarantee stability and security. It is common
> knowledge that one should not expect too much even from one's
> neighbours … Accordingly, the view in Southern Italy is that the
> executive, the legislature and the judiciary are so corrupt that the
> division of power is merely a fiction of the 'ruling class'. The public
> institutions are therefore not perceived as instruments in the service of
> the citizen; instead, the citizen is seen simply as the victim of the power
> of the state.
>
> *(Giordano, 1990, p. 39ff.)*

Such attitudes are based largely on historical experiences which are part of the
complicated national history of Italy. However, they also have something to do
with that inherited system of economic and social patron/client relationships
which structured life in the feudal society of Sicily and continues to structure life
even today in many respects. Proof is offered again and again that the government
helps the powerful, but not the poor. A Sicilian farmer from a valley hit by an
earthquake who had been waiting in vain for public assistance expressed this in
the following words:

> The judiciary is a net which entangles the mass of the people. But it is
> a net full of loopholes for the racketeers who steal from the farmers and
> the workers.
>
> *(ibid.)*

While this Sicilian example is an extreme case of the imprint of history on the relationship between citizen and authority, fragments of similar historical legacies
can be found in the collective memory of all European societies. They are
reflected in everyday culture when 'people' and 'state' encounter each other in the
persons of the average citizen and an employee of the state. Symbolic rules operate in these encounters, governing manner, speech and even gesture. We all know
and share these rules, albeit unconsciously. For this reason every encounter with a
bobby, a *flic*, or some other nationality of policeman is a piece of practical political culture. The symbolic structure of the encounter will demonstrate how much
help or stupidity, how much respect or arrogance, how much fairness or highhand-
edness we expect from our own or the foreign political system.

When we get involved in an encounter with authority on holiday or in the course
of our travels, we become part of a cultural experience, a participant in an adventure of everyday life. So we have to stop and think how far the home rules of the
game apply or whether there are rules that are foreign and unfamiliar to us. It is
not just because the language is different that communication is difficult at times
like this. The social and cultural rules of the game produce international misunderstandings, too. In this way the history of different nations catches up with our
everyday European experience again and again.

This market scene – photographed on a Sunday morning on the Quai des Celestins in Lyons – could have been taken virtually anywhere in Europe as far as the body language and general activity are concerned (credit: Barnabys Picture Library/Ray Roberts).

Everyday situations and routines

Our everyday life is made up mainly of routines which lend it its special rhythm and continuity. Some things we do every day, some every week, some irregularly and sporadically; some we like doing more than others. Anyway, it is the sum of these regular activities which makes up and determines the character of a considerable part of our lives. Knowledge of these rhythms and rules is what constitutes the largest part of our cultural capital. Without them we are helpless, insecure, irritable and vulnerable. This becomes apparent when we leave our normal space and get involved in a 'foreign' environment.

Of course, we are not entirely without help, since the various social and national scenes have certain structures in common, despite their diversity. Situations that occur in the street, in shops, or in the cinema resemble each other irrespective of whether they take place in Paris, London or in an Italian village. Though they resemble each other, they are not the same and their rules are not identical.

Alongside the common elements there is always something special that lends the scene its specifically local, social and national colouring. Nor are we neutral, passive participants; we always have the rules and rituals of our own experiences and everyday practices at the back of our minds and we compare our foreign encounters with them.

Subjectivity and bias affect scientific research and the observation of everyday life. We cannot observe in a totally objective way, let alone slip into an Italian, French or Dutch skin; part of us always remains caught up in our own culture. You should keep this in mind when considering the following small everyday scenarios.

On the move

As far back as the 1920s, the journalist and sociologist Siegfried Kracauer wrote in his observations of everyday life in industrial societies and in large cities: 'As members of the masses, people are only tiny elements which together make up a composite character, not individuals who think of themselves as formed from within.' According to Kracauer, this character is imposed on people by the rationality of production and the uniformity of culture. In other words, human everyday life is choreographed or runs along on fixed lines and the basic figures are always the same. Individuals believe themselves to have free choice of movement and behaviour, but in actual fact all they are doing is following the movements of the masses, who appear to be manipulated as though by remote control. Kracauer calls the figures in the choreography 'the ornament of the masses', made up of 'thousands of bodies' which have lost their individuality without knowing it (Kracauer, 1977 p. 51).

Without being quite so pessimistic in cultural terms, the 'mass experience' does seem to be the dominant motif in everyday life, especially in urban society. Our urban culture offers promise and disappointment at one and the same time. It presents an immense diversity of impressions and opportunities for encounters, which cannot usually be realized, because they remain anonymous, without communication. At home, one is so used to it that one hardly notices it any more. But abroad one is powerfully conscious of this 'mass experience'. This is the impression made on a foreigner by industrial Birmingham, England's second largest city:

> There you stand, totally helpless in this desolate city where the latest
> street maps and guides are already out of date because some fly-over
> has turned into a subway or even a building. People hurry past as if
> shopping were hard labour and you're lucky if you happen to end up in
> New Street, the only old-style street where it's still possible to take a
> stroll and where the houses date from the start of the century.
>
> *(Berliner Tagesspiegel, 13 January 1991)*

Experiences like this of the overcrowded maze of a city make a specially deep impression when you encounter them literally en route in bus, tram or underground. When you see its main thoroughfares through the windows of its transport system, the city becomes an adventure, the scene for an expedition. Such an expedition can be arduous and may consist of experiences like being wedged in the middle of a mass of people, making your way in queues of passers-by or being washed to and fro in floods of people. It is, of course, also possible to gain something else: the pleasure of observation.

A German traveller gives the following report of a visit to London in 1847:

> London is on a much grander scale than Paris; the traffic, which
> consists of all types of carriages and of pedestrians in the main streets
> and also the traffic of vessels on the Thames, surpasses everything that
> exists in any other city. A sight-seeing trip through all the hurly-burly
> on the top deck of an omnibus through the City and the West End is
> highly attractive; no less so is a trip on one of the countless steamers on
> the Thames, past the city and down towards Greenwich or beyond. It is
> instructive and entertaining to spend more time in places like the
> Thames or the docks where the main flow of traffic is found.
>
> *(Elben, 1931, p. 85)*

It seems as though this practice of 'taking a trip through everyday life' has been part of the tourist programme when visiting cities for more than 150 years (Kaschuba, 1991).

Without actually getting into conversation with your fellow travellers, this travelling around a big city can create shared experiences, memories and associations that are, despite all anonymity and inarticulateness, a form of closeness. In the middle of a crowd, your neighbour suddenly becomes an individual with his or her own unique outline, who makes personal statements, even if only in your imagination.

The way in which people behave in a queue also has its own laws – social and cultural traffic rules which are partly general and partly specific to countries and localities. There are the general rules about leaving others in peace, keeping your distance, and avoiding all but the most fleeting eye contact (though there are always people, mostly men, who don't obey that one). Other customs have a more specifically national orientation: the disciplined queuing at a London bus stop is completely different from the restless jostling for places in public transport in Rome. There the queue is constantly on the move and it seems like a form of sport to secure your place in the front row with a bold, arrogant gesture. Anybody exercising genteel British restraint in this situation would have to put up with a long wait or even go on foot. For foreigners in particular coping with these traffic rules represents the real adventure in their encounter with a different culture:

> The really heroic feats are not climbing Kilimanjaro or crossing the
> Sahara in a Land Rover, but travelling from the flat to the airport,
> getting one's suitcase to the check-in desk, choosing the right terminal
> …
>
> *(Bruckner and Finkielkraut, 1981, p. 140)*

At the checkout

The most deepseated differences in everyday life in Europe probably relate to food shopping, depending on whether you use the supermarket or the corner shop.

The supermarket is a mass enterprise, organized and rationalized down to the last detail. You could visualize supermarkets as the artfully contrived slopes of a mountain of standardized, mass-produced and pre-packaged goods. The fact that you can buy the same brands in Lyons or in Amsterdam, in London or in Zurich demonstrates just how international food manufacturers and their goods are. Foreign visitors don't have to worry about not being able to communicate, since the prices are printed and the labels multi-lingual. You can pick everything up and inspect it. And the whole shopping trip can be done without uttering a word from start to finish, when the customer can read the total off the display.

The corner shop, on the other hand, is often a place where food is exposed to the world, where local vegetables and types of bread can be bought in small quantities and still have to be weighed. Usually you can't just take what you want, you have to ask for or order it. Here shopping is still a communicative activity, a dialogue between people rather than between display shelves and trolley. It is not surprising that when people are abroad and feel uncertain about the language and everyday customs they prefer to use the supermarket rather than risk the corner shop.

The origins of the shop go back far into the past. It was the first stationary point of sale, gradually replacing itinerant merchants and pedlars who supplied the medieval rural population with essential goods that their farms and households could not produce. The next stage was that shops were set up in towns; they offered a limited range of goods for local needs and were, at first, not much more than sales outlets for local craftsmen.

The supermarket, on the other hand, represents the present. It made its first appearance in the eighteenth century, developing out of the covered and open air markets of the city; the history of Parisian supermarkets demonstrates this very clearly. The temples of consumerism that we know today gradually came into being during the second half of the nineteenth century.

The department store and the supermarket could be described as a 'world of goods'; the small shop, on the other hand, is a world of looking, smelling and talking, more a 'world of people'. A German schoolgirl writes of her impressions in Italian shops:

> Things were all the livelier in the many small shops … The goods are
> arranged close together on the shelves, packed in bright paper bags,
> cartons, boxes and glasses. The many varieties of pasta on offer took up
> a particularly large space, of course, and it took a long time to make up
> my mind which to choose … But what I particularly liked about these
> *salumeria* (delicatessens) was that they are clearly the meeting place and
> centre of conversation for all the local people. The shop owner often has
> his whole family in the shop and between looking for things and paying
> for them the latest news passes back and forth. One has a chat and a
> laugh and no-one is in a hurry.
>
> *(Frankfurter Allgemeine Zeitung, 6 March 1986)*

These young people who visited Leningrad had some similar, some different experiences when they went shopping:

> If you need cheese, sausages and milk you have to visit three different
> shops and not only that, you have to look first to see if what you need

is available and then take a note of the price for the quantity you want. After that you get into the queue for the cashdesk and pay. Although there is usually a cash register, the amounts are almost always calculated on an abacus first and then entered on the cash register. Receipt in hand, you then queue at the goods counter and after another wait you get what you want. We encountered the openness and helpfulness of the local people for the first time in the shops of Leningrad. Without being asked, they helped us to choose food and took care that we were served properly. And the shopping process, which seemed time consuming and laborious in comparison with our experience of shopping in supermarkets, also had its good side: a friendly chat enabled us to make our first contacts and pick up some valuable tips.

(Studienkreis für Tourismus, 1986, p. 327)

What shopping is actually going to be like clearly depends on the type and size of shop, on the goods on offer in that country, on its rules, and maybe also on differences between town and country, since these sometimes seem to give rise to a different type of behaviour as far as consumption and communication are concerned. Overall, however, the differences between various kinds of shopping have become less marked, both nationally and internationally.

Then there is that very central shopping experience, the weekend family shopping expedition, which takes place every Friday night or Saturday and follows the same routine each time. This is not a leisurely trip, a chance to wander round looking at things and enjoying yourself, but a purposeful dash round different shops, car parks and checkout queues, crossing off items on a long shopping list. Although there are signs of change among the younger generation, this is still a major shopping event right through Europe, particularly for women. They bear the responsibility for ordinary shopping, which men are keen to avoid because it's so tedious, involving planning, searching for the cheapest offer, queuing and waiting to be served. The reason men often give to get out of this more stressful and humdrum kind of shopping is that they've earned most of the money to pay for it. They also consider that this can give them the right to have the final word about household spending. The following situation in an Irish farming family is not typical solely of the Irish:

> Peter gives Joan the money when she needs to pay her bill. He is also the one who works out how to pay the builders of their new house. If Joan wants to buy anything for herself or the children, like a dress, she has to go to Peter and ask him for money. 'Well, sometimes he starts arguing, but usually he gives me what I want. When it's something like the washing machine he almost always agrees. And in any case, I don't suggest anything we don't really need. In most cases we reach agreement.'

(Hallerstein-Teufel, 1984, p. 140)

It clearly depends on what you buy as to how much you enjoy shopping. Shopping for groceries seems to be regarded as work all over Europe, while buying clothes, books or records is usually seen as something you do as part of your leisure time. This kind of consumption brings with it a hint of freedom, of not actually 'needing' but 'wanting' something, something from a tempting array of goods. Paying for luxuries – brightly-coloured tiles from the mosaic of a desirable lifestyle – is less enjoyable, since the warm glow of consumer democracy fades at the cashdesk. Supermarkets cater for different social classes and this is, of course, reflected in the prices charged. People with limited budgets rarely stray into the luxury world of expensive gourmet tastes epitomized by Harrods Food Hall or Fortnum & Mason. They are more likely to patronize their local Co-op or Kwik-Save. Despite the democratization of advertisements, people's styles of consumption are still class-related.

Consumption styles also have national characteristics. If you compare shopping lists across Europe, you will soon see that there are quite considerable variations between countries, despite Europe-wide conformity of certain brands of clothing and shoes, perfumes and cleaning agents. The grocery list reflects the main differences – those between national food cultures. This doesn't mean that the Spanish, the British and the Italians eat entirely different kinds of food, but rather that they have preferences for certain ways of eating and traditions to do with food. The German shopping list, headed by sausages and meat followed by large amounts of baked goods and beer to help get through the weekend might sound a bit strange to the Italian housewife, whose list consists of vegetables, cheese and pasta, complemented by wine rather than beer. The French housewife might not think very much of the food her British counterpart buys for Sunday breakfast – she would probably consider bacon, eggs and sausages to be more suitable for an evening meal. So European variety is alive and well – in shops and shopping baskets, at any rate.

'Mahlzeit!'

The word *Mahlzeit*!, meaning literally mealtime, is used in Germany around the middle of the day as a form of well-wishing or greeting. It is popular with civil servants, office employees and workers who use this expression to voice their desire that the middle of the working day should be marked by a longer break for relaxation and recreation. Although it sounds rather abrupt and command-like, it expresses something common to other cultures – a wish that the midday meal should be a peaceful and enjoyable occasion. Of course, not everyone has a proper lunch, this varies from one individual or nation to another. It depends to a large extent on the customs and traditions which have determined our respective food cultures.

What we eat and how we eat it is not something which has simply happened by chance – historical influence has had something to do with it. Research into the nutrition of the last two decades in particular has made it possible to reconstruct in broad outline the evolution of that combination of foods and table manners which makes up today's food culture or cultures. We know that our modern eating habits have been influenced by many factors, such as particular working and living conditions, improved transportation systems and food production technologies, home-grown products and foreign imports, traditional ways of preparing food and new eating habits, tastes which are acceptable and those which are not. We also know that experiments in new ways of eating usually started at the top of the social hierarchy. Money, time and staff facilitated the quest for refinement and distraction, using sophisticated cuisine to create a special life style which would set the upper classes apart from the normality and conformity of other people's diets. Poor people, on the other hand, had neither the time nor the money to cope with anything more than the question of how their daily hunger could be stilled most effectively and cheaply – up to this century, at any rate. Today's fashion for food which was the diet of yesterday's poor is a relatively recent development.

While the European food culture underwent many changes in the course of history, it is possible to sketch in some important dividing lines. To this day, for instance, there is an equator dividing the continent between southern European pasta and northern European potatoes. We know that pasta arrived in Italy as far back as the middle ages, coming from Arabian countries via Venice. As early as the fourteenth century different types of spaghetti, macaroni and other variants of pasta found their way first into the households of the upper classes and then became more generally popular. Pasta became known and valued in other European countries via trading connections and the pilgrimages of the eighteenth century. Food production on an industrial scale, tourism and the spread of Italian restaurants during the post-war years have helped it to become a truly European dish (Tannahill, 1973, pp. 280–2).

The potato arrived much later, imported first from America in the sixteenth and seventeenth centuries by the Spanish and Italian colonial trade; it became known in England and Germany during the seventeenth century. There was, initially, a great deal of prejudice against the potato on the grounds that it was inedible, poisonous and only good for pig food. This was gradually overcome in western and northern Europe during the periods of severe famine of the late eighteenth century. Eventually, after many unsuccessful attempts to persuade farmers that it was a new high-yielding crop rich in nutrients, the potato became part of the regular diet in town and country households. It replaced porridge and meals based on bread, and was eaten with other vegetables and meat. In the nineteenth century the potato was food for rich and poor: prepared in various ways, it was a mainstay of the French *haute cuisine* which dictated European standards of taste and, at the same time, it was the 'bread of the poor', the staple food of the working population in the age of industrialization (Sandgruber, 1982, p. 145ff.).

Chocolate, first as a drink then as eating chocolate, spread from Italy to France and then throughout Europe. In the case of coffee, this was introduced to Europe from Arabia in the sixteenth century. By the seventeenth century it had become a fashionable drink in the aristocratic houses of western Europe and spread from there via bourgeois households until it finally reached the cups of the lower classes. The only difference was that the coffee cups of the wealthy upper classes and the affluent middle classes steamed with an infusion of real coffee beans. All that could be found in the cups of the lower classes was a brew of some coffee substitute such as chicory enriched by the addition of just a few genuine beans (Schivelbusch, 1983, p. 25ff.).

The outcome of all these innovations and changes is that the contours of a gastronomic map of Europe have gradually emerged, with a mixture of common elements and national specialities. The publication and distribution of cookery books and recipes has also played a part. Since the eighteenth century they have set certain standards of food culture, especially for middle-class households. These standards, which laid down how food should be prepared and the order of the courses to be served in the 'respectable' German, French, British or Dutch household, came nearest to representing a 'national cuisine'. A look into the kitchens of farming and working families, on the other hand, is more likely to have revealed a more regionally based diet. This began to change only gradually with the industrialization of food production and the changing living conditions of the family in the nineteenth century.

From the historical point of view, European eating culture underwent two main phases of innovation. The first was the period between about 1770 and 1840 when a veritable revolution took place in the eating habits of large sectors of the population. Coffee, cocoa, sugar, white bread, potatoes and fresh meat began to displace traditional everyday dishes like soup, porridge and dried or preserved food stuffs and food was increasingly bought rather than grown. The second began at the start of our century with the industrialization of food production and the creation of cross-regional markets; it reached completion when imported mass products became available in fresh or preserved form.

In addition to these changes in nutrition and consumption, European food cultures have been influenced, perhaps even more strongly, by the 'refinement' of taste preferences and table manners. The 'civilization of eating' is a significant feature of the European process of civilization which changed everyday culture decisively from the sixteenth to the eighteenth century. The cultural sociologist and historian, Norbert Elias described this turning point as follows:

> People who ate together in the way customary in the Middle Ages, taking meat with their fingers from the same dish, wine from the same goblet, soup from the same pot or the same plate ... such people stood in a different relationship to one another than we do. And this involves not only the level of clear, rational consciousness; their emotional life also had a different structure and character. The way in which their emotions were regulated meant that they were conditioned to forms of relationship and conduct which, by today's standards, are embarrassing, or at least unattractive.
>
> *(Elias, 1978 I, p. 69)*

Elias goes on to describe how the old ways of behaving at table changed among the upper classes, particularly with regard to table linen and table manners. Eating with a spoon or, even worse, bare hands, gulping food down, wiping hands, mouth and nose on the tablecloth (if there was one) and many other kinds of coarse behaviour were replaced by new, more 'civilized' table manners. It is not just the food on the table, but the way it is consumed and enjoyed that signals the 'civilized life style' now (Elias, 1978 I, p. 104ff.).

Civilizing eating in this way demonstrates how change is brought about by setting external norms of behaviour which are gradually transformed into inner values, becoming second nature. The new attitude towards eating which has developed reflects fundamental changes in the handling of human needs: it mirrors the

The food for the banquet, which is being prepared in this engraving from Bartolomeo Scappi's Opera *(1570), seems to have a variety of ingredients and to involve complex preparations (credit: British Library, London).*

'modern' control of instincts and emotions which has become the standard for our everyday behaviour. This is why the countless books on etiquette which even now

227

try to teach us the proper way to handle cutlery and china are there not only to guide us through the eating jungle, but also give pointers to the training of the whole character.

We can afford to be a bit sarcastic nowadays about etiquette and those stern rules for table manners, since there has been a certain liberalization in this respect over the last few decades. People no longer pay so much attention to the right way to eat certain dishes, which wine goes with which course or when it is permissible to use your fingers, either around the lunch table at home or in a restaurant. Strict etiquette has given way to an informal and permissive approach to table manners based on the premise, that while there are certain basic rules as to the 'proper' way to eat, a preoccupation with the correct use of knife and fork and napkin should not get in the way of the enjoyment of food.

No doubt this change has also something to do with the fact that the traditional concept of the communal meal, which had a central function in the old code of table manners has now given way to a whole multitude of different ways of eating.

> It certainly makes a difference whether I organize a picnic with some friends in the summer or whether I join a queue at the self-service counter in a canteen; whether I have a lavish working lunch 'on expenses' with business contacts or whether I take a bite of my sandwich in the car while the traffic lights are red; whether I am attending a wedding breakfast or eating a hot dog at a disco; whether I'm having mashed potatoes spooned into my mouth in a hospital or whether I am sitting in a bar in Hamburg; whether I join a course for connoisseurs or have breakfast at home ...
>
> *(Rath, 1984, p. 140)*

The rules vary according to the situation, there is less compulsion to do certain things, the norms have been relaxed. This doesn't mean that the way we eat has been de-regulated and de-ritualized: there is a basic type of acceptable behaviour associated with each kind of eating. To eat fish with your fingers as though it were a curry-sausage is still not the done thing, and the crowd in a snack bar would find it odd if you dissected a hamburger with a knife and fork.

There is still room for misunderstandings when national food cultures clash. A German exchange student, for instance, reports from her stay in Marseille:

> I had a small room in a students' hostel. There was to be a party with crêpes. Like the other German students I expected that with so many people in that small room, everyone would make themselves comfortable and eat on their knees or standing up as they used to do during my student days in Germany. To my utter amazement, this was not the case. With a lot of effort the room was cleared and a table was organized which was so big that very little space was left between the table and the walls. The whole evening was spent very uncomfortably sitting round the table ... For my French friends a celebration meant a communal meal and for a communal meal a communal table was needed. The table, the communal meal at the table, continuing to sit there until long after the actual food has been eaten, symbolizes *convivialité.*

In turn, a French student reported about her German eating experience:

> I was invited for a meal by my landlady by way of welcome and as a preliminary to closer contacts in the future. I was very irritated by the way in which the evening worked out. Apart from the food and the sequence of courses I was horrified by the whole atmosphere, particularly by the way each course was cleared away almost before the last person had put down his fork and because as soon as everyone had finished eating they got up straightaway, went into the living room and carried on drinking …

Even if the written rules of eating have been relaxed, this does not mean that informal rules have ceased to be important. Our eating culture is particularly rich in gestures and symbolic acts by which we signal enjoyment, well-being, readiness to communicate and closeness. Conversely, understanding breaks down if signs and signals do not come from the same cultural code. But this is brought home to us only when we are plunged into an alien situation, when we suddenly realize what adventures of gastronomic culture lie in store for us in a different social milieu or with foreign hospitality.

Just this small row of restaurants, photographed in London in 1992, shows how many different 'national' cuisines are available in large European cities (credit: Marshall Aver).

The same is true of the meals and dishes themselves, of course, as well as the rules of behaviour. There seems to be a contradiction between the much publicized notion of national cuisine, with restaurants in different European cities offering typical Spanish, French or Italian dishes, and the historical perspective, which proves that truly national eating cultures barely exist. This fiction of a 'national cuisine' is to a large extent the product of modern mobility and mass tourism. It is no more typical of country and people than the holiday brochure image of beaches, hotels and tourist restaurants, who then have to do their best to make the internationally uniform food they offer look a bit different by giving it a 'typically national' tinge. When you step into the real world outside tourist ghettos and tourist menus, it is often surprising how difficult it is to find these 'typical dishes' in normal eating places and restaurants.

On the other hand, there are still some dishes and eating traditions which are associated with certain countries and can be found there in different regional variations. A dessert like *Kaiserschmarren* will probably taste best in the kitchens and dining rooms of Austria, where it comes from, though you will probably find it on the menu in most central European countries. Steak and kidney pie is most likely to be found in Great Britain, while (according to gourmets) the best bouillabaisse can be found on the French Mediterranean or Atlantic coasts.

It is noticeable that what we might cautiously label 'national' dishes are based on ingredients and recipes which were formerly thought of typically as poor people's food. More often than not it is the country tradition of making the best use of local ingredients and left-overs which determines our images of European gastronomic culture. Such images belong among those 'myths of the everyday world' which Roland Barthes (1964) has described so graphically for French culture. And we are only too pleased to believe that a tasty plateful of Russian bortsch, Hungarian goulash, British fish and chips, Italian minestrone, Irish stew or German sauerkraut will not only make us feel full, but give us a dollop of unspoilt national culture into the bargain.

One of the most successful myths of all time is the Italian pizza. Starting out in the seventeenth century in the south of Italy as a marriage between dough, tomatoes, cheese and spices, its empire is now world-wide. The Italian paper *La Repubblica* (13 April 1983) carried a report of a conference of Italian pizza bakers, who were in no doubt that, despite the success of the Italian fashion industry and others, the pizza convey the most powerful image of Italy all over the world, even if the ingredients used in other countries weren't always authentic. So in the long term it is not the specific flavour or ingredients that achieve success, but rather the name and perhaps the colourful appearance. The Hungarians would certainly say the same about their goulash and the French often despair at the sight of the 'French' *pommes frites* offered to them abroad.

Paradoxically it is this very trend of erecting (or inventing) barriers between different kinds of food and cooking which has given rise to the internationalization of restaurant menus. The 'typical' Italian, French or Swedish dish seems to have become classed as such because it can not only be found and eaten in its region of origin, but also holds its own abroad as a foreign speciality in competition with local foods. Nowadays it is commonplace to find there are quite a few French or Indian eating places in a British restaurant guide, that Algerian and Chinese cuisines are almost completely at home in France and that the German gastronomic scene consists mainly of Greek and Italian restaurants in many regions. As far back as the nineteenth century, Brillat-Savarin warned that the emergence of restaurants would even out and eventually eliminate the differences between national and regional foods.

The influence of international food manufacturers and the desire for exotic foods awoken by foreign travel have combined to produce much more open minded attitudes towards food in the more affluent countries. And what we haven't yet brought back as tourists is gradually being imported by different ethnic groups, since ingredients for Turkish, Arabic, Greek and Chinese recipes are becoming freely available to us in shops run by immigrants.

Often forgotten in the pleasure of finding some new gastronomic delight is the past connection between food and religious eating observances. We know from Jewish history in Germany and France, for instance, how much Germans and French felt the kosher cuisine of their Jewish fellow citizens to be alien and divisive, since their Jewish friends would not always eat and drink what was offered to them in friendship. In the past, anti-semitism has constantly stressed this deep division in everyday life, and it seems we still may not be immune from this xenophobic reaction. After all, do we really appreciate the immensity of the problem represented by the predominance of pork in restaurants and works canteens for those millions of Muslims who live in England, Germany or France today? At worst we make jokes about it, at best we ignore it. And do we consider how important Ramadan is for our colleagues? These four weeks in spring are a time not only of special abstemiousness, but also of nightly feasts and family celebrations, so cultural and religious traditions are marked by particular food observances. Since this phenomenon is hardly marked by the host countries and barely acknowledged by companies and universities, how else is this culture to survive and develop, but by withdrawal into the ethnic community?

The most up-to-date food phenomenon, fast food restaurants, seems to be the reverse of eating apart from others. There were, of course, historical precursors: the idea of the sausage stand, for instance, is supposed to go back to the Middle Ages. And there were always stands and booths in weekly markets and annual fairs in the eighteenth and nineteenth centuries, where passers-by could get a snack without losing their 'ambulatory rhythm':

> Here the act of consuming is common to all the people, the snack-bar seems to exercise a democratic and egalitarian influence: the worker in his overalls stands at the counter eating side by side with the elegant lady in her fur coat with her little finger crooked. This is what you might call the 'true poetry' of the fairground.
>
> *(Tolksdorf, 1981, p. 122)*

At the start of the twentieth century a network of booths for snacks and drinks grew up around factories and in working class districts in particular. You could get a quick, cheap snack standing up, because the time schedule of the factory would not permit a more leisured way of eating.

The growth of car ownership and a change in the use of leisure time in subsequent decades brought about further changes in the way food is produced and distributed.

> The concentration of snackbars around stations, bus terminals, motorways and exit roads from large towns, around large car parks and tourist attractions etc., clearly showed the connection between motorization and snackbars. Admittedly, these developments did not

> happen as fast in Europe as, for instance, in the USA where drive-in
> restaurants and coin-operated restaurants are a well-established part of
> the 'car-culture'. The Americans give this provision of goods and fast
> foods the logical name of 'roadside food'.
>
> *(Tolksdorf, 1981, p. 126)*

Today, the international hamburger culture has conquered practically every country and continent. McDonalds, the biggest restaurant chain in the world, currently boasts 11,480 outlets, of which only 10 per cent are in the mother country of the USA. Being named by connoisseurs as 'the arch enemy of all gourmets' has not prevented them and the other fast food chains from ruining European taste buds.

Presumably it is not so much the taste of the food which has made this phenomenon so attractive and successful, but rather current eating-out fashions. A snack bar is not just a place where food is provided, but somewhere with a special atmosphere. What matters is not whether hot dogs, hamburgers, doner kebabs, Chinese spring rolls or fish and chips are on offer, but that you can eat, look, drink, and even speak in a certain way, without having to think of complicated table rules and ways of eating. Buying food like this means you don't have to interrupt work or leisure by allowing time for a proper meal. The visit to the snack bar imposes fewer obligations. You can come and go as you please, gobble your food down or eat at a leisurely pace, have a chance to see and be seen. While it is a way of avoiding traditional food rituals, it is not without its own ritualistic framework. What dominates here is a youthful culture (though you can be as old as you like) which offers conscious enjoyment of the chance to combine the fun of eating with that of watching, the opportunity to live for the moment, giving yourself up completely to the stimulus of the taste and the situation. This is epitomized in the American concept of 'fast-food happiness'.

There is, I suppose, an underlying motif here which actually links McDonalds with such temples of indulgence as the Parisian *Tour d'Argent*. The Europeanization of our food culture has made most progress in the refined cuisine of sophisticated and speciality restaurants and in fast-food, since both are truly international as far as raw materials and products, table manners and eating rituals, levels of taste and the type of furniture used are concerned. Anyway, neither of them has much connection with national characteristics and styles. But traditions, idiosyncrasies and regional characteristics are much more in evidence in the good plain food and farmhouse dishes served in villages and small towns. Here they are not aiming to offer 'national' dishes, but rather 'regional' ones. Provence and Alsace, Bavaria and the Rhineland, Cornwall and the North of England might as well be different continents as far as food is concerned.

Prost, cheers, santé!

Much that has influenced and brought about change in past and present food and eating habits also applies, of course, to drink and drinking. Apart from what you need to quench your thirst, there are two types of drinking: with meals and social drinking. What you choose to drink with meals depends not only on what you actually want or need, but also on the influence of certain cultural rules. One drink goes better than another with fish, meat or poultry; you are more likely to drink alcohol on festive occasions than every day; some foods seem to need a long slurp of drink to wash them down, while others require only little sips; in some places it is usual to drink beer with a meal, in others wine. So there is much overlapping and intermingling of customs and rules which, while it rarely adds up to the strict rules of *haute cuisine*, still indicates quite clearly that not everything is permitted or customary. Social group, gender, age, regional or national characteristics determine which kind of behaviour is most appropriate. Even the all-purpose drink Coca-Cola is not totally acceptable everywhere.

Social drinking may take place in private rooms and clubs, but is typically done by men in *Wirtshäuser* (simple restaurants), pubs, cafés or bars. The public places where people meet over an alcoholic drink are mainly male territory. Rules of behaviour here are not as refined as in a sophisticated restaurant, though the interaction of alcohol and sociability is organized with just as many rituals. This applies not only to the world famous (or infamous) German *Bierzelte* (beer tents) and the Polish and Russian vodka clubs, but also to the pint at lunchtime or the glass after work.

Leaving aside the solitary drinker, imbibing alcohol in public is to a large extent a communicative and interactive pastime. It takes place in line with well-established

Unspoken rules as to who may occupy what space in a café or bar may sometimes be more relaxed out of doors (credit: Mike Levers).

233

routines that determine the choice of drink, the manner and pace of drinking, the words you use when raising your glass and the way you join a group. Having a drink together emphasizes and strengthens a feeling of community, buying a round automatically attracts rounds in return because this is how mutual appreciation and the equality of the situation are expressed symbolically. In the course of our adolescent and adult drinking life we learn norms and rituals such as who should buy the first round, how fast one has to drink to keep up with the group, when it is OK to quit without breaking up the group and when not and so on. You find variations from country to country and from place to place, but all these groups of drinkers demonstrate the same basic patterns of male sociability, which cross national and class boundaries. Two men meeting by chance on some foreign railway station can communicate after a fashion through the dialogue of their glasses and the rhythm of their drinking, even though they may not speak the same language or know each other's social class.

Unlike food, the culture of drinking is strongly gender-specific. Women are largely excluded and tolerated only on the periphery, at any rate in ordinary pubs and bistros. They are perfectly welcome to 'take a little drop' at parties and special festivities (preferably in private, within the family circle). There are also cultural expectations of the type of alcoholic drink appropriate to each gender.

> In our modern society there is virtual agreement about who drinks sweet
> liqueurs and who hard spirits; all you have to do is to watch the waiter
> in a café as he spontaneously serves the drinks which have been
> ordered, to see how the glasses of liqueur end up in front of the women
> and the glasses of brandy in front of the men.
>
> *(Fabre-Vassas, 1989, p. 13)*

Attitudes of this kind have become more relaxed among the younger generation, especially in affluent areas of northern Europe; in general young people pay less attention to rules and norms. There are still special moral and aesthetic connotations where women and alcohol are concerned, however. It is not done for a woman to drink as much or as often as a man. And when a man is drunk, he is usually the object of indulgent tolerance or even amusement, while a drunken woman is treated with scorn and derision. This gender norm seems to be the same in all cultures, almost like an anthropological pattern.

So even though alcohol seems to promise a legitimate diversion from our everyday world, it is, to a large extent, bound by rules. In addition to the separation of the sexes, clear social distinctions can also be found. Working-class sociability and drinking rituals are very different from corresponding middle-class occasions and these are different again from those of high society. These distinctions apply to type of drink and where it's drunk, social conventions and body language, to the kind of invitation offered and what it represents. The basic rule still seems to be consistent: the common man drinks in public, while the gentleman indulges either in the exclusive reservation of his expensive club or, preferably, at home in private.

Here, too, the rituals and forms of group behaviour can be traced back to historical precedents from the cultures of both the aristocracy and agricultural or industrial workers. There was social drinking centuries ago in groups of people working together or among friends. There were also examples of so-called 'instrumental drinking', when small groups deliberately set out to get drunk so as to reach a common emotional high, and the rituals of raising glasses and greeting each other which display mutual respect. This suggests that the consumption of alcohol has a cultural background, that it once had a ritualistic function and was used in religious ceremonies involving the confirmation and invocation of a community spirit. Another reason why people drank a lot was to aid the consumption and digestion of foods which were rich in fats and carbohydrates, of the kind normally eaten in northern and eastern Europe. The efficacy of drink as a digestive aid was recognized even then and people were quite happy to put up with the stimulating effect of the alcohol as well. But it was much more difficult and involved to produce alcohol at that time. The phenomenon of large-scale, regular alcohol consumption as we know it today is relatively new. Alcohol only became part of everyday life once it was produced on an industrial scale. This is true not only of schnapps, cognac and whisky, which only became widely available through modern methods of production and distribution, but also of wine and beer, even though they seem to have been around a long time, historically speaking. For economic reasons they weren't within everybody's reach all the time. It is a well-known fact that even the wine-growers, especially in the traditional wine-growing areas, could only drink the occasional glass of wine because they had to sell the whole of their output to make a living. Their own wine was too expensive for them and they had to make do with other drinks.

Until the last century certain types of drinks predominated in certain regions because they were grown and produced there. Since there has been an international market for alcohol, there are no such clear dividing lines, though you can still trace the after-effects of certain traditions. Locals – though more likely, foreigners – have favourites among the types and brands available which are regarded as 'national drinks'. And there are still certain drinking customs that have been influenced by different national conditions, so that it is not always easy to set up social occasions and festivities which cross cultural boundaries. You often have to keep a careful eye on your host to find out which drink local people regard as suitable for food, a toast or drinking someone's health. And even then you may have cultural clashes as, for instance, when a French host found that his German guests wanted to go on drinking wine after the meal. In France wine is drunk with food and not afterwards. In Germany, on the other hand, they often don't open the second bottle until after the meal. No such communication problems arise in the fizzy drink or Coca-Cola culture, of course.

After work

Since the beginning of the 1980s we have been living in a leisure oriented society. That, at any rate, is the thesis which underpins social scientists' discussions about the development of our everyday culture and identity. It assumes that our main concerns in life are no longer to do with work, but how to spend our leisure in a meaningful, enjoyable and varied way. If you reckon that there are 168 hours in a week, less 56 sleeping hours and 40 working hours, this leaves 72 hours of leisure time.

Now while this calculation may be correct in a strictly mathematical sense, it is not true in terms of everyday culture. The amount of time which is freely available for leisure is considerably less. An investigation in Switzerland, for instance, found that working people have only 2.6 hours per weekday free of firm commitments, though men do slightly better than women. The Swiss spend almost a quarter of this free time in front of the television. Excursions, reading, hobbies, visiting friends and relatives and finally sport come some way down the list (Mäder, 1990, p. 23ff.). It is likely that the use of leisure time in other European countries will be roughly similar. So whether the French, Italians or Scandinavians are winners of the 'world leisure championship' is difficult to decide, even irrelevant.

In any case, from a historical perspective, the concept of leisure is a relatively recent one in European societies. In the pre-industrial way of life of farmers and craftsmen, work and recreational activities were combined in a daily rhythm in which there was no separation in space and time between work and leisure. Measured solely in terms of time, a working day consisted of up to 12, 14, even 16 hours. Closer inspection of these working days shows, however, that they included considerable potential for relaxation and breaks in the form of conversations, interruptions, conviviality and phases of working at a very much slower rate. In the mid-nineteenth century, during the early stages of industrialization, fundamental changes were introduced that divided the sphere of work from the private areas of life, as far as location and organization were concerned. The old, familiar ways of relaxing and communicating then disappeared from the working day. Everything not immediately connected with work was banned, especially from the factories, and relegated to out-of-work hours.

This meant that the way in which each day was structured was completely changed, even though it had been practised and enshrined in social custom for centuries. Separation between work and leisure was emphasized when the working day was shortened to 10 or 12 hours and, starting after the First World War, gradually to 8 hours. Bedtime is no longer 7 or 8 o'clock but has moved two or three hours later into the night. There are consequently longer opening hours for pubs and places of entertainment and the working population in particular has a longer consecutive period of leisure in the evening to meet its own private needs. There is now a cultural separation between people's perception of 'working time' and 'living time' and in the organization of their everyday life. This, in turn, creates the conditions necessary for new patterns of conviviality and consumption to develop, along with new intellectual needs for entertainment, education and knowledge, and new commercially-oriented ways of organizing leisure time. It has been possible to shape and develop systematically the way we organize our leisure time only in the last seventy or so years.

In the abstract then it seems possible to speak of today's leisure society, since throughout history there has never been such a large part of the day without work. In practice, however, we may well wonder whether we really have reached a stage where we can relax and enjoy ourselves as much as we wish. The whole of our everyday life, including our leisure time, has become increasingly hectic and stressful.

We suffer more and more from shortage of time. The time spent at work is being increasingly condensed through the rationalization of processes and the allocation of tasks; the growing amount of time spent travelling to and from work as well as to leisure pursuits means there is less time available for recreation; new demands on our roles with our partners and with the family make new claims on the time available for relationships; our leisure behaviour gets more and more hectic thanks to an obsessive search for a change of programme and scene because we are hell-bent on using our leisure time 'actively' and 'purposefully'. Our leisure time thus turns into an exhausting cross country gallop of spare time activities that has to be completed on schedule, demanding a whole new method of allocating and rationing time.

In addition, people are finding it more and more necessary to give out frequent signals of how busy they are. The constant glance at the watch and at the appointments diary, the ever-present car phone, mobile phone and bleeper, the complication of agreeing times for social engagements in which adults and now even children are involved – all this may well be necessary, but at the same time it demonstrates how indispensible you are, how constantly in demand. The person who does not suffer from a shortage of time falls under suspicion, with himself and others, of having difficulty in making friends or being of low social standing. The traditional work ethos is still alive, dominating the way we perceive our leisure time and preventing it from having its own identity, so that we see it only as complementary to our work. Effort is a necessary prerequisite of relaxation, laziness of hard work. Leisure time is not an end in itself, therefore, but a way of rewarding oneself for work done.

It is no accident that we tend to establish routines and rituals for our leisure time as well, all those little ways of 'switching off', getting our breath back when we get home after work, for example. But there does not seem to be an overwhelming choice of different forms of relaxation. On the contrary, all research suggests that the same thing happens almost everywhere: people sit down in front of the television. According to a survey in the *Radio Times*, British people spend more than half their spare time in front of the television. Every eighth person spends as much as 90 per cent of their spare time in front of the small screen, which is switched on immediately they return home. Statistics for Germany and France are not much lower. It looks as though the shock-horror scenario foreseen by critics twenty years ago might actually have come to pass: the uniform culture of the box, collective images and feelings experienced second-hand via American TV serials and soap operas. What those critics deduced would happen was an irresistible decline into a passive mass (media) culture which would render people inarticulate and unable to think for themselves; it would be so totally naïve and boring as to transcend all frontiers of country and taste.

In one respect they were right if you consider the quality of some of today's TV programmes. But in other respects their fears do not seem to have been completely realized. It is true that the small screen offers the same standard diet from London to Moscow; but people draw their own conclusions from it.

Dallas is seen and experienced differently in Paris than in Stockholm. Television pictures are seen through different colour glasses according to the images people have of the world. Nor has 'mass communication' lost its voice. Audience surveys show again and again that television programmes present material on important contemporary issues, providing the subject matter for discussion at work and in the family. They create new fantasies, new myths of everyday life, which are bound up with individual experiences and dreams and are thereby transformed. The dialogue is not simply internalized by the viewer, but rewritten, as it were. Communication via the media is continued in the form of personal communication. Although television watching may look antisocial at the time, when people turn away to stare at the box, uttering only the odd word such as 'Another beer!' or 'Idiot'! interspersed with the crunching of peanuts and crisps, it can actually have a positively stimulating effect on communication, in that it carries on after what has apparently been a wasted hour. The next day may see the retelling and evaluation of the whole storyline of a film in the workplace or at school; opinions, preferences and dislikes are voiced, heroines and crooks discussed. Television also features in everyday experience as part of the relaxation routine. It reflects everyday experiences, not only in the news and documentary programmes, but also by the way television material is drawn into the collective everyday world and everyday fantasies.

That is undoubtedly the advantage of this medium compared with books. Television presents us with concrete images rather than abstract ones, unlike books, where the reader has to create the images in his or her own head. This is, no doubt, one of the main reasons why viewing has increased so considerably at the expense of reading as a form of relaxation after work. In addition, it is available all the time, a wide choice is offered and access is easier compared with a book. In France, less than half of the population still reads a paper every day, let alone highbrow literature. And other countries are not very different. The only variation is peak viewing time; in France this is between 8.30 pm and 11 pm, while in Great Britain and Germany the best time starts around 6.30 pm (Große Peclum, 1990, p. 189).

As you might expect, watching TV has ousted quite a few other ways of spending the evening, but these have by no means vanished completely. Many still prefer more convivial forms of sociability. The nightly visit to the 'local' or the café promises them more variety and a chance to relax, or perhaps they're just in the habit of doing it. Here is a typical account of one of the old cafés in Vienna:

> There are customs to be observed in the café, little rituals to be cultivated: you have your own special place there. You look round to see who else is there (and if anyone is missing). You have a laugh when the waiter goes through his routine: in fact, you laugh before he does it, because you know what to expect. You fetch something to read. 'Is that paper free?' The boss of the coffee house group, who works for the publishers, Falter, replies 'Show me the paper that's free!' in a thoroughly relaxed and unhurried tone. His is a philosophical nature, responding to the intrusion of the practical world. Suddenly everything is an intrusion, everything which is not the coffee house, the whole wide world outside, whilst inside it gets quieter, bit by bit more calm, more sleepy.

(Die Zeit, 19 April 1991)

There are many other after-work scenes and activities that could be described as well as cafés: the disco-culture of the young or the nightly activities of a sports club, the visit to the cinema or the theatre, the lonely model ship maker or the friendly group of card players. Which leisure activities you choose to fill the evening after work depends on class and gender, on whether you live in the country or in town, on your age and on personal preferences.

Personal style is not, however, determined solely by the leisure activities available and by individual needs. It is influenced by the way we want to present ourselves to the people around us. Aware of it or not, we make a public statement about our life style through our choice of leisure activities by telling the world, as it were, who we are, what we can afford and what our interests are. Leisure activities have to do with social prestige, as well. They epitomize our life style – the stereotype of the fashion and trend conscious young adult demonstrates this particularly well. Visits to certain films, concerts, restaurants, and the kind of sport you choose are proof that you belong to the scene. These are routines as well, demonstrating how leisure activities provide an opportunity for tradition and trend to reunite in routine and in ritual.

If the theory suggested above is valid, that is, that our leisure activities directly or indirectly echo the forms and norms of our working life, then an important question remains to be answered. How do the large numbers of people in western European societies who are unemployed deal with an everyday where the core work time is missing? How can they develop leisure behaviour without the counterbalance of work, unable to feel that they are part of an 'active' environment and its shared values?

In fact, relevant sociological research shows that unlimited free time cannot be converted into an endless life of leisure. This is not just because of the lack of funds or actual poverty which usually goes with unemployment. More important is the feeling that, unless you have legitimized your leisure by earning it in the form of work, you may not reward yourself with the pleasure it brings. In an environment where social identity is defined to a large extent by characteristics of employment and income, the unemployed are always in danger of being unable to find the attributes that establish their identity. The unemployed person seems socially superfluous, can no longer take part in conversations about stress and lack of time, and loses the social reference points to the world of work which are so important, even for leisure activities. He or she doubts the purpose of life itself.

So what seems like a wonderful dream for those in work – not to have to go to work and to have time to do whatever you want – is in reality impossible to achieve when time is suddenly available in abundance. That is why you get those cases where unemployed people carry on for months leaving their house every morning, briefcase in hand, and coming home at the usual time in an attempt to keep it from those around them (often including their own family) that they have lost their job. This is also why young people search so desperately for ties to groups which will enable them to develop concepts of identity for themselves, in defiance of society and its norms if needs be.

Sociologists in the United Kingdom have paid especially close attention to the connections between unemployment amongst young people and youth peer-group cultures. By studying young people's styles and their copies of other styles, they have been able to show how vital participation in such a youth culture is to the individual young person:

> Youth culture also offers a collective identity, a reference group, from which to develop an individual identity, 'magically' freed from the ascribed roles of home, school and work. It provides cognitive material from which to develop an alternative career, kept sacred from, and in rebellion with, the adult world. It is a free area between the control and authority of the adult world and freedom among one's peers. For a temporary period during youth, an alternative script can be performed, outside of the socializing forces of work, and before those of marriage become important. Young people need an identity which separates them from the expectations and roles imposed on them by family, school and work. Once they have made this separation, which makes a dramaturgical statement about their differences from those expectations imposed upon them by others, they feel free to explore and develop what they are.
>
> *(Brake, 1980, p. 166)*

The social safety net represented by the peer-group catches many a young unemployed man and saves him from utter despair and isolation. This net is missing for most unemployed girls and young women. They have to deal with the situation by themselves.

Sport

If you think that watching television is a very passive way of using your leisure time, then presumably sport counts as a particularly active way. People regard sport as healthy, a purposeful leisure activity, a good way of making friends, character- and personality-forming, especially for the young.

Recreational and sporting activities have always had a special part to play in the context of the western process of civilization. Not only do they exercise the body and develop agility, they also teach ways of controlling aggression and behaving in socially competitive situations. When you do some kind of sport, you also learn the social rules of a game and accept their validity. The idea of fair play was encouraged in the forms of sport practised by English gentlemen and in the English boarding schools; it was taken up by European sports clubs, other schools and also by the workers' sports movement in the second half of the nineteenth century.

In parallel with the expansion of leisure time, especially after the First World War, the sports movement turned into a real mass movement which had a major influence on the way millions of people spent their spare time after work and at weekends. Football, athletics, cycling, rowing, swimming and gymnastics became mass sports which, until the fifties, were practised mainly by young men. Girls and young women were admitted only grudgingly to these new kinds of leisure activity. At the same time, sports assumed different social profiles. Soccer, cycling and boxing gradually came to be regarded as proletarian sports, while the upper classes restricted themselves to more expensive kinds of sport, such as riding, tennis, sailing, or golf. Earthy, physical sports were associated with the lower elements in society, while the cleaner, more elegant sports were for the top end of the social scale.

So while the hundred years from the 1850s to the 1950s could be described as the era of mass sport, the last thirty years have seen sport take on a new quality and dimension. Sport no longer represents just one possible leisure sector among many: instead, it has become the central motif of the whole of our everyday culture. Whole societies are becoming obsessed with sport. Having an interest in sport has become a new, comprehensive value of primary importance for society. If you add the billions who are interested enough to watch sporting events on television or gather at sports grounds every day or every week to the millions who are actively pursuing a sport, then it is clear that sport is no longer a minority hobby, but a theme of central importance for the larger part of society.

This has been taken for granted for so long that we have hardly noticed these changes to our everyday culture. And yet, up to only a few years ago, we might have interpreted certain everyday scenes completely differently: someone running in the street was simply in a hurry; anyone who flexed his muscles to lift or move something did so in the context of physical labour. We interpreted things in that way because of our experience, on the basis of an historically-generated logic. Today's logic, however, is different. People who run are jogging; people lifting weights and using exercise machines are bodybuilding. The joggers are not running because they are in a hurry – on the contrary, they devote a lot of their time to sport, and the bodybuilders work with and on their muscles when they may not normally undertake any physical labour.

It is necessary to spell out this new interpretation of events so as to make it quite clear how our everyday consciousness (in cultural-anthropological terms) has been stood on its head. Today, taking an interest in sport permeates everything and is taken for granted. People playing, running and dressed in sports gear are part of the normal everyday scene in our streets, parks and on public footpaths. This is something else which is different: sports activities are no longer confined to clubs and sports facilities but have taken up a central position in society, claiming public space and public recognition.

Sport-related behaviour patterns therefore are a normal part of our everyday awareness – it is no longer necessary to justify or explain them. Another important aspect is that the sports craze cuts right across the whole population; maybe the distribution isn't completely even, but it includes both sexes, people from the most diverse social strata and age groups, city dwellers and country folk. A third observation is that there is another sports movement, with its own rules and rituals, which has grown up outside the school and club tradition. It has created its own commercial and non-commercial organizational forms – town marathons, sponsored walks, athletic studios and fitness centres. Fourth, the new sporting trend has developed its own styles and symbols: nowadays you simply have to have special clothes and equipment, rather than just a pair of gym shorts which can be used for any kind of sport, as used to be the case. Children and adolescents are particularly adept at finding their way round this new world of brands and badges. It is impossible to enjoy the game without the special trainers, the tennis racket made by firm X and the tracksuit with the special stripe, because otherwise they would be shown up as amateurs in front of the other children.

The number of those who practise sport in Germany is the same as for the other western European societies, with similar growth patterns. In the mid-1950s 47 per cent of 15 to 24-year-olds practised a sport (60 per cent of males and 35 per cent of females); in the mid-1980s more than 72 per cent of this age group took part in sport (75 per cent of males and 69 per cent of females). So nowadays nearly three out of four adolescents of both sexes are actively pursuing some sport on a daily or weekly basis (Zinnecker, 1989, p. 137). Critics claim that the scale of the leisure culture shows that what was once just something you did in your spare time has been distorted now into an organized, manipulative cult for the masses. They suggest that, rather than creating new freedoms and body awareness, this cult produces their opposite – a new set of norms and pressures: physical strain, added stress instead of relaxation and the addictive qualities of the drug 'sport'. And it seems likely that the responses most frequently given in surveys, such as 'enjoying exercise', 'health benefits' and 'a greater awareness of living' show only part of the social reality and truth. The other compulsions that motivate us are very much more complicated and convoluted. We ourselves are hardly conscious of them. The millions who exercise don't look as though they are doing it for fun: they pant and sweat, they are out of breath, their faces contorted with effort. Clearly, it is not just exercise they are after, but rather the feeling they get of winning a victory over themselves – self-discipline and willpower are the real motives.

This addiction to the physical experience is what is meant when sport is described as a drug. People use exercise as a way of surpassing their own limits, both physically and psychologically, as part of a search for self-confirmation. The sociologist, Agnes Heller, speaks of the cult of the body, which has replaced that of the spirit and which, as an axiom for health – Get Fit and Live Longer – has reached truly mythical proportions. Just suggesting that sport will improve your health is no longer enough; nowadays, the requirement to keep fit has become an imperative, a social obligation. Anyone who does not conform is taking a reckless gamble with their life chances.

The work you have to do on your body corresponds closely to the industrial concept of performance and work. Even looked at superficially, sport echoes certain features of industrial work. Rhythm and timing is no longer subjective, determined by the spirit of the game, but reflects performance-based norms. The exercise routines carried out not only by sportsmen and women at the top, but also those lower down the scale, are just as abstract and normative as the time and motion studies of the industrial assembly line. The words 'I want to make it' contain a give-away linguistic image – the body that can perform is a capable and willing worker. When you expend energy in sport, you are not only achieving physical fitness, but – and this is perhaps more important – you are demonstrating that you have the will and the subjective readiness for performance for its own sake. When you say yes to the sporting principles of fight and competition, you are behaving in the

The loneliness of the long-distance Power Jogger ...
(credit: Marshall Aver).

same way as in the traditional world of work. Although it seems at first as though you're just working at a 'voluntary', 'recreational' leisure pursuit, sporting ideals then take over in life as well; the jogger is Marathon Man, even when he is at work in his office.

These are not, of course, the only reasons why sport is so popular today. There is much in leisuretime sport that does not fit in with this theory. Nevertheless, it is something which seems to feature very large just now and, if this is the case, the question of the social dimension and the cultural importance of taking part in sport assumes special significance.

Sports sociologists maintain that jogging is a new sports fashion peculiar to the middle classes. The emphasis on its effect on health and fitness, the showy demonstration of easy movement, immediately contradicted by a glance at the stop watch on the wrist to make a check on performance, the conviction that one has an entirely individual approach to one's hobby – these are cultural gestures which look revealingly like the claim to individuality and self-conscious posturings of the dynamic entrepreneur, the success-oriented executive or the senior lecturer in his mid-life crisis. Dynamic young executives in industry, management and the professions do not consider it at all unusual to recover from the day's work and get fit for the next at one and the same time, perhaps even to jog to work so as to arrive at the office 'fresh'. On the other hand, try telling a worker that he or she should get fit for their everyday working life by practising sport in their spare time; you'd probably get an unequivocal gesture in reply. Sport has a different emphasis; it is still a game and has a lot to do with sociability, with being in a group, with beer or coffee afterwards. And the sports practised are considerably less performance-oriented and do not involve the same degree of self-inflicted torment. The working day is physically strenuous enough – there is no need to do the same again in your spare time.

The way in which tennis has developed seems to indicate a quite different set of cultural phenomena. Originally played exclusively by the upper middle and upper classes, tennis seems to be well on the way to becoming a new mass sport. Facilities such as communal tennis courts, tennis sections within other sports clubs, make-shift tennis courts on school playgrounds or car parks have made it easier for children of less well-off families to take part. In addition, a change has also taken place in the way the sport looks. The 'white' sport has long since turned into a 'coloured' sport. Loud colours and cut-off jeans are allowed. The great tennis tournaments are staged in a highly-charged emotional atmosphere against a backdrop of noise not very different from the kind you hear in a football stadium.

Conversely, football has long since left its proletarian past behind to become a nationwide TV spectacle which transcends social identifiers and boundaries. Football provides those 'community experiences' for which there seems to be an increasing need in our modern, isolating and communication-starved society. People seem to want emotional identification rather than rational objectivity. Imaginary 'we-identities' can be created that, for two hours at any rate, give spectators the feeling that they are part of a great whole which blurs everyday problems and makes everyday life seem better.

The new cult of bodybuilding and body styling generates an exceptionally individualistic and narcissistic attitude. Young men and now quite a few young women are inspired by a strange form of narcissism to shape their bodies into a muscular work of art which represents for them an aesthetic self-image; they literally create themselves according to their own own ideas.

> These are training activities where no opponent is present or, at least, where no opponent is needed. Whoever goes jogging, does body building, yoga exercises, fitness training, or even karate has no need of an opponent or a sporting partner. Exercises are aimed primarily at one's own body, its ability to perform, its health, its aesthetic shape, the dynamics of exercise. The basis of this sport-related exercise is strictly individualistic; its narcissistic character can scarcely be ignored. The exercise serves one's self-esteem, the meditative search for meaning, the experience-related enhancement of personal well-being.
> *(Zinnecker, 1989, p. 153ff.)*

These are just a few spotlights on a phenomenon that has systematically engulfed our everyday culture. Fitness and the outfits associated with it are new cultural tenets which have achieved the eminence of real cultural values. In the same way that knowledge of books or visits to the theatre used to be socially prestigious, the same is now true of things to do with sport. You don't have to stop discussing the latest Wimbledon tournament in favour of the latest opera performance. It is just as valid to discuss sport as culture.

The prophecies made by the supporters of sport now seem to have been fulfilled. Sport is the ultimate democratic leisure culture, never before achieved. Through the culture of the body and its self-expression in sport and games, we seem to have achieved equality of the classes and sexes, the dream of the classless society. But is that really true?

To find out more, French cultural sociologists have begun a detailed investigation of body culture in contemporary French society; they have come to some astonishing conclusions (Boltanski, 1976). Different and idiosyncratic class styles are clearly apparent in the attitudes of different classes to illness and medicines, and to sport. Workers still have a somewhat instrumental relationship to their bodies – illness is acknowledged only at the point where it physically inhibits their ability to work. This is completely different from the self-indulgent, narcissistic relationship that white collar workers and intellectuals develop to every symptom of physical malaise, which they can describe to their friends and their GP in eloquent detail. They differed in the way they related to sport with regard to motives, the aesthetics of the body, the preference for group or individual sport as well as in the relationship between sport and everyday life. To emphasize the point, most workers would regard fitness training at or for work as a mild form of mental derangement. Sport is for pleasure, not for work. It fulfils social, sociable and group-related functions.

What can we conclude from this? Body culture is class-related. If you tell me what you wear, what pills you take, what kinds of sport you like, then I shall tell you where you belong in society. Sport has become yet another example of class-specific value orientation and, as such, is directly relevant to the interpretation of everyday culture.

'We' identities: the group

If the social scientists are right with their forecasts that the 1980s and 1990s are years of a fundamental change in social values, then we are facing a new age of individuality. What is meant by this is not so much a new stage of personal freedom, but rather the loss of social ties and security. According to this view, there were three factors, or dimensions, which brought about the change from the modern to the post modern period. These were:

> … disembedding, *removal* from historically prescribed social forms and commitments in the sense of traditional contexts of dominance and support (the 'liberating dimension'); and – here the meaning of the word is virtually turned into its opposite – a re-embedding, a *new type of social commitment* (the 'control' or 'reintegration dimension').
>
> *(Beck, 1992, p. 128)*

This theory should be put into perspective. It is true that the traditional systems of classification by class and social strata have lost much of their power. Community and family ties have become looser. Nevertheless, there is still a basic underlying anthropological structure which validates our need for company and membership of a group as forms of collective identity construction.

> We are born into social classes, themselves complexly stratified, possessing distinct 'ways of life', which are modified perceptions, values, behaviour and institutions which affect the social relations of these groups. The values and social meanings embodied in these make up the culture of the group. We are formed and also form (collectively at least) a series of social relations necessary to reproducing our social existence. We start to build an identity contained in this nexus of social relations and meanings, and the culture transmitting this meaning to us both aids us to make sense of the world, but also retrains our development. We draw upon existing cultural patterns, and from this make ourselves, including our relation to the dominant culture. We create ourselves, but bound by distinct patterns of possibilities, we do not have freedom in any absolute sense, but a series of choices bound by a distinct social framework.
>
> *(Brake, 1980, p. 6)*

And when we have to discard the old patterns for orienting ourselves within society, we look for new group relationships to define our identity. These serve one particular purpose – the symbolic construction of community. Four such relationships are to be addressed here. They are the construction of we-feelings in the youth culture, at neighbourhood communication level, in the local community as defined with an historical interpretation and, finally and regrettably, in the erection of barriers to exclude all things foreign.

Youth cultures

The traditional image of youth, and the youth culture, was of 14- to 20-year-olds and their way of life. Since the so-called youth rebellions of the 1950s and, in particular, the late 1960s, we have lost this cohesive, narrow concept of youth. This is because the generation-specific social canon of styles and values has been broken up at the same time.

> Previously each period in life, each stage in one's career was marked by its particular style of dress which symbolized one's achievements … These distinctions were rejected by a generation whose predecessors were clearly suffering under the strain of no longer being able to make an instant identification of the status or sex of the person sitting opposite them. Whole battalions of managers in big hotels and expensive restaurants had to learn the hard way that the louse-ridden, long-haired creatures they had just indignantly thrown out were, in fact, rock musicians rolling in money.
>
> *(Stephan, 1985, p. 65)*

There is a new cult of youthfulness which is not limited to the young in age, but permeates all age groups in society through styles of dress, mannerisms of speech or musical preferences. People in their thirties or forties seem to feel themselves to be part of, or at least in sympathy with, the life style of youth, so perhaps it is possible to speak of a provisional concept of youth in which the core of the youth culture consists of those between the ages of 16 and 30. It applies in particular to the young adults who are still undergoing training, or are at the start of their career and are not yet married.

If you just consider the history of the past four or five centuries, the idea of a special age called youth and of special cultural practices confined to young people is relatively new. The well-known French historian, Philippe Ariès, summarizes the situation up to the end of the seventeenth century as follows:

> Childhood was defined as covering the child's most tender years, namely, the period when the small creature cannot survive without help from others. The child had barely achieved physical independence when it was suddenly and without any transition numbered amongst the adults to share their work and their games. From being a very small child it became a young person, without passing through the different stages of youth, which ... have become important features of the highly developed societies of today.
>
> *(Ariès, 1978, p. 46)*

This is why it is reckoned that youth was invented, as it were, in the eighteenth century. What is meant by this is the creation of a special stage in life of youthful attitudes and identity formation which represents a kind of pause between child-like dependence and adult independence. This had consequences not only for the interpretation of family roles and hierarchies, but also for the new awareness of youthful patterns of behaviour and cultural practices.

> The transition to adolescence was particularly strongly marked in traditional society by acceptance into an organized youth group, often accompanied by ritual. This was most important to young men; for girls, admission to the social occasions for young people was more relevant. The age of acceptance into youth groups varied considerably. Rural fraternities rarely accepted members younger than 16, sometimes there was a minimum age of 20 ... The completion of an apprenticeship was the precondition for joining an urban trade guild. This was rarely achieved before the age of 17 or 18 and often later.
>
> *(Mitterauer, 1986, p. 74ff.)*

The initiation ritual was part of the rites of passage, a form of symbolic reception into new social roles and groups which permitted young males to practise new, freer forms of behaviour. They also learned to sound out and respect collective social norms. Groups of both urban and rural youth have typically used practical jokes and rebellious attitudes to test out the norms and boundaries of the rules of collective everyday life in a fairly light-hearted way. At the same time the group built up its own personal systems of rules and relationships, whereby it took on social and territorial identity.

> The gang or the clique is the real street community of young people; it is not only the product of the street but also takes possession of it

> symbolically … Against this background the territorial characteristics of communities of children and young people appear as an age-specific variant of the symbolic acquisition of space. They also transform constructed space into a lived-in one, where they explore the direct environment, establish meeting points (street corners, squares, kiosks etc.), look for hiding places (sheds, cellars, lofts etc.) and thus develop a feeling for their locality.
>
> *(Lindner, 1983, p. 201ff.)*

The Swedish psychologist Erik Erikson, a follower of Sigmund Freud, posits an important stage in the genesis of personality: adolescence, both in the sense of sexual maturation and the formation of the I-identity, compels young people to leave the emotional safety nets of their early childhood behind and to establish new forms of contact for their social orientation. This process of moving on is frequently brought about by detachment from the context of the family and involvement with a new adolescent peer-group.

These peer-group structures represent the central authority for the process of youthful enculturization. Peers, that is, young people of roughly the same age, develop their own collectively-organized youth subculture: this has firm rules of gesture and style which sometimes challenge adult culture. In this way they create for themselves the 'psychosocial moratorium' (Erikson) of a prolonged phase of youth. This phase is, however, no longer so sharply divided from adulthood and not based to any great extent on traditional rites of passage. A French study found that:

> In the context of our society sexual initiation hardly counts as a rite of passage to adulthood any more … What has become of marriage, which in the traditional society was probably the most important rite of initiation into the 'serious business of life'? This is no longer a clear step towards achieving an 'established position in life'. Young middle class people, in particular, often live together without being married, which seems to them to offer the advantages of both married and unmarried life. This makes marriage seem a simple formality … The acquisition of the first motorbike or car no longer signals a change of status, and these days you can get married without solid material prospects – though a large proportion of those concerned can, of course, count on the support of parents or society.
>
> *(Béjin, 1988, p. 186)*

As I have already said, breaking away from the family belongs mainly to the tradition of male youth culture. Female youth culture is less publically evident because it has always been played out in the home or perhaps school, rather than in the street or the pub. So far as women are concerned, growing up took place under close parental supervision and it was because of this that release from the family and family control was withheld from girls for longer. While this has eased up a lot today, the peer-group culture has not lost its essentially male style.

At any rate, young people meet through that culture rather than in the parental living room or at the church dance of yesteryear. This is confirmed by French research into how the way in which young people make contact has changed: partners now meet for the first time mainly in public places.

Couples meet in the street, in the neighbourhood, next door, in the café, at the baker's, in the park, in the shopping centre, in hospital, on public transport.

(Bozon and Héran, 1987)

In addition, the ways in which people get to know each other have loosened up. They no longer get acquainted gradually in the cautious, ritualistic manner prescribed by tradition. Instead, strangers meet by chance and immediately start looking for ways of getting together with an openness that was unimaginable in the past.

This move away from tradition has also been strongly influenced by the way that modern youth cultures have become standardized and internationalized by the adoption of similar fashions, music and fast food, ways of behaving and talking, values and symbols – all those things that older generations deplore as the 'Americanization of youth'. Concurrently, the comparatively recent commercialization of youth culture has caused local-regional characteristics to become weaker; taste and style have become so uniform, that many phenomena appear almost interchangeable.

Yet all these developments have not altered the fact that young people still find it necessary to construct their identity by distancing themselves from the 'world of grown ups' and the strategy they use to do this is frequently one of social conflict. This is not just the usual intergenerational conflict long since identified in research into this age group, but rather the reflection of larger, quite fundamental social conflicts involving work and training opportunities, chances in life and life perspectives; various aspects of social experience are mirrored in the different kinds of youth culture. Class-related profiles have been worked out in an apparently homogeneous youth culture.

> ... a quasi-delinquent male-dominated sub-culture in a district ... with a high immigrant population, has its origins in structural contradictions, and is mediated by class, race and gender, and further modified by the local working-class community and the local political economy. As such it is a far cry from a quasi-bohemian sixth form culture, whose roots are in the progressive middle-class intelligentsia, and whose concern is with liberal or radical criticism, and motivated by self-growth and individuality. Prospects for this group are not only different in terms of opportunities and alternatives, but also at the levels of personal life, emotions and social relationships.
>
> *(Brake, 1980, p. 165)*

These different social problems are also spelt out in forms of cultural self-presentation such as dress and hairstyle, badges and emblems, gestures and body language; in short, in one's own aesthetic and symbolic codes.

> In our society youth becomes new only if it causes problems. Official investigations, concerned or outraged comments and news reports as well as so-called unbiased studies by social scientists reach for the word 'youth' only if and when young people draw attention to themselves by kicking over the traces. Then they put on bizarre rituals, dress in exotic clothes, take on strange poses, break conventions, bottles, windows and

Cultural self-presentation can take a wide variety of forms and change very quickly. This group of teenagers from the early-1980s would doubtless present themselves quite differently today (credit: Mike Levers).

skulls and provoke the forces of law and order. Once young people adopt this strategy, they can be assured of headlines and of having their anger taken seriously. They are then arrested, prosecuted, warned, lectured, taken into custody, defamed but also applauded, imitated and listened to ... When dissatisfied and unemployed young people in cities become violent, whether symbolically or physically, they exercise the only means of power at their disposal, that is, to cause confusion. Their power is the threatening gesture. They may have taken leave of their senses but their agitation conforms to extremely clear rules.

(Hebdige, 1986, p. 186)

However chaotic protests by punks, heavy metal addicts or skinheads may seem, they are inspired by clear ideas of how society can be made aware of a specific, individual situation, since individual experiences and frustrations are being articulated through the protest. The more hopeless you perceive your situation to be, the tougher your symbolic or militant protest.

It is no accident that there has been a recent upsurge of ethnocentric and nationalistic trends in the subcultures of young people. Anti-foreigner and Nazi-type slogans abound in the United Kingdom and France, in Germany and Italy. This phenomonen represents the clash of two militant gestures of hopelessness. On the one hand, young people who are native to the country want to defend the minimal opportunities they have for training, careers and pay; so they use racist acts and slogans to try to keep 'their' territory free of immigrant youths from other countries and continents who, in their experience, can only mean competition. On the other hand, and often in response to this threat, young immigrants from Africa, Asia or Turkey resort to similar measures to forcibly draw attention to their desperate situation. Research in the United Kingdom confirms that the more immigrant groups hark back to their ethnic culture and origins, the more intense racism becomes in the host society.

Especially extreme forms of hostility against foreigners are apparent in the hooliganism which has been spreading throughout western Europe for some time, in football in particular. A skinhead from Berlin readily volunteers this information:

> We meet in discos and have a few drinks; after that we mess around a bit in the streets, sing a few songs, *Deutschlandlieder* (nationalistic songs) and so forth. If the fuzz rolls up, we clear off ... Or we do a bit of vandalising on the trams. Or we go to the football match just to stir things up, start a fight or two and that sort of thing.
>
> *(Stock and Mühlberg, 1990, p. 26)*

The problems that young people are acting out in such a dramatic way are the same problems that already beset the whole of society, such as the struggle for work and prosperity, the fear of 'alien' groups, the cultural and social problems of orientation in a consumer and media society, the dissolution of family ties and social networks. Young people used to have a hopeful and expectant attitude, they were basically optimistic; now their existence is subverted by a feeling of anxiety and uncertainty about the future. A Swedish study established that young people in Scandinavia feel 'materially satiated but socially starved'; that they complain of the lack of emotional and social ties; that they have lost belief in their own visions.

> The peer group is more significant for the development of norms, morals and values in one's life style than adults. In all societies interactions within one's own age group have played a part next in importance to the cooperation between adolescents and adults. In today's society, however, the peer-group is increasingly becoming a refuge.
>
> *(Henriksson, 1985, p. 146ff.)*

While the principle of youthful protest is well founded in historical tradition, the conditions of social tension and situations of conflict it expresses today can no longer be sorted out simply in biographical or biological terms. You can no longer expect that young people will sort themselves out, just by growing older.

Neighbourhood communication

You don't have to draw an idyllic picture of friendly neighbourhood life based on the country village to demonstrate that social contact with our immediate environment (or the lack of it) is still an important reference point for our identity, even in today's urban society. We need the communicative structure of everyday encounters to provide some kind of 'echo' of ourselves, a confirmation of who we are and what we are like. Communication with our neighbours reassures us of our local and territorial identity. Particularly intimate or profound conversations are not necessary; it is often enough simply to exchange greetings, a few sentences and eye contact. When we move into a new neighbourhood, the absence of these small signals makes it seem to us at first like a social vacuum.

A lot of neighbourhood communication is what is called *Klatsch*, *chiacchiere* or gossip. This might make it sound as though this kind of communication also has its malicious, indiscreet and socially manipulative side, where people are checking up on each other. But you could interpret this as a statement of group responsibility, of concern for the wellbeing of individual members, since they are including the individual in the community's circle of inner discourse and showing interest in his or her everyday problems. Gossip comes from the time of tightly knit urban neighbourhoods and local communities, and may still be a rural reality.

> To this day, everyone in the village knows, for instance, by whom and with whom which illegitimate child was conceived and because it is known, there is no longer any need to talk about it. Keeping to the principles of social control means, therefore, that you can get on with everybody, that you are well integrated and can talk with anybody in the way he expects.
>
> *(Brüggemann and Riehle, 1986, p. 182ff.)*

In one of his studies the sociologist, Jörg R. Bergmann, calls gossip a 'discreet indiscretion'; he speaks of a proper 'communicative species' with its own cultural history (Bergmann, 1987, p. 36). It is true that many images from the past which relate to gossip are common currency. The term *Kaffeeklatsch* (coffee/gossip) comes from the early forms of café of the sixteenth century when men met for a social or business chat. When people are compared to gossiping washerwomen, this refers to the fact that women met at wells, at the waterside or in laundries, which were special places for communication between females. 'Below stairs gossip', where the private lives of the masters were raked over and 'office gossip', born of the employee culture of our century, are also descriptions which are commonly used.

In 1986 a press agency from Reykjavik used the headline 'There's nothing better than a gossip over a cup of coffee' to report how Icelandair stewardesses completely forgot to report for duty because they were so busy drinking coffee and chatting: the plane lifted off without them. Such reports raise a smile mainly because of the traditional assumption that it is women who go in for *Klatsch und Tratsch* (gossip and scandalmongering).

Of course, this stereotype could survive only so long as it remained unresearched. We now have evidence to prove that the so-called 'female love of gossip' was essentially a male prejudice. A glance at the *circoli*, the groups of Italian men who meet to talk on the piazza or in the bars, shows that almost any topic under the sun is discussed there: work and money problems, questions of family and relation-ships. Italian women are more likely to discuss such things at home, or during the evening *passeggiata* where groups of women friends walk together in the main street. The groups of regulars that meet in German pubs (*Stammtischrunden*) have just as much information at their disposal as the infamous ladies' coffee mornings. It is possible to verify such impressions statistically.

> In an exploratory study based on discrete observations in the student foyer of an American university J. Levin and A. Arluke recorded that ... women gossip slightly more than men (71 per cent against 64 per cent) and are much more prepared to gossip about close friends and family members. Statistically there was no significant difference between women and men as far as the use of a denigrating tone and the subjects discussed were concerned. It is possible to conclude from the present investigations ... that gossip is in no way the sole prerogative of women. There may be differences of degree and style ... and these differences might at times be considerable. But overall, the theory that gossip is a typically female form of communication can be refuted ...
>
> *(Bergmann, 1987, p. 81ff.)*

No-one would dispute that there are differences between male and female conver-sational behaviour and the speech configurations involved. But the decisive differ-ence does not seem to be at this level. It relates, rather, to how such conversational situations are perceived and how they are interpreted, since this may well be with a gender-specific bias. Knowledge and communication were and are cultural means of dominance, so when men gossip, it is described as a 'public virtue', but when women do it, it is a 'private addiction'.

> The fact that a tendency to gossip is attributed to women as a categorical characteristic is basically due to the fact that women, as a result of the gender-specific organisation of the division of work, find themselves in the position of potential producers of gossip to a much greater extent than men. Many indications suggest that women and men do not differ significantly in their actual ability to produce gossip.
>
> *(Bergmann, 1987, p. 91)*

Or, to put it more succinctly, as yet men are still able to produce better justifi-cation for their love of gossip.

'Our history'

Searching for clues and influences that have determined the course of local, re-gional and national history is very popular today. Newspapers, books and tele-vision programmes all debate the question of the historical identity of our society. Critics are quick to criticize this craving for nostalgia. They reckon that present-day society is so confused that we are harking back to a past which we believe to be clearcut and reassuring, offering refuge from this world by escaping into his-tory. On the other hand, supporters of the historical movement maintain that it is a basic human need to be reasssured about our origins, that the past is necessary to enable us to balance the present with a perspective of the future.

Whichever stance you support, there seem to be two possible explanations of this search for history. One is that we are aware that our accepted images of history are disintegrating and that conventional interpretations no longer meet our need for an explanation – the concern for a new history of everyday issues and experiences probably reflects this. Another explanation, and this seems to me to be the main reason, is that the traditional history of progress and civilization is being called into question because of the current crisis of orientation within society.

If it is correct that attempts to seek meaning and to establish value orientations within society are useful only as long as they give us the feeling that we are achieving something new and realizing hopes, then this search for meaning in history is probably an expression of a crisis over meaning in the present.

There is, of course, nothing new about this desire to search for meaning in the past. In the period at the end of the eighteenth century and the beginning of the nineteenth, which was a decisive phase in the establishment of the European nation state, the national idea was bathed in the light of historical tradition and a historical task. To support the myth of the nation, they had to seek out ancient myths of pre-national tribal and folk history which were supposed to provide an ideological underpinning for the nation's foundations. Scholars and writers then described this 'patriotic' history in such a positive and influential manner that the imaginary national unity of society gradually became a reality. Within a short space of time some newly-formed nations felt themselves to be united by the invisible ties of a community with a common fate in history which had 'always' been in existence, despite differences of language, old territorial lines of division and ethnic disunity: the history of German national consciousness is a particularly good example. In addition, regional history and tradition were preserved in innumerable ways in a frantic attempt to construct historical memorials to landscapes and the peoples who inhabited them.

The manufacture of national history carried on into this century, right up to the post-war period. The mechanisms for giving meaning to history and invoking history are always reactivated in economic and social crisis situations, so as to compensate for crises of meaning in the present by creating meaning out of the past. In the 1950s, the socialist countries provided a prime example in their desperate search for the traditions of a democratic 'folk culture' whose songs and dances, village customs and costumes were cultivated by national folksong and dance ensembles and presented in performances of folklore. The 1960s saw a shift of opinion, condemning folklorism as 'traditional primitivism', reactionary and an impediment to the construction of a united society and state. The western countries also indulged in a wave of folklorism in the 1950s and 1960s, especially in those areas where it proved especially attractive to tourists, who can find an abundant programme of cultural and regional evenings on offer from the Bavarian to the Austrian lakes, from Italian to Swiss Alpine villages. Folksy dances and folk theatre performances bring them closer to 'age old traditions' and make their stay more interesting. Nature and culture sell well together – and even the locals have their regional consciousness raised.

Some of that nationalistic fervour has survived to this day, especially when linked with national jubilees or the interests of the tourist industry. At the *Bicentenaire*, the celebration of the 200th anniversary of the French Revolution, there seemed to be almost more foreign guests than local people taking part in the celebrations in Paris.

The new history movement of today does not have close connections with this official historicism and its patriotic and exotic aberrations. It has a totally different direction and is of a different quality, trying to take a critical approach to the nostalgic nuances and commercially exploitable images of the past. In contrast to earlier trips back into history, it is more like a movement from below, searching for the small experiences of regional culture and history rather than the great myths. There have been many social shifts and cultural changes: these include the pressure for industrial revival during the two post-war decades, a new wave of migration into the towns in almost all European countries, the shock of post-war modernity linked with the effects of the mass medium of television and a new mobility brought by the car and, finally, the new waves of immigration, particularly in the 1960s and 1970s. The outcome is that it seems as though people are not turning nostalgically to the past but rather making a thoughtful attempt to gain critical insights and create a balance for the present. This is exemplified first of all in the emphasis on a 'democratic' image of history; secondly, in the local and regional shape of the history movement, which goes against the official idea of the centralization of culture and, thirdly, in the close link between themes of political and cultural history, where the regions with their specific history and their current social and ecological problems are presented as homeland.

The subjects that these new regional and historical movements choose to research are not 'perfect worlds' or 'cosy corners'. There is little that is idyllic in the history of Nazi Germany, a French history of women or a British history of the working class. You are more likely to find a painful grappling with themes of power, experience of authority, injustice, and anger. This search for a more open image of history, more amenable to discussion and interpretation, is no longer controlled solely by official historians and history teachers. History workshops, school groups, adult education classes and unions are trying to reconstruct a 'collective memory' which up to now was preserved only in isolation and 'privately', in accounts of people's lives and experiences. This democratic historical research can be counted a success, since it is not only great men who make history, but ordinary men and women; macropolitics can be reflected in the microcosm of local history; your own locality may be rediscovered as a 'theatre of history'. This approach is a way of secularizing history and dissolving myths: it forms a transition to a new way of dealing with the past.

This doesn't mean though, that we don't lapse into little historical indulgences and nostalgia from time to time. In the eastern European countries, for instance, there are problems implicit in the way they are looking backwards at dreams of history. Historical traditions and ethnic feelings of belonging – as demonstrated through language, religion, regional histories – are used to legitimize political-territorial strivings for autonomy. Every surviving tradition, be it a revival of Baltic languages or Uzbec folk dances, marks its exponents out and comes across as a symbolic declaration of independence. Laying claim to a special historical and ethnic identity highlights the peculiarity and originality of certain areas and peoples, providing justification for political and cultural rights to existence and autonomy.

The dramatic nature of the developments in eastern Europe should not, of course, make us overlook the fact that in the short space of a few years people there have to catch up with what has evolved gradually over decades in the societies of western Europe. This is a return to regional traditions and identities which had almost vanished within a vast uniform culture. And the people of eastern Europe should not keep looking backwards at history, but must turn to a future where a new balance is developed between culture and politics, between the region and the centralized state. The future does not lie in history, but builds on it.

'Turks out!'

During the last two decades most western European countries have become immigration countries, though not officially and in most cases not willingly. Asian, African and Caribbean immigrants in the United Kingdom, North African and Spanish groups in France, Turkish and Greek families in Germany, unloved Italian 'guests' in German-speaking Switzerland – the decline in prosperity has caused millions of people to be on the move. And in the light of changes in eastern Europe, it is not difficult to predict that we are on the threshold of a new mass migration.

This new mobility of people and of cultures carries with it the potential for economic, social and cultural conflict – we can only guess at its explosive power. The societies of the new host countries are already marked by economic struggles for a share in work and life opportunities, by cultural conflicts between indigenous and foreign languages, skin colours, religions, food cultures. The British sociologist, Stephen Castles, says:

> Migration is one of the central experiences of the modern world. It involves not only millions of international migrants, but also the even larger number of people who, in the course of economic restructuring, have to migrate from village to town or from one industrial area to another within a country. Even the population groups which stay where they are (for the moment) are affected by the cultural and ethnic interactions caused by migration. The migrations are but one aspect of the ever increasing speed of the transformation processes impressing themselves on our consciousness ... Thus, suspicion and defensiveness in the face of migrants is often less a reaction to their own characteristics than a general feeling of insecurity among the population of the host countries.
>
> *(Castles, 1986, p. 37)*

At the beginning of this development in the immediate post-war period, it was assumed at first that the migrant families would either become integrated quite quickly into the new host societies, or that – after a limited period of working abroad – they would decide to return to their home country quite soon. This hope

This shop, with its stock of Turkish specialities, is in the centre of Hanover in northern Germany. It is typical of many such enterprises which have been set up to cater for the needs of minority immigrant populations (credit: Deutsche Presse-Agentur).

turned out to be naïve. It is impossible for immigrants to arrive at such 'planned' life decisions on the basis of the experience they have. The horizons of orientation move and change, according to the length of time migrants have spent in the new country. What was once alien becomes familiar and vice versa.

Because they don't know whether to stick to their origins or look to the future, the immigrant groups in western Europe develop an ambivalent attitude to assimilation in their new countries. They often evolve a double strategy, adjusting to the local culture at a public level, in the world of work and in education but separating off their private, family lives, pursuing folklore or religious practices within an 'ethnic colony'. Faced with exclusion and class demotion in the 'new homeland', foreign workers often keep open the option of whether to stay or leave, even in the second generation. It is necessary to do this because it is impossible to resolve the feelings of being alien in the new country and of becoming estranged from the old home country and transpose them into a decision based on hope. So migrants are forced to accept a life on the edges of both host and home societies, without being really accepted in either.

257

This uneasy situation is nurtured by the fact that the European host countries still consider ethnic origin or foreignness to be of the utmost significance. Deviations from what is considered normal by the native population, that is, strange languages or religions, differences in everyday culture and mental attitudes, are automatically declared to be 'alien'. However many concrete personal experiences of cultural dialogue and cultural understanding take place at work, in the neighbourhood or on public transport, they will always be counteracted by the dialectic principle which renders interethnic experiences anonymous and stereotyped. This is the divisive Them and Us which has had such an important influence on the history of the formation of the European nation states.

Another contributory factor is 'that for most of the immigrants the contrast between the old home country and the country to which they have emigrated is not only ethnic or national, but also involves a difference in the degree of modernity' which is not so easily assimilated (Bausinger, 1986, p. 154). Then there is the inclination to seek safety in one's own cultural traditions, which can also create misunderstandings. What the host country perceives as a nostalgic form of exotic, cultural indulgence often means the exact opposite to the foreign worker, for whom it is a defiant affirmation of non-acceptance and social disadvantage. For them, folklore is not a consolation for homesickness but a protest culture. The Rasta culture in the United Kingdom is therefore 'not an attempt to recreate a slice of the Caribbean under the grey skies of England, but a cultural explanation of the experience of institutional discrimination within a class society' (Castles, 1986, p. 42).

The locals in Germany, France, Switzerland or the United Kingdom mostly react to a flood of foreign immigrants with fear of too much foreign influence. And this is a not unreasonable reaction, when you consider that the local residents may be in the minority in neighbourhoods, in factories or school classes.

> Out of a population of 1.2 million in Seine-Saint-Denis, 250,000 inhabitants are registered as non-European immigrants. The number of illegal immigrants is estimated at 50,000 to 60,000. The people from Guadaloupe and Martinique and the children of Algerians and Maroccans born in France are seen as undesirable foreigners by the majority of the population, even though they have French citizenship. The indigenous population feel that they are in the minority in these quarters. They suffer from the noise, the smells, the general dilapidation … The high rate of population movement shows how dissatisfied they are. Anyone who can afford to, whether a member of the indigenous or foreign community, will move on as soon as possible. Those staying behind are the dregs of those unable to make good.
>
> *(Frankfurter Allgemeine Zeitung, 12 January 1991)*

The fights that break out in cities between ethnic groups of young people or the radical national rights movements hostile to foreigners are but the tip of the iceberg. They are just extreme examples of something which is part of everyday: xenophobia, or a prejudice towards foreign culture which amounts to hostility towards foreigners, is clearly firmly established in the minds of many people. We react irritably to people who look foreign, responding patronizingly to foreigners in Pidgin English. Our immediate expectation is of 'foreignness' rather than the experience of cultural commonalities or differences.

Immigrants are thus constantly made aware of their foreignness in the new world. And for those who decide to return, many people, especially women and children, find it difficult to find their way back into the more traditional life forms and norms after the experience of estrangement from their own country and their own culture. Many who return home find that 'There we were Turks – here we are Germans'. Those who decide to stay on in the new society lose the consolation and relief of the 'myth of returning':

> The moment one has decided to settle for good, there is little sense in pretending that a return to the country of origin will automatically bring happiness and fulfilment. This change of behaviour also means that immigrants start to expect more from the host society and no longer accept discrimination against them as a matter of course. Perhaps the best evidence for this change in affiliation is the transference of rituals which mark the turning points in life from the countries of origin to Great Britain. Southern Asians and Chinese perform their own wedding ceremonies and even their own funeral ceremonies in Great Britain. It would have been unimaginable in the past for a male immigrant from India or Hong Kong to perform his wedding ceremony outside the boundary of the parental village ... South Asian and Chinese immigrants have started to settle as minorities next to other similar groups who form an integral part of British society.
>
> *(Watson, 1980, p. 44ff.)*

What is most difficult for both sides to accept is that the condition, which both thought of at first as only provisional, is actually permanent – they will have to live side by side for a long time.

European everyday life – prospects for a multicultural society?

At the end of this cross country gallop over the territories and situations of the European everyday, the picture of our cultural world has become not simpler, but more complex. There is obviously no simple answer to the question 'What is everyday life?' Indeed, the discussion just raises new questions and problems. And this is a good thing, since it helps us to grasp that it is only possible to get a sensible idea of the relationship between past and present if we learn how to ask the 'right' questions and in doing so come to accept the multiplicity of different answers.

What it comes down to is a question of perspective. Are we to regard the familiar and trusted everyday life as a 'situation', where we are passive, at its mercy, drifting helplessly with the tide of social forces, duties and routines? Or should we interpret our everyday life as offering more active opportunities, as a particular means of handling experiential situations and habits and coordinating them in cultural patterns? Do we conceive of the everyday as an independent series of reflex actions or as a chain of activities which requires a concise sequence of acts of decision and orientation, interactions and communications from each of us? Regarded from this active point of view, everyday life would thus be a 'locus of balance', an environment which constantly needs to be balanced anew at any one time, where we model our own social and cultural identity. In the words of Agnes Heller

> In everyday life the person objectivizes himself in many forms. He shapes his world (his immediate environment) and in this way he shapes himself.
>
> *(Heller, 1984, p. 6)*

Everyday culture signifies a mode of active interaction with societal development and transformation processes: with changes of dialect and languages, relationships with the neighbourhood and other people, forms of attachment to a particular place and mobility, notions of near and far, of class and gender specific roles, of ethnic and national identities. Culture in the sense of a life culture like that would have to be understood as a

> commonly shared system of symbolic meanings, which is generated more or less concurrently in all activities of life. This culture is the outcome of interaction with, and accommodation to the material conditions of life according to certain production relationships, and is created anew every day by association with existing relevant traditions. In other words, it is not a finished entity, but capable of change. It is class specific, ethnically specific in early forms of societies and nationally specific since the transition to a bourgeois society. It is objectified in rituals, traditions, customs, standards, institutions, in clothing, language, music etc. and it lives in the cultural practices of the groups in question. The functions of culture are to constitute perceptions and form identity (for groups or for the individual).
>
> *(Auernheimer, 1984, p. 23ff.)*

If we are able to look beyond our own ethnic or national concerns to consider the very diverse landscape of European everyday cultures, then we certainly are left with an ambivalent picture.

On the one hand contacts between cultures have become closer, they seem to have come to resemble each other. Because of the effects of modern technology and modern media, through travel and everyday intercultural contacts, through the experience of different patterns of everyday behaviour and standards, many differences seem to have become relative and reduced to common factors. If you are travelling from Paris to London, or from Amsterdam to Rome, you no longer get out at a station or an airport into a completely foreign, closed world; you have enough knowledge and cultural competency to be able to organize a hotel bed, supper, excursion programme, trip to sights and daily necessities. We have learned to operate to some extent in a 'multicultural' manner, because experiences with other cultural styles and customs are part of what we are used to dealing with at home, before going on a journey.

On the other hand, this 'natural' convergence and mixing of cultures also generates defensive attitudes. Some of these come about because of the infiltration of foreign elements into our everyday environment, but some are also the result of the planned coalescence of Europe. Even the unification of different forms of government, legal standards, administrative regulations and education systems that is intended may reinforce that fear of not being able to locate yourself in a common European culture. We are still very much dependent on the idea of cultural autonomy, which now seems to be threatened both by too much variety and too much uniformity.

> The things we take for granted culturally (without which life would be extremely complicated, not to say impossible) have fallen into decay for the most part; to a great extent people no longer live within horizons of firmly established group cultures and the more someone becomes entangled with modern possibilities, the more likely it is that he will become the plaything of contradictory information and instructions for action.
>
> *(Bausinger, 1986, p. 142)*

So the concept of multicultural societies in the context of a Europe which is becoming more and more integrated contains both anxieties and opportunities. We have lived too long in historically constituted societies in which national symbols and ethnic attributions formed important cornerstones of our identity, for us to be able to disperse it all in favour of an accepted cultural pluralism. Fears of foreign control are therefore part of our historical inheritance. Yet we are also aware of the possibility of a different future.

> Naturally, a successful multicultural society is also nourished by the positive gains that its members see for themselves in diversity. But that is only *one* aspect among many, and it serves little purpose to behave as the advocates of multiculturalism do, who assume that foreigners are important simply as a 'living resource for exotic appetites', as 'sentimental clowns who are there to chase away our boredom'. It is true that many of the currently promoted concepts of multiculturalism are surrounded by illusions and much naïve enthusiasm crumbles in the face of real problems, if the foreigners don't measure up to the virtues which have been attributed to them. But who is to say that we have reached the end of the road? And are there any other viable concepts? A multiculturalism which has to be lived with is founded in the first instance on tolerance. Postmodernity recommends us to see variety as opportunity. This makes the possibility of an all-embracing ideology, religion or philosophy more and more unlikely. In this sense, the task of cultural politics would be to promote the coexistence of different cultures as the real chance for survival.
>
> *(Hofmann, 1990, p. 176ff.)*

Once upon a time we had an identity; today we are searching for one. That, at any rate, is the general impression when we take a rather lachrymose look at our confusing experiences of the present. Of course, we cannot even be all that certain that earlier generations and societies had not already come to the same conclusion.

References

ARIÈS, P. (1978) *Geschichte der Kindheit,* München.

AUERNHEIMER, G. (1984) 'Kultur, Identität und interkulturelle Erziehung', *Demokratische Erziehung,* no. 12, pp. 23–6.

BARTHES, R. (1964) *Mythen des Alltags,* Frankfurt am Main.

BAUSINGER, H. (ed.) (1986) *Ausländer – Inländer: Arbeitsmigration und kulturelle Identität,* Tübingen.

BECK, U. (1992) *Risk Society: towards a new modernity,* London, Sage Publications.

BÉJIN, A. (1988) 'Ehe ohne Trauschein und Post-Adoleszenz: Anmerkungen zu einigen Mythen des "Nicht-Ubergangs" ', in LÜSCHER, K. (ed.) *Die 'postmoderne' Familie,* Konstanz.

BERGMANN, J. R. (1987) *Klatsch. Zur Sozialform der diskreten Indiskretion,* Berlin/New York.

BEUTEL, M. (1976) 'Fenster in Holland – Holland im Fenster', *Notizen,* no. 4, pp. 85–104.

BOLTANSKI, L. (1976) 'Die soziale Verwendung des Körpers', in KAMPER, D. and RITTNER, V. (eds) *Zur Geschichte des Körpers,* München/Wien.

BOURDIEU, P. (1979) *La distinction. Critique sociale de jugement,* Paris, Éditions de minuit.

BOZON, M. (1982) 'La fréquentation des cafés dans une petite ville ouvrière', *Ethnologie française,* vol. XII, pp. 137–46.

BOZON, M. and HÉRAN, F. (1987) 'La découverte du conjoint I – Evolution et morphologie des scènes de rencontre', *Population,* no. 6, pp. 943–86.

BRAKE, M. (1980) *The sociology of youth cultures and subcultures,* London, Routledge and Kegan Paul.

BRUCKNER, P. and FINKIELKRAUT, A. (1981) *Das Abenteuer gleich um die Ecke: Kleines Handbuch der Alltagsüberlebenskunst,* München/Wien.

BRÜGGEMANN, B. and RIEHLE, R. (1986) *Das Dorf: Uber die Modernisierung einer Idylle,* Frankfurt/New York.

CASTLES, S. (1986) 'Migration und Gesellschaftsstruktur – Klasse, Ethnizität oder Community', in BAUSINGER, H. (ed.) *Ausländer – Inländer: Arbeitsmigration und kulturelle Identität,* Tübingen.

DEVAUX, K. and HALVA, H.-J. (1986) 'Die ehrbare Familie – Veränderungen im Zentrum sizilianischen Selbstverständnisses', *Notizen,* no. 24, pp. 237–70.

ELBEN, O. (1931) *Lebenserinnerungen 1823-1899,* Stuttgart.

ELIAS, N. (1978) *The Civilizing Process: the history of manners. Sociogenetic and Psychogenetic Investigations,* translated by JEPHCOTT, E., Oxford, Basil Blackwell.

FABRE-VASSAS, C. (1989) 'La boisson des ethnologues', *Terrain,* no. 13, pp. 5–14.

FERGUSON, A. (1966) *An Essay on the History of Civil Society 1767,* edited by FORBES, D., Edinburgh University Press.

FLADE, A. and ROTH, W. (1987) *Wohnen psychologisch betrachtet*, Bern.

FREMDE DEUTSCHE (1986) *Alltagskultur aus der Sicht ausländischer Studierender*, Ludwig-Uhland-Institut (ed.), Tübingen.

FREVERT, U. (1986) *Frauen-Geschichte: Zwischen Bürgerlicher Verbesserung und Neuer Weiblichkeit*, Frankfurt am Main.

GIORDANO, C. (1990) 'Wege der Gefahr. Zur Typographie süditalienischer Gefahrvermeidung', *Zeitschrift für Volkskunde*, **86**, pp. 37–52.

GROSSE PECLUM, M.-L. (1990) 'Gibt es denn europäische Zuschauer? – Fernsehnutzung in einem internationalisierten Programmangebot', *Zeitschrift für Kulturaustausch*, **40**, pp. 185–94.

HALLERSTEIN-TEUFEL, N. H. VON (1984) *Die Familie ist mein Nest: Irische Frauen im Spannungsfeld von Arbeitsteilung, Autoritätsstruktur und Wohnumwelt*, Frankfurt am Main.

HAUSEN, K. (1977) 'Die Polarisierung der "Geschlechtscharaktere" – eine Spiegelung der Dissoziation von Erwerbs– und Familienleben', in CONZE, W. (ed.) *Sozialgeschichte der Familie in der Neuzeit Europas*, Stuttgart, pp. 367–93.

HEBDIGE, D. (1986) 'Versteckspiel im Rampenlicht', in COHEN, P. *et al.*, *Verborgen im Licht. Neues zur Jugendfrage*, Frankfurt am Main, pp. 186–205.

HELLER, A. (1984) *Everyday Life*, translated by CAMPBELL, G. L., London, Routledge and Kegan Paul.

HENRIKSSON, B. (1985) 'Materiell übersättigt – sozial ausgehungert: Diagnosen und Perspektiven aus Schweden', in HENGST, H. (ed.) *Kindheit in Europa*, Frankfurt am Main.

HOFFMANN, H. (1990) *Kultur als Lebensform*, Frankfurt am Main.

KANT, I. (1975) *Anthropologie in pragmatischer Absicht* (A309/B307), Vol. VI, Darmstadt.

KASCHUBA, W. (1991) 'Erkundung der Moderne: Bürgerliches Reisen nach 1800', *Zeitschrift für Volkskunde*, **87**, pp. 29–52.

KRACAUER, S. (1977) *Das Ornament der Masse*, Frankfurt am Main.

LINDNER, R. (1983) 'Straße – Straßenjunge – Straßenbande', *Zeitschrift für Volkskunde*, **79**, pp. 192–208.

MÄDER, U. (1990) *Frei-Zeit: Fantasie und Realität*, Zürich.

MITTERAUER, M. (1986) *Sozialgeschichte der Jugend*, Frankfurt.

MOOSER, J. (1984) *Arbeiterleben in Deutschland 1900–1970*, Frankfurt am Main.

NIETHAMMER, L. and BRÜGGEMEIER, F.-J. (1976) 'Wie wohnten Arbeiter im Kaiserreich?', *Archiv für Sozialgeschichte*, **XVI**, pp. 51–134.

PROJEKTGRUPPE CURRICULUM FAMILIE (ed.) (1978) *Familie in der Gesellschaft*, Pt. II., Bonn.

RATH, C.-D. (1984) *Reste der Tafelrunde. Das Abenteuer der Eßkultur*, Reinbek.

ROUSSEL, L. (1988) 'Die soziologische Bedeutung der demographischen Erschütterung in den Industrieländern der letzten zwanzig Jahre', in LÜSCHER, K. (ed.) *Die 'postmoderne' Familie*, Konstanz.

SALLINEN-GIMPL, P. (1988) 'Die Rolle der Mutter als ethnologisches Forschungsproblem', *Ethnologia Scandinavica*, pp. 134–41.

SANDGRUBER, R. (1982) *Die Anfänge der Konsumgesellschaft. Konsumgüterverbrauch, Lebensstandard und Alltagskultur in Österreich im 18. und 19. Jahrhundert*, München.

SCHARFE, M., SCHMOLZE, M. and SCHUBERT, G. (eds) (1985) *Wallfahrt. Tradition und Mode*, Tübingen.

SCHILD, A. and SYWOTTEK, A. (eds) (1988) *Massenwohnung und Eigenheim. Wohnungsbau und Wohnen in der Großstadt seit dem Ersten Weltkrieg*, Frankfurt am Main/New York.

SCHIVELBUSCH, W. (1983) *Das Paradies, der Geschmack und die Vernunft. Eine Geschichte der Genußmittel*, Frankfurt am Main/Berlin/Wien.

SEGALEN, M. (1986) *Historical anthropology of the family*, translated by WHITEHOUSE, J. C. and MATHEWS, S., Cambridge University Press.

STEPHAN, C. (1985) *Ganz entspannt im Supermarkt. Liebe und Leben im ausgehenden 20. Jahrhundert*, Berlin.

STOCK, M. and MÜHLBERG, P. (1990) *Die Szene von innen. Skinheads, Grufties, Heavy Metals, Punks*, Berlin.

STUDIENKREIS FÜR TOURISMUS (1986) *Wettbewerb Jugend reist und lernt Europa kennen*, Studienkreis für Tourismus, Starnberg.

TANNAHILL, R. (1973) *Food in History*, London, Eyre Methuen.

TOLKSDORF, U. (1981) 'Der Schnellimbiß und The World of Ronald McDonalds', *Kieler Blätter zur Volkskunde*, **XIII**, pp. 117–62.

WARD, A. H. (1987) 'Gender relations and young people', *Cultural Studies*, no. 2, pp. 211–17.

WATSON, J. L. (1980) 'Arbeitsimmigranten in Großbritannien – neuere Entwicklungen', in BLASCHKE, J. and GREUSSING, K. (eds) *"Dritte Welt" in Europa: Probleme der Arbeitsimmigration*, Frankfurt am Main.

WILLIAMS, R. (1963) *Culture and Society 1780-1950*, Harmondsworth, Penguin.

WILLIAMS, R. (1971) *The Long Revolution*, Harmondsworth, Penguin.

WINCK, M. (1986) *Britain Today. Living*, Tübingen, DIFF.

ZINNECKER, J. (1989) 'Die Versportung jugendlicher Körper' in BRETTSCHNEIDER, W.-D. (ed.) *Sport im Alltag von Jugendlichen*, Schorndorf.

Acknowledgements

Grateful acknowledgement is made to the following sources for permission to reproduce material in this book:

Essay 1

Figures

Figure 1: Milne, A. A. (1979) *Winnie-La-Pu*, translated by Kellerman, I. and Lewin, R. A., New York, E. P. Dutton and Co. Illustrations from Milne, A. A. (1926) Winnie the Pooh, illustrated by Shepard E. H., New York, E. P. Dutton and Co. Used by permission of E.P. Dutton Children's Books (a division of Penguin Books USA Inc.) and Curtis Brown, London.

Text

Extract from *The European*, 20–26 February 1992

Tables

Tables 1 and 2: Finkenstaedt, T. and Schröder, K. (1990) 'Sprachenschranken statt Zollschranken? Grundlegung einer Fremdsprachenpolitik für das Europa von morgen', in *Materialen zur Bildungspolitik 11*, Stifterverband für die Deutsche Wissenschaft; Table 3: Finkenstaedt, T. and Schröder, K. (1990) Studienkreis für Tourismus e.V; Table 4: *Statistische Mitteilungen des Deutschen Volkshochschulverbandes, Arbeitsjahr 1987*, Deutscher Volkshochschulverband e. v. Pädagogische Arbeitsstelle

Essay 2

Figures

Figure 1: Ringer, F. (1987) 'On segmentation in modern European educational systems', in Muller, D. K., Ringer, F. and Simon, B. (eds), *The Rise of the Modern Educational System*, Cambridge University Press; Figure 2: Lukacs, P. (1989) 'Changes in selection policy in Hungary: the case of the admission system in higher education', *Comparative Education*, **25** (2), p. 226, Carfax Publishing Company

Tables

Table 2: Description Papers of the International Seminar on *Core Curriculum in Western Societies*, SLO, Enschede, the Netherlands, November 1985; Table 4: Courtesy of the Georg Eckert Institute; Table 5: Federal Ministry of Education and Science (1990/91) *Basic Structural Data. Education Statistics From The Federal Republic of Germany,* Bundesminister für Bildung und Wissenschaft; Table 6: Courtesy of Eurostat; Table 7: Reprinted from Wilson, M. (ed.), *Girls And Young Women In Education: a european perspective,* Copyright 1991, with permission from Pergamon Press Ltd, Headington Hill Hall, Oxford OX3 0BW, UK; Table 8: Clancy, P. (1989) 'Gender differences in student participation at third level', in Hussey, C., (ed.), *Equal Opportunities for Women in Higher Education*, University College, Dublin; Table 9: Statistical Yearbook of the German Federal Republic (1988), Statistiches Bundesamt

Essay 3

Tables

Table 2: Sinus (1988) *Sowjetische und amerikanische Politik im Urteil der Deutschen in der Bundesrepublik*, München, Gesellschaft für Sozialforschung und Marktforschung mbH; Table 4: Luyken, G. M. (1989) 'Europa 1992: Auch ein Binnenmarkt für die Medien?' *Rundfunk und Fernsehen*, **37** (2–3), pp. 167–79, Hans-Bredow-Institut; Tables 5 and 6: Kessler, M. and Schrape, K. (1990) 'Fernsehmarkt Westeuropa', *Media Perspektiven,* 1, pp. 25–32; Table 7: Kleinsteuber, H. J. (ed.) (1991) *Radio: das unterschätzte Medium: Erfahrungen mit nicht-kommerziellen Lokalstationen in 15 Staaten*, Vistas Verlag GmbH; Tables 8a and 8b: From *The European Newspaper Minibook* (1990) courtesy of Carat International; Tables 9 and 10: Sonnenberg U. (1990) 'Programmangebote und Programmproduktion in den Ländern der Europäischen Gemeinschaft', in Kleinsteuber, H. J., Wiesner, V. and Wilke, P. (eds) *EG-Medienpolitik: Fernsehen In Europa zwischen Kultur und Kommerz*, Vistas Verlag GmbH.

The work of the Humanities Programme Committee of the EADTU has been carried out with the support of the Commission of the European Community within the frameworks of the ERASMUS Programme and the Jean Monnet Project.

Notes on contributors

Wolfgang Kaschuba

Wolfgang Kaschuba (b. 1950) studied political science and empirical cultural studies at the University of Tübingen and was then researcher and lecturer at the Ludwig Uhland Institute for Empirical Cultural Sciences. In 1992 he was appointed Professor of European Ethnology at the Humboldt University, Berlin. His major interests and publications are on cultural-historical and socio-cultural questions; the history of rural society; social movements in the 19th and 20th centuries; working-class culture and mentalities; life-styles and cultural practice of present-day society.

Hans J. Kleinsteuber

Hans J. Kleinsteuber (b. 1943) studied political science, economics, cybernetics, American studies and political journalism in Berlin and Medord (USA) from 1962 to 1968. From 1969 to 1975 he was a lecturer at the John F. Kennedy Institute at the Free University of Berlin. Since 1975 he has been Professor of Political Science specializing in comparative politics at the University of Hamburg. He is head of the Media and Policy Centre at the University's Institute for Political Science. His publications are on politics and the media in the USA and Europe, on

266

the development of national media systems and on changes in radio. He has carried out several research projects on aspects of European media policies.

Bob Moon

Bob Moon has been Professor of Education at the Open University in the UK since 1988. He began his career teaching in London and later was headteacher of two comprehensive schools. He was a founder member of the International Association for the Development of Adolescent Schooling, which co-ordinates the work of experimental schools across Europe. He has been consultant to a number of European governments and has acted as an expert adviser to the OECD Centre for Educational Research and Innovation. His research interest is in the comparative development of educational systems in Europe, a theme on which he has published a number of books and articles.

Torsten Rossman

Torsten Rossman (b. 1963) trained as a naval officer. Between 1984 and 1990 he studied political science and Scandinavian studies in Hamburg and has been self-employed as a journalist. Since 1990 he has taught at the University of Hamburg and since 1991 has been on the staff of the Media and Policy Centre of the Insitute for Political Science at the University. His publications are on media politics in Europe and on radio in Scandinavia.

Konrad Schröder

Konrad Schröder (b. 1941) studied English, pedagogy, Romance languages and French at the University of Saarbrücken. He has worked in schools in the Saarland and in Bavaria and as a lecturer at the teacher training colleges in Ludwigsburg and Karlsruhe and the University of Frankfurt. He is currently Professor of English at the University of Augsburg. He is a consultant to the German government on education, co-editor of the journal *Die Neueren Sprachen* and holds offices in numerous learned bodies. His major interests are in the theoretical basis of foreign language teaching, foreign language politics and language planning and the history of foreign language teaching. He has published extensively on the teaching of English and other languages.

Monica Shelley

Monica Shelley is currently a Lecturer in Modern Languages (German) at the Open University. She has contributed to a wide range of Open University teaching materials, including packs and courses on such diverse subjects as parent and health education, consumer affairs, recycling and local and family history. Her translations from German into English include work by Bertolt Brecht as well as more technical reports and articles. She is currently carrying out life history work with people from the former DDR.

Volkert Wiesner

Volkert Wiesner (b. 1953) trained as a printer, studied political science and journalism between 1981 and 1985 in Hamburg and worked as an editor. He gained his Ph.D. at the University of Hamburg in 1990. From 1988 to 1992 he was on the staff of the Media and Policy Centre and a lecturer in the Institute for Political Science at the University of Hamburg. Since 1992 he has been adviser on ecological questions of environmental policy to the Ministry for the Environment in Lower Saxony. His publications cover politics and the media in Canada and Europe, the development of national media systems and radio in the Federal Republic of Germany.

Margaret Winck

Margaret Winck (b. 1946) graduated in English Language and English Literature from Leicester University. She has 25 years of experience in distance education in Germany, having contributed to numerous courses on the teaching of English Language, English Literature and Cultural Studies developed at the German Institute for Distance Education in Tübingen. She is co-author of several English text books for schools and has a particular interest in the interface between language teaching and cultural studies.

Index to Book 2